DANCE
WITH THE
DEVIL

DANCE WITH THE DEVIL

A MEMOIR OF MURDER AND LOSS

DAVID BAGBY

FOREWORD BY ELLIOTT LEYTON

KEY PORTER BOOKS

Library and Archives Canada Cataloguing in Publication

Bagby, David
Dance with the devil: a memoir of murder and loss / David Bagby.

ISBN 978-1-55263-819-4

1. Bagby, Andrew David—Death and burial. 2. Turner, Zachary Andrew—Death and burial. 3. Turner, Shirley Jane. 4. Filicide—Newfoundland and Labrador. 5. Suicide—Newfoundland and Labrador. 6. Criminal justice, Administration of—Newfoundland and Labrador. 7. Social service—Newfoundland and Labrador. 8. Child welfare—Newfoundland and Labrador. I. Title.

HV6533.P4B33 2007   364.15209718   C2006-906411-3

ONTARIO ARTS COUNCIL
CONSEIL DES ARTS DE L'ONTARIO

The publisher gratefully acknowledges the support of the Canada Council for the Arts and the Ontario Arts Council for its publishing program. We acknowledge the support of the Government of Ontario through the Ontario Media Development Corporation's Ontario Book Initiative.

We acknowledge the financial support of the Government of Canada through the Book Publishing Industry Development Program (BPIDP) for our publishing activities.

Key Porter Books Limited
Six Adelaide Street East, Tenth Floor
Toronto, Ontario
Canada M5C 1H6

www.keyporter.com

Text design: Martin Gould
Electronic formatting: Jean Lightfoot Peters

Printed and bound in Canada

09 10 11 5

To Zachary,
to Edward Shaw,
and to all potential bail-release murder victims

CONTENTS

If we cannot find the truth, what is our hope of justice?

—Scott Turow, from *Presumed Innocent*

FOREWORD

By Elliott Leyton,
Professor Emeritus of Forensic Anthropology,
Memorial University of Newfoundland

Dance with the Devil tells a story so achingly vile and contemptible that everyone has a duty to read and consider its contents. The book documents how the system of social work, law, and psychiatry arrogantly facilitated the tragic murder of a child, Zachary Turner.

We Canadians may be proud of our peaceable kingdom, but we rarely pause to consider its defects, and few of us understand how inhuman and incompetent our major institutions can be. Read this book to see how the "professionals" who are paid to serve and protect our interests systematically fussed over and pampered a murderer, ignoring all warnings that she would kill again. When she did kill for a second time, murdering her baby and herself, the professionals acted only to protect themselves, blocking all inquiries into how this dereliction of duty could have happened. Thus, you will learn how the "caring professions" of social work and psychology treated an endangered child with an ignorance and indifference that would prove fatal; how the "healing profession" did nothing to foresee the coming rampage; and how the judges and attorneys in the Department of Justice were incapable of grasping the most elementary principles of criminality, let alone "justice."

David and Kate Bagby are among the most gentle and lovable people you could ever hope to meet; they are also among the most trusting, a quality that was shared by their son, Andrew. Alas, their innocence would soon end in the annihilation of their entire bloodline.

David, an engineer in California, and his devout English-born wife, Kate, must have been delighted that their only child, Andrew, had been accepted into medical school at the Memorial University of Newfoundland in Canada's windswept easternmost province. They could not have known that while he was in medical school, Andrew would have a college romance with a fellow medical student, Shirley Turner, an older woman with a long history of mental instability and many children from previous marriages. Most of Turner's fellow students and professors recognized that she was a volatile, even dangerous woman. Turner was known to have made several suicide attempts when lovers had rejected her, and she was also infamous for her rages whenever her plans were thwarted (so threatening was she that a senior physician and professor in the medical school had taken out a restraining order against her, forbidding her to contact him). All of this information was available, but none of it was exchanged among the social workers, psychologists, lawyers, judges, and psychiatrists who were later to be responsible for Turner and her child, despite official policies insisting such information be shared.

After she murdered Dr. Andrew Bagby because he had ended their relationship, she then fled to Canada. Through a fantastical display of bumbling incompetence and indifference that goes to the very heart of the senile Canadian bureaucracy, the brutal killer used her personal powers of evasion and manipulation to fight extradition for almost two years. The Newfoundland police officer whose job it was to liaise with the

Pennsylvania police read the file and interviewed Turner. He was one of the few to recognize what a dangerous woman she was and tried to warn the social workers and attorneys (as had the Bagbys) who were responsible for Turner and her soon-to-be-born child, Zachary.

Turner was temporarily placed in a correctional institution to await extradition to the United States, and Zachary was turned over to the Bagbys. The Bagbys said nothing, revelling in the love of their grandson and fearful that if they interfered with the process of justice they might lose him.

The Bagbys' fears were justified. In fact, a kind of "conspiracy of indifference" was growing among the "professionals," an unconscious agreement between the social workers, the legal system and the psychiatrists involved in the case, based on a shared inability to see the killer who was sitting in front of them. Ultimately, this incapacity would release Turner on bail, return Zachary to her care, and grant Turner the freedom to murder her child. Turner manipulated her psychiatrist, as well as two impecunious new friends into standing bail for her (in Newfoundland, a preposterous system exists in which no money need be put up to bail out a person, merely a promise). At the critical bail hearing, neither the Crown attorney nor Turner's defense lawyer questioned the wisdom of releasing an indicted murderer from institutional control. Worse, no one had explained to those posting the bail that if they later changed their minds about Turner's reliability (as at least one of them did), they had the right to retract the bond. Most damning of all, if true, is that it remains unclear whether or not the presiding judge even read the airtight file on Turner prepared by the Pennsylvania Police.

On the loose and fighting extradition, Turner now came under the care of the social workers and psychologists in the

Department of Social Services and the Department of Child and Youth Services. Turner deftly manoeuvred the young and inexperienced social workers, who were utterly lacking in direction from senior bureaucrats, into using public money to provide her with welfare housing and income—even a daily cleaning lady. Clearly, the social workers saw Turner as their sole responsibility and they treated her and Zachary as social-service recipients, rather than treating Turner as a dubious person with a child in need of protection. The Bagbys counted for nothing.

David Bagby writes with passion about the murders of their only child and only grandchild—murders that destroyed, perhaps for all time, any hope that he and his wife might ever have for peace of mind. But he also writes to a noble social purpose. His hope in writing this is that such bureaucracy-facilitated killing will never happen again in Canada; that someone awaiting extradition on serious charges of murder will never again be allowed out on bail and in control of a child; and that the practices of bail and child protection will be radically changed. It is David and Kate Bagby's desperate hope that never again will the justice industry trample on all morality, intelligence, and natural justice.

In the wake of the killings and the suicide, Newfoundland's Child Advocate's Office sparked an enquiry that, in late 2006, issued a stinging three-volume report by forensic pathologist Dr. Peter Markesteyn, with David C. Day as legal counsel. It remains to be seen if the provincial government has the courage and the energy to implement their superb and necessary recommendations and to crush the incompetents who orchestrated this tragedy.

Author of *Men of Blood: Murder in Everyday Life* and *Hunting Humans: The Rise of the Modern Multiple Murderer*, Dr. Leyton served for fifteen months on the Child Advocate's initial Advisory Panel reviewing the death of Zachary Turner.

PROLOGUE

November 6, 2001—The body of twenty-eight year old Latrobe Area Hospital physician Dr. Andrew Bagby was found Tuesday morning in Keystone State Park, several miles north of Latrobe. He had been shot five times with a small-calibre weapon.

October 4, 2006—A review has found that Newfoundland and Labrador's Department of Social Services failed a thirteen-month old boy who was drowned by his mother in a 2003 murder suicide.

The province's child advocate says the mother, Shirley Turner, who was facing extradition to the United States on a murder charge, should never have had custody of the child.

CHAPTER 1
MURDER

Andrew had been trying for many months to peacefully end his two-year romance with Shirley, but she kept wedging her way back into his life. On Saturday, November 3, 2001, over lunch at the tiny Latrobe, Pennsylvania airport, he finally convinced her that their relationship was over. She boarded her flight and returned to her home in Council Bluffs, Iowa.

Twenty-four hours later, on Sunday afternoon, Shirley took her .22 calibre pistol, her cellphone, and some cash, and she headed east on Interstate 80. Early Monday morning, Andrew was getting ready for work when she presented herself at the door of his apartment, located across the street from his workplace, the Latrobe Area Hospital. He allowed her into his apartment and left her there while he walked across the street and reported for work.

At his 7:30 morning report Andrew told his supervisor, Dr. Clark Simpson, the chief resident in family practice medicine, about his early morning surprise visitor: "Guess who showed up on my doorstep this morning."[1]

Clark, who already knew something of Andrew's troubles in trying to end the relationship, offered the only plausible guess: "Shirley?"

"Yup. That psychotic bitch was on my doorstep!"

"So what did you do?"

"I let her in."

Clark tried to convey his concern about Shirley's erratic behaviour: "Andrew, are you sure about this?"

"Oh, yeah. Everything's fine."

Andrew finished his morning duties at the main hospital, drove twenty miles north on Route 981, and reported for the afternoon shift at the satellite clinic in Saltsburg, a neighbouring town. In a quick chat late in the afternoon, Clark thought Andrew said that he was planning to meet Shirley after work in a "bar" and send her on her way again. Clark offered to go with him, just to help keep things cool, but Andrew once again assured him that all was well. They agreed that, after Andrew finished sending Shirley home again, he would pick up a six-pack of beer and go to Clark's apartment for the evening.

A little before 5 p.m. Andrew left the Saltsburg clinic, picked up a six-pack at a convenience store, and went to meet Shirley. Unfortunately, the meeting took place in an isolated park, not in a bar, as Clark had remembered Andrew saying.

From the parking lot of Keystone State Park, just off of Route 981, Andrew used his cellphone to call Shirley's cellphone.

A witness later reported seeing a lone car in the parking lot at around 5:30 p.m., "dark blue or black."[2] The description was consistent with Andrew's black Toyota Corolla.

Another witness reported walking through the parking lot a few minutes after 6 p.m. and passing two cars parked side-by-side, "a small dark colored car and an unknown color sport utility vehicle."[3] The descriptions of both vehicles were consistent with Andrew's Corolla and Shirley's Toyota RAV4.

Forensic analysis later disclosed the sequence of wounds to Andrew's body. The first two slugs, in quick succession, entered the left side of his chest and his left cheek. The second slug exited behind his left ear. He spun halfway around and fell on his face in the gravel, shoulders hunched forward. Shirley carefully aimed the next two shots at his rectum. Then she stepped forward, bent slightly, and placed a final round in the back of his head—an execution shot close enough to singe the hair. The gun was empty, so she kicked him in the head.

She returned to her car and headed back to Iowa. The relationship was definitely over.

The same witness who reported seeing side-by-side cars on Monday evening was up well before dawn Tuesday morning, walking through the trees near the parking lot. He saw "the small dark colored car parked in the same location as the night before but the SUV was gone."[4] He shined a flashlight at the car, noticed nothing unusual, and kept walking.

Just before 6:00 a.m. a man searching for aluminum cans in the park dumpster found Andrew's corpse, covered in a thin layer of frost, face down on the blood-soaked gravel.

CHAPTER 2
BACKGROUND

According to Andrew, Shirley called herself a welfare brat and declared that he was born with a silver spoon in his mouth, to which he replied, "My dad's not a Bill Gates, so it couldn't be silver…bronze, maybe." That seemed to be a good figurative summary of their differing backgrounds.

ANDREW

I met Kate in October of 1967, a few months before my discharge from the navy in Long Beach, California. I had always assumed that marriage would be somewhere in my future, but not so soon, because my first priority as a civilian was to earn a degree in engineering and establish a career. Besides, I hardly knew any women. They still scared me.

Kate had firmly decided against marriage long before immigrating to California from England. Her plan was to circle the globe, working as a nurse for two years in America and two in Australia and then settle into spinsterhood as a district midwife somewhere in Devon, a beautiful county in southwest England.

After a blind date at Disneyland, we couldn't keep away from each other. In the next two weeks we went out together twelve more times. Though our union was inevitable, it took me four more months to recognize that fact and propose marriage. She accepted and three weeks later a judge declared us an official couple. Several birth control methods served to forestall little baby distractions while I earned an engineering degree, but as I neared graduation, we dropped the precautions and enthusiastically set about making a baby: great fun, but not reproductive. After a year, we worried that we may not be able to conceive a child of our own, and Kate started taking a fertility drug. It worked. A year later, in the spring of 1973, Kate was finally pregnant.

I discovered that one of life's sweetest pleasures was the feeling of pressing my close-shaven cheek onto my pregnant wife's smooth, soft tummy where I could listen to the gurgles and thumps that go on in there. As my son grew, I could sometimes hear the baby's heartbeat, and could certainly feel him squirm and kick. There was a primordial connection between that new Baby life in there and pleasure zones in Daddy's brain out here.

After a tough labour ending in a Caesarean section, Kate and our beautiful baby boy were brought out into the hallway. Kate and I hugged and kissed and cried tears of joy. We named him Andrew David Bagby and took him home to live and grow with us.

The next twenty-two years were only remarkable for their lack of significant problems. Kate's and my careers progressed very nicely; hers as an OB/GYN nurse practitioner and mine as a computer engineer. Andrew performed his job—growing up—to near perfection. He was a bright and eager baby and toddler, a good student from kindergarten through college, and an Eagle Scout, both figuratively and literally. He was a good kid.

He was not, however, a perfect kid. For several years in early grade school, his classmates found that he could be easily goaded into violent reaction with the slightest of insults. Kate and I must have sat Andrew down on a monthly basis to deliver some variation on the non-violence speech: "Andrew, somebody's *words* don't hurt you. Let them *say* anything they like; it won't hurt you. But the one who *hits* first is *always* wrong. The first rule, the last rule, and all the rules in between: *don't touch anybody without their permission!*" He eventually accepted the wisdom of this advice, cooled his temper, and developed many good strong friendships throughout his school years. He matured into an easygoing personality who could fit in with any crowd and aspired to become a doctor.

After graduating with a degree in biological sciences from the University of California at Irvine, Andrew failed to get into medical school. Choking down the disappointment, he got a job and repeated the application process—this time he applied to about sixty schools. He also became engaged to a lovely young lady named Heather Arnold, but left the wedding date unspecified because he didn't know when, where, or even if, he would be going away to school.

In the spring of 1996, persistence paid off and Andrew was accepted into the class of 2000 Faculty of Medicine at Memorial University of Newfoundland in St. John's, Newfoundland, Canada: MUN MED, for short. I confess that I had to check an atlas to locate that easternmost city in North America. In late summer, Andrew and Heather drove the four thousand miles from California to Newfoundland, where his medical studies progressed very well; he passed the first year of medical school.

Cohabitation fared less well. When they came home on break in the summer of 1997, Andrew and Heather announced that the engagement was off. A common story: two good people who couldn't live together in peace and harmony. But there was no animosity in their parting; in fact, Kate and I had

Andrew's blessing to continue our love and support of Heather. When he returned to St. John's, Heather moved in with us and became something of a surrogate daughter. She got a job and struggled to get her head on straight and identify her life's work. Two years later, in July 1999, Heather had settled on a career in medicine and entered her first year of training at MUN MED. By that time Andrew, in his last year of training, was often seen in the company of a family practice resident named Shirley Turner.

SHIRLEY

Shirley Jane Turner was born on January 28, 1961, in Wichita, Kansas, to an American father and a Newfoundland mother. Her parents separated when she was about seven years old, and she went with her mother to live in the tiny seaside village of Daniel's Harbour on the west coast of the island of Newfoundland. At the age of sixteen she enrolled in Sir Wilfred Grenfell College, a satellite of MUN located in Corner Brook, on the west coast of Newfoundland. She was, according to fellow student Rene Pollett, "by far one of the most intelligent and funny people I'd ever met... She would get 98s and 100s on chemistry exams... All in our circle of friends were amazed by her academic abilities."[1]

Pollett, who grew up in a "comfortable middle-class home" in Corner Brook, became fast friends with Shirley, whose childhood was spent in "desperate poverty in rural Newfoundland." Near the end of their college friendship, talking of future plans, Shirley considered a career in nursing. Pollett set her friend straight: "Forget that. With your marks, you should be a doctor."

In 1981, less than a year away from an undergraduate degree in chemistry, Shirley's medical ambitions were temporarily sidetracked by marriage. Even without a degree, Shirley had enough background to qualify as a high-school chemistry teacher in Deer Lake, another small community in western Newfoundland. Shirley and her then husband had two children: a son in 1982 and a daughter in 1985.

Shirley divorced in 1988 to marry her high school sweetheart. They had a daughter in 1990. This second marriage was effectively over when the couple separated in 1991, although the divorce would not be official for another six years. After the separation, the father retained physical custody of their year-old baby, while Shirley's son and her older daughter, aged eight and five, lived with their mother in St. John's.

About two years after the separation, the son and older daughter went to live with their father and his parents, leaving Shirley once again free to pursue her life's ambition—a career in medicine. She quickly completed her bachelor of science in chemistry at Memorial University of Newfoundland and was immediately accepted into medical school, beginning her studies in the fall of 1993.

Shirley's exceptional brain served her well through the academic trials of medical school and her family-practice residency, but her innate confrontational style gave her a reputation as something of a witch among her fellow students, as well as the doctors and nurses on hospital staff. Her love life was also characterized by bouts of extreme confrontation, alternating with periods of normal intimacy.

ANDREW AND SHIRLEY

Andrew first mentioned Shirley to me and Kate during one of our regular weekly telephone chats, sometime in the summer of 1999. She was a resident and he was a clerk on one of his medical school training sessions; they began dating occasionally.

While Andrew was home in California in August 1999, Kate asked if Shirley was his girlfriend. He vehemently denied it, explaining that she was twelve years older than he, with two ex-husbands and three children, and she didn't want another committed relationship—only a friend to party with. Andrew was in perfect agreement, as he needed to focus on finishing school and landing a residency in the intensely competitive field of surgery. Party on! No strings.

Kate had her first direct contact with Shirley when she called our home and asked to speak with Andrew, who was out at the time. Over the next hour, she hardly drew a breath as she related her life story to Kate.

Shirley's stepfather had died and she needed somebody to talk to. This man had been like a father to her, and her mother had abandoned him when he became ill. Shirley did not get on well with her mother, but she loved her stepfather. She could not attend the funeral on the west coast of Newfoundland because of residency commitments.

Kate heard all about the trials and tribulations of the MUN residency program, and about Shirley's two marriages to men who tried to hold her back from her ambition to be a doctor. She wanted nothing more of marriage. She only wanted a friend in Andrew, who she described as such a good listener.

She said she did not have her two oldest children with her because they were so well looked after by their grandparents. Shirley's youngest child, a daughter, was living with her (the child's) father, Shirley's second husband, and his new partner. Shirley had originally planned to work in Labrador after residency, because the provincial government had sponsored her financially through medical school, but had since changed her mind. She decided instead to go to America, because she could earn more money and have more freedom there. She would be farther from her children, but she could always pay for them to visit if they wanted to come. None of her children had wanted to join her to live in America because, she said, they were scared of the prospect of big towns.

When they finally hung up the phone, Kate said, "Phew! She seems nice enough, but it's tough to end the conversation."

A few days later I answered the phone and was soon swamped in Shirley's patter. About thirty minutes into her monologue, I lost patience and excused myself with a false declaration that someone was at the door. We uttered hurried goodbyes and hung up the phone. After that, Kate and I nearly always screened our telephone calls.

Andrew worked out his own solution to this dilemma, as I learned one evening when he was visiting us in California. Shirley called and he went upstairs to speak with her in private, using our bedside phone. Not knowing that, I went upstairs and found him sitting on the bed with the phone at his ear, reading a book. When he heard me come up, he turned, smiled, raised his eyebrows, and gently shook his head. Later he explained, "I don't have to say much—an occasional 'yeah, uh-huh', just to let her know I'm still there."

Kate and I first met Shirley in person in September 1999 when she took a side trip from a job-hunting excursion to visit Andrew in California. He picked her up at the airport and brought her directly to the wedding reception of a friend. I thought she was quite attractive, sort of cute, and just about the same size Kate had been when we were married: five feet tall and a little under a hundred pounds. The conversation was all light and fluffy and, since I could wander in and out, it didn't feel like purgatory. That was the only occasion in which Andrew and Shirley were in California at the same time. She would visit Kate and me twice more, but never again while Andrew was there.

During the Christmas break of 2000, Shirley took her three children to Disneyland, and asked if she could stay with Kate and me for a couple of days on the way there and a couple more on the way back. We readily agreed, and the two stopovers were pleasant enough, but we gained no additional insight into her character. At the time, we didn't know how important her character would turn out to be.

The following summer, 2001, Shirley again asked if she could stay with us for a few days, accompanied by her college chum Rana, Rana's husband Greg, and their five-month-old baby, Aaron. Again, Kate and I agreed, and quickly liked Greg and Rana, and vied for cuddle time with Aaron. Shirley didn't seem much interested in the baby, but we didn't mind; it gave us more time with him. I think it was Rana who observed that, when our time came, we were going to make wonderful grandparents. Kate and I had often talked about it and the timing would have been just about right: when Andrew finished his residency, settled into a medical practice, married some lovely young lady and had some bouncy little babies, we would be ready to retire and move near him to act as the wonderful grandparents we couldn't wait to be. That had been the general plan for the last few decades of our lives.

One Sunday evening during Shirley's visit, driving back to our home in Sunnyvale from a day at the wineries in Napa Valley, Shirley delivered a very strange announcement: "I'd like to have another baby. I think I could do a better job as a mother now." Rana and Kate simultaneously voiced their astonishment, saying something along the lines of, Are you nuts?! You already have three children who don't even live with you, the medical career you've been after all your life is finally underway, and you want to have another baby! She had no definitive answer to that, except that she wanted the father to be a doctor.

Our first personal experience with Shirley's erratic emotional swings came that evening. Greg and I had taken turns paying for meals the previous evening and throughout the day, so Shirley declared that she would treat us to dinner at a fondue restaurant that Andrew had told her about. Kate pointed out that it was very expensive, but Shirley insisted that it was no problem, so off we went.

Newfoundlanders bear the brunt of a great many jokes in Canada, based largely on a stereotypical dumb fisherman—a "Newfie"—who is the product of too much inbreeding, eats strange food, and drinks a foul rum known as "screech." Newfoundlanders' responses to this term vary dramatically; some laugh it off, some consider it an endearing part of their heritage, and some are deeply offended.

Sitting around the table watching our fondue cook, Shirley got a perverse kick out of putting a Newfie twist into whatever we talked about. After a while, Greg had heard enough and said something like, I grew up in Newfoundland and it's a good place to live and work and raise a family, and I get a little tired of the negative stereotype that gets thrown around sometimes.

He said it gently, trying not to poison the atmosphere, but Shirley stormed out of the room. After a few minutes of uncomfortable silence, Kate excused herself and went in search of Shirley. She was in the ladies' room, literally crying on the shoulder of a complete stranger. She turned to Kate and said, "Greg and Rana are using you as a cheap hotel! I hope you realize that!"

Obviously, it had not occurred to Shirley that, if Greg and Rana were abusing our hospitality, so was she. They both returned to the table and we struggled through the remainder of an uncomfortable dinner.

When the check arrived, Shirley grumbled about the huge total: "I guess you all expect the rich doctor to pay for this!"

Even though the dinner had been her idea, Greg and I each put roughly our share of money on the table.

Before our guests returned to Canada, Shirley gave us one more glimpse into her extraordinary sense of values. On Tuesday morning, September 11, 2001, Kate, Greg, Rana, and I were gaping at the television, horrified by the images of two airplanes successively barrelling into the World Trade Center. Shirley strolled into the living room, glanced at the television, and enthusiastically announced that she had just arranged the telephone connection at her new apartment in Council Bluffs, Iowa. The rest of us turned as one to stare at her, unable to comprehend how the murder of thousands of people could be overshadowed in her mind by the successful arrangement of a routine telephone hookup.

Five weeks later, on October 20, we saw Shirley when she accompanied Andrew at the Pittsburgh wedding of his long-time friends Karl and Marci. Kate noticed that Andrew seemed slightly ill at ease during the reception, but neither of us noted any exceptional behaviour on Shirley's part. We hugged Andrew and said goodbye several days later, before our return flight to California.

CHAPTER 3
NOTIFICATION

Tuesday morning, November 6, 2001, began as a normal work-day. Kate treated OB/GYN patients at Santa Clara Valley Medical Center while I wrote telecommunications test procedures for Ditech Communications Corporation.

At 8:40 a.m. California time, Kate was between patients when a call came in out of the blue from Shirley. She obviously knew that Kate was working, yet she engaged in idle chit-chat, telling Kate that her hospital privileges had been approved, and that she was going home to wash her hair and tidy up before returning to the hospital clinic for an 11:30 appointment with a patient. Then Shirley casually asked if Kate had heard from Andrew lately. Kate hadn't. Shirley said that she had been home all day Monday with a migraine headache that had started on Sunday, and she asked if Kate was busy. With two patients wait-ing, Kate was, so they hung up the phone.

Twenty minutes later, Shirley called Kate again and asked if she had heard from Andrew, adding that she had tried his home and cellphones with no luck. She said that she had last spoken with Andrew by telephone on Sunday, and that he had sounded "very happy." After a little more chit-chat, they hung up again.

In a third call a short time later Shirley initiated a long rambling conversation. The Pennsylvania State Police had called her boss seeking information on her recent whereabouts. Her boss had reported that she called in sick with a migraine on Monday, but was back at work today, Tuesday. Kate speculated that perhaps Shirley had lost a credit card the last time she was in Pennsylvania and suggested that she call the Pennsylvania police and find out exactly what the problem was.

Shirley then asked Kate to call Andrew's hospital and have him paged. She could not do it herself, she said, because she "had a history" with the switchboard operator.

Kate heard a voice in the background on Shirley's end of the line. Shirley said that it was her nurse and she told the nurse (with Kate overhearing) that she had heard nothing else from Pennsylvania. Then Shirley told Kate that she had spoken with her nurse the night before and that, because of her migraine, the nurse was the only person she had spoken with. Kate thought that seemed an odd piece of information, but still made nothing significant out of it.

Shirley then referred to the policeman's call in a way that finally aroused Kate's concern: "If it's Greensburg, it must be about Andrew, mustn't it?" Perhaps it was the connection of "policeman," "Greensburg," and "Andrew," or perhaps it was a subconscious recognition of the phony innocence in Shirley's voice. Whatever the cause, Kate's anxiety reflex kicked in—her bowels started to churn.

They promised to call each other if they learned anything and then they hung up the phone. Then Kate made two quick trips to the restroom.

Around 2:30 p.m. California time, a Sunnyvale, California police officer called Kate at work and told her to phone the coroner's office in Greensburg, Pennsylvania. Kate put it all together—"policeman," "Greensburg," "Andrew," and now "coroner"—and drew the worst possible inference. Fighting panic, desperately hoping there was some other explanation, she asked, "Is my son dead?" The officer said that he could not tell her, that she should call the number, and that there was dreadful news.

In full panic now, Kate called the number and a gruff voice told her that this was the courthouse, which was closed, and she would have to call back the next day.

Straining for control, Kate called back the Sunnyvale police officer and was given a second number in Greensburg, this time for the Pennsylvania State Police barracks.

She dialled, identified herself, and was connected to a Sergeant Krulac, who told her as gently as he could (there is no *good* way to give a parent such news) that Andrew was dead "under suspicious circumstances." Kate collapsed, unable to focus, unable to think—only to feel a terrible crushing helpless hopeless despair. When she recovered enough to function at a minimal level, Krulac told her that Andrew had been murdered, and that it had taken place in a park. Kate hung up the phone and dialled my work number.

I picked up the phone to hear Kate's desolate cry, "Andrew's dead! He's been murdered!"

I screamed, "No!" threw the phone down on the desk, jumped out of my chair, and started to hyperventilate.

Recovering enough to snatch up the phone again, I asked something practical: "Where are you?"

Kate's voice was weak but clear: "At work."

Then I suggested something truly stupid: "Stay there. I'll come to you." I could not have driven my car out of a parking space, much less across town to Kate's office. I probably could not even find my car.

Kate was a step ahead of me: "Get someone to take you home; I'll meet you there."

I hung up the phone and stumbled out of my cubicle and around the corner looking for Paul, my boss. His cubicle was in the next hallway and I met him coming around to see what the commotion was about. I moaned, "Andrew's dead. Can you take me home?"

He was stunned, but took control, saying, "I don't have my car at work today, but I'll get you a ride," and he turned and disappeared back up the hallway.

Paul couldn't have been gone more than a few seconds, but I was seething in a high-energy cauldron of rage and despair. I had to do *something*, so I straight-ahead heel-kicked a six-foot grey metal storage cabinet.

He came back with Jon, a co-worker, who led me out to the parking lot and helped me into the passenger seat of his van. All the way home, I could only think, "No!" and twist and squirm in the seat. The pain would not go away. I was marginally aware of what we were doing and where we were going, so even in this state of agony I was able to give Jon simple hand-signal directions to my house.

Kate wasn't home yet when we arrived. I unlocked the front door and went in and threw myself on the living room floor and moaned, "No, no, no!" over and over again. Denial still didn't work—the pain *would not* go away.

I got to my feet and stumbled across the street to a friend's house. Barbara answered the doorbell and I told her, "Andrew's dead!" She couldn't take away the pain, either, and added her own to the mix. She came back across the street with me and we waited for Kate to come home. I wanted to hold her, as if that would somehow ease the pain. I have no recollection of how long Jon stayed, of who brought Kate home, or of how long they stayed. I was focused entirely on Kate.

When she finally arrived, we held each other and sobbed and moaned and tried to think, but nothing was distinct through the blind fog of despair. One of us cleared our head enough to decide that Kate and I had to go to Andrew. I gave my credit card to Barbara, who used the upstairs phone to get Kate and me a 10 p.m. flight to Pittsburgh, the closest major airport to Latrobe.

Kate called Shirley and learned that a Pennsylvania policeman had called and told her of Andrew's death, and that he had asked Shirley not to talk to us until we had been officially notified. She had agreed, she said, and had "gone to the mall to try and forget." She said that it must be awful for us, as she knew how much we loved him, but that she had loved him, too. She said that Andrew had been happy on Thursday (November 1) when they had been to a hockey game. Kate promised to call her when we got to Pittsburgh.

The next few hours were a blur, but some critical things got done. Family and friends were notified, some clothes and a toilet bag were stuffed into a suitcase, someone brought Kate's car from her work, someone brought my car and briefcase from my work, the current bills were piled on the kitchen table, and we cried and wailed and moaned until we could not physically stand to cry any more. And then we cried some more.

A couple of hours before flight time, Barbara and her husband Virgil loaded us into their car and headed for the San Francisco airport. On the way Virgil thought of our meaningless will, which left all our worldly possessions to Andrew. If the plane to Pittsburgh crashed we would thankfully be free of our misery, but our net worth would be distributed who-knew-how, so outside the terminal at SFO we scribbled a brief new will, dividing our assets among our siblings and their families.

Once the plane was in the air, most passengers tried to sleep, but we had far too much tortured energy to relax. We cried as quietly as we could and talked out what we wanted to do next, coming up with a new and very simple plan for our lives: get Andrew's body and take it home, settle our estate formally, and kill ourselves. Throughout the five-hour flight we went through variations on the same theme: "I don't need this. There's nothing else I want to do without Andrew in the world. Fuck this. I'm done. I don't want to get out of bed every day without Andrew somewhere in the world."

At one point we became dimly aware of a controversy among some other passengers across the aisle and a few rows up. Some people on a business trip were complaining about the lack of pillows on the flight, spawning the same thought for both Kate and me: "I wish I could consider that a problem."

We were met in the Pittsburgh airport lobby by two Pennsylvania State Police officers, one in uniform and one, Trooper Ray Andrekanic, in plain clothes. They led us out to the main lobby where we spotted Karl and Marci (Andrew had been best man at their wedding three weeks before) and fell into another round of hugs and tears. Their names had already come up in the investigation and the police wanted to interview them, so they agreed to go straight back to the police's Greensburg barracks, where Trooper Andrekanic was taking Kate and me.

On the way, he gently asked a few questions about Andrew's friends and workmates, and whether he had any interest in guns. It wasn't a detailed interview, but he got a little information from us. In hindsight, it was the first of several talks with the police in which nearly all information flow was from us to them. That was the way it should be: they needed information fast, and they needed to avoid contamination of information by revealing as little as possible about their current thinking. They also needed to handle us with silk gloves to prevent further damage to our shattered psyches.

At the Greensburg barracks we were ushered into the office of Lieutenant Robert Weaver, who came around his desk and enfolded Kate in a huge hug and said, "I don't know exactly how you're feeling, but my son committed suicide seven years ago, so I guess I have some idea."

"Good God," I thought, "that's the only thing worse than this!"

More officers came into the room, a sequence of faces blurred through tears: Trooper Mike McElfresh (the lead investigator), Corporal Donna Defelice, Sergeant Krulac, and Renee Kidney (victim and witness assistant). They all sat in a rough semicircle facing Weaver's desk while he gave a synopsis of what they knew: Andrew's body had been found early yesterday morning (Tuesday). He had been shot five times. Nothing had been stolen, so it wasn't a robbery. There were two shots in the rectal area and a wound on the head, so the killer was angry—it was a crime of passion. It had been a quick and painless end.

Kate and I listened and cried, and I swore a lot. Kate asked if they had a suspect in mind. "Shirley Turner," Weaver said. Kate asked if he wanted us to talk to her, or not, since she had promised to call Shirley once we were in Pennsylvania. He said, "I can't advise you on that."

Then Weaver said that Deputy Coroner Dennis Johns wanted to talk to us. Everyone but Kate and I left the room and Johns came in. He sat in the lieutenant's chair and gave us a brief report on the cause of death: gunshot wounds, quick and painless. We told him we needed to see Andrew. He didn't think that was a good idea. We insisted. On this point there was no room for compromise.

It was at this point that Renee Kidney, the victim support officer, took charge of the arrangements, leading me to a different room where I first had to select a mortuary. She was not allowed to suggest one, and I knew nothing about them and cared even less, so she held up the Yellow Pages and I pointed to one at random: Bacha Funeral Directors in Greensburg. Kidney said it was a good choice.

Next, we had to decide if we wanted to have Andrew embalmed. Kidney intimated that we would probably not want to see him in his current post-autopsy condition. I was, and am, absolutely certain that she was right about that.

With those arrangements made, I felt a new surge of rage boiling up again and, afraid that I was about to lose control completely, I ran out the side door of the barracks. I remember throwing my coat at the ground and screaming obscenities at the universe: "You goddamned son-of-a-bitch! You mother-fucking bastard!" And so on until most of the pressure was released. I had not heard Weaver's reference to Shirley as the prime suspect, so I had no clue who this bastard might be, but I hated him or her with all my soul. Once the rage abated I picked up my coat and went back inside.

Trooper Andrekanic drove us to Latrobe Area Hospital where Andrew had worked. We were ushered into the office of Dr. John Bertolino, head of the Family Practice residency program. More hugs. More tears. I lost it again, ran outside, shook the high chain-link fence and raged against the universe once more. Dr. Bertolino came out right behind me, waited for me to settle down a little, and led me back to his office, saying something on the way that struck me as very odd: "You gave me your son and I didn't protect him."

At the time, Dr. Bertolino was a complete stranger to me and I wasn't the least bit analytical, but hindsight has allowed me to reconsider his comment. It wasn't odd at all. Decent people strive to do good things and hate to see bad things happen anywhere around them. And they most hate bad things to happen in their domain, what they consider their sphere of influence. He could not have foreseen Andrew's killing or done anything to prevent it, but in his gut he felt it happened *on his watch*, so he felt some hint of responsibility. Not justified, but part of the character that is built into decent people.

Another blurred sequence of faces came through Dr. Bertolino's office. Bill DiCuccio, one of Andrew's fellow residents, and Clark Simpson, the chief resident, were the only two I remember, because they stayed longer than the others. They turned out to be among Andrew's closest friends at the hospital and soon became our good friends, too.

Dr. Bertolino asked if they could hold a memorial service for Andrew, and we absolutely refused; he was ours! We would see what the police found out, take Andrew home to California, hold a service there, and then think of something to do with the rest of our lives. (Double suicide had already receded as our foremost goal, with nothing yet to replace it.) Dr. Bertolino graciously dropped the subject.

Latrobe Area Hospital maintains a group of houses and apartments for use by young doctors in their residency programs, and Andrew had lived in one of these directly across the street from the Family Practice office. Dr. Bertolino offered to put us up in another of these houses that was currently vacant. We accepted and were led to a small cottage on Tacoma Street, less than a two-minute walk from his office. He and his secretary, Rhonda Anderson, made sure we had the basic necessities and then left us to our private misery. Karl and Marci appeared for a short time and then went off to buy some groceries, as this was to be our home until the police finished their investigation.

Many years before Andrew was murdered, Kate had done some volunteer work with an organization called the Centre for Living with Dying, which provided emotional support and counselling to people who had lost a loved one to death. After an intensive training program, she took on several clients over a period of several years, listening to them vent their sorrows, frustrations, fears and anxieties; and providing succour plus practical advice on coping with severe loss. One of the coping tools Kate recommended to some of her clients was journaling, and here in Latrobe, twenty-four hours after learning of our son's murder, she recognized that we would probably benefit from the exercise. She also had a vague feeling that the details of our daily activities since Andrew's murder might have some significance in the police investigation, although she did not yet crystallize these feelings into thoughts about Shirley Turner's behaviour. Once Kate determined that we should keep journals, a phone call to Rhonda yielded several pads of paper and pens. Since that day, we have semi-religiously put our thoughts and feelings on paper, and these journals have provided not only an emotional outlet to help keep us sane, but invaluable source material for this book.

Sometime in the early afternoon Lieutenant Weaver and Corporal Defelice picked us up at the Tacoma Street house and drove us to the crime scene, which was a gravel parking lot about two hundred feet off of Route 981, at Keystone State Park a few miles north of Latrobe. Weaver showed us where Andrew's body and car had been found, and gave us a brief description of the search activity. Forensics had finished with the scene, collecting spent shell casings, cigarette butts, and tire castings, but so far no weapon had been recovered. The bloody area where our baby had lain was covered in a thin layer of sand. Kate knelt and prayed for him. We milled around in desolation a few more minutes and then rode back to Tacoma Street.

Troopers McElfresh and Andrekanic and two hospital representatives appeared at the door late in the afternoon and led us over to Andrew's house, where Kate and I had trouble focusing on anything practical; all we could see was Andrew's absence. Upstairs, McElfresh and I went through a pile of photos, some of which were of Andrew's friends. With no particular emphasis he asked if any of these photos was Shirley Turner. I went back through the pile and there were none.

Down in the living room, Kate and I slumped onto Andrew's sofa while McElfresh conducted a gentle but thorough interview. He and Andrekanic took detailed notes as we talked about what we knew of Andrew's relationships with his family, friends, and especially his workmates. Clark Simpson had been a financial analyst before medical school and had complimented Andrew on his IRA investments. He was also the owner of a collector's edition of Tolkien's *The Lord of the Rings*, one of Andrew's favourite collections of stories. Bill DiCuccio was a kindred spirit who shared Andrew's sense of humour, including the enjoyment of some light heckling of the speaker during group meetings. Shawn Bell was a deer spotter, a position that Andrew was amazed to find he—a California city boy—also enjoyed. Bridget O'Rourke was very shy, so Andrew usually tried to include her in whatever social activity was underway, and they had recently joined a local health club together.

McElfresh took a history of Andrew's career as well, but focused primarily on his friends and lovers. That meant Shirley Turner. We gave him a brief history of their relationship, including her attendance at Karl and Marci's recent wedding and yesterday's phone calls to Kate. During later reflection, we noticed that, as in the ride from the airport, nearly all information flow was from us to the police. Again, that was as it should be.

I read somewhere that, religion aside, the practical function—the psychological roots—of a funeral or a wake or any death ritual lay in the fact that the survivors knew the deceased was really gone, because they had seen the body with their own eyes. Without this personal confirmation there might be a lingering hope that it was all some outrageous mistake. This apparently happens sometimes when a soldier is listed as "Missing in Action." "Maybe my beloved wasn't really killed; his body was never found. Maybe he sneaked away somehow and is evading the enemy until he can slip back over the line to our side. Maybe he was captured and is now slowly wasting away in a POW camp, waiting and praying for rescue. Maybe he will come home to me after this horrible war is over. Maybe this agony will be replaced with a glorious joy and blessed relief when I can see and hold my beloved again!" In virtually every instance, these fragile hopes are eventually shattered on the stone face of reality. But the only way to extinguish them, and thus be free to adjust to the new state of the universe, is to see for yourself. *Look at the body.* Know, from the evidence of your own two eyes, that he is gone. Kate and I didn't think all this through at the time, but we instinctively felt that we had to see *our* beloved.

In the evening, Clark and Bill drove us to Bacha's Mortuary to say goodbye to our baby. Although we had wanted to do this—absolutely had to do this—it was the most dreadful experience of our lives. Mr. Bacha led us to a small conference room and gently told us some things about the arrangements, but I can't remember a single word of that conversation. Then he handed Kate a Bible and took us down a flight of stairs ending in a hallway leading off to the left. At the far end stood a gurney with a body entirely covered in a white sheet, except the head. Kate and I went to him.

When the face was clearly visible, I murmured, "It's really him." Until that moment, there must have been a subconscious kernel of irrational hope, but it was gone now. We sobbed and wailed and moaned. I kissed Andrew's cold dead forehead— like kissing a stone. He was pumped full of embalming fluid and caked with makeup to fill the bullet hole in his face and to mask the autopsy and the pale grey of dead Caucasian skin. The only thing about him that seemed natural was his hair. I wept and I hated. I still did not know who I hated, but I hated them as much as it is possible for one human being to hate another.

Kate clung to Andrew in desperation. She tried to look for something to read for him in the Bible, but couldn't see. She kissed him and caressed him and wept her tears onto his face. Thinking it was one of these tears, she gently wiped a spot on his left cheek, but it wasn't a tear; the mortician's plug that had filled the bullet hole came loose. She gently pushed the plug back in place and wailed even louder and clung to him even tighter. She *could not* let go of him. She seemed to be *willing* him to wake up and grin at her and say, "Lighten up, Mom! Let's go get some dinner! I'm famished!"

Cremation was set for the next day so we knew this was the last time we would ever see our baby. It was excruciating to leave him lying there in a basement covered by a sheet, but it would have been no less excruciating to leave him in a glorious mausoleum. Eventually we did allow Clark and Bill to lead us back up the stairs and out the door and into the car. As in our meeting with Mr. Bacha, I have no memory of anything anyone said on the ride back to Tacoma.

Bill had his favourite photograph of Andrew (with a smile on his face and a beer in his hand), which he planned to put on display in the resident's lounge at the hospital. He also had some of his dad's homemade wine, which we put to good use washing down a roast chicken dinner while we mourned Andrew and got to know each other. Like Kate, Bill was a devout Christian who lived in hope that we would all see Andrew again. Like me, Clark disavowed religion, believing that this life is all we get. On the major practical point, we all agreed: whoever took Andrew away from us was a monster who had to be stopped.

It was during this first in-depth conversation with Clark, in which he recounted Andrew's story of Shirley's Monday morning appearance on his doorstep, that our suspicions of her began to solidify.

Despair is utterly exhausting, so we fell into bed hoping for our first few hours of sleep since yesterday's phone calls had yanked us into this nightmare. But the word was spreading among relatives and friends, so the phone kept ringing with offers of sympathy and support. We answered the first few calls, explaining each time what little we knew and weeping all over again with a different friend or relative. After a few repetitions we unplugged the phone and tried to sleep. There was an image in my mind of physically pushing the horror away—my right hand reaching forward, palm out, slowly sweeping it aside. With the help of this image, exhaustion finally won out over my wildly racing brain and I drifted off.

CHAPTER 4
TLC

As soon as I was conscious again, shortly after dawn on Thursday morning, my first thought was, "It's still true," and the full force of the pain flooded over me again. Images built of words don't come close, but they're all I have: a kick in the head or the solar plexus…a virulent flu burning every muscle of the body, especially the heart.

Kate awoke at about the same time, with the same thought and the same feeling. In seconds, we were both back into tears and rage; in minutes, we were both completely exhausted again, as if we had not slept at all.

In the lulls between meltdowns we managed some practical communication. Did I sleep okay? Most of the night. Kate? Hardly at all. Did we want a cup of tea? I guess so. Shower? Why not. Brush your teeth? Same logic.

Soon the phone calls and visits began; dozens of calls to and from Kate's family in England, mine in Missouri, and long-time friends in California, telling and retelling what little we knew and weeping and raging together. Like us, they were horrified and outraged, but they also provided immeasurable emotional as well as practical support: Carol would collect our mail and pay our bills, Barbara and Virgil would look after the house and water the plants, and Mary Ann would tend Kate's garden. Our bosses would keep our jobs open as long as we needed.

Andrew's fellow residents came by in twos and threes to try and console the grieving parents of their new friend. Together we tried to comprehend how *murder* could happen to our baby and to their friend; we tried to integrate murder's vicious truth into our view of the universe. Denial? Not available, unless we traded away our sanity, which might have been worth the pain relief. God? Kate did not believe that God had orchestrated Andrew's killing, but she wondered why He could not have stopped the killer. Luck? This was my preferred explanation: there is a very small percentage of the population who kill, but they don't display a scarlet K on their foreheads. Andrew just happened to run across one of these people. He had rotten luck.

A proper meal was delivered to our door every evening, thanks to a sign-up sheet posted at the hospital. Sometimes our benefactor would stay and eat with us and sometimes not, but all had some connection to Andrew, so that we quickly discovered the depth of anguish that was circulating around the hospital in the wake of his murder.

It was soon apparent to Kate and me that, although he had only been with them a few months, Andrew had become an integral part of the hospital community. He wasn't only ours; he was partly theirs, too, and they needed to say a proper goodbye. They needed the memorial service we had denied them on our first day in Latrobe.

Jan Mills, whose husband Steve had worked with Andrew, arranged the church, the reception, and the pastor. Reverend David Batchelder conducted the service and delivered a wonderful eulogy in which he first searched for an appropriate word to describe what happened to Andrew. Passing up "tragedy" as inadequate, he settled on "atrocity," which was still far too weak, but came as close as language could get to the awful reality.

Four more services were planned—one at Andrew's medical school alma mater in Newfoundland and one for each of his far-flung homes. A third of his ashes would be buried with those of his grandparents in Missouri, a third in England, and a third in his native California.

Our days in Pennsylvania formed a pattern: wake up, realize that Andrew was still dead, weep and rage, make some tea, read the newspaper, talk for hours on the phone with distant family and friends, and be consoled by a wonderful group of new local friends. Next to pain, pure love is the strongest impression we took away from Latrobe—a place where we now have new friends who will be with us for life. They have known us in the bottom of our pit, and we have known them at the peak of their generosity. As Jan Mills put it, "Our paths, once crossed, can never be uncrossed."

In the midst of all this tender loving care, my rage began to crystallize. At first, I had simply hated, without any firm image of how that hatred might translate into action. At some point I began to envision my hands around a throat, thumbs pushing steadily deeper into a windpipe. There was no body below the throat and no face above, and no struggle, and no sound—just the throat and my hands, and I could feel the soft flesh slowly giving way under the constant pressure of my thumbs. I desperately wanted to know whose face should sit above that throat. Only the police could find that out.

CHAPTER 5
INVESTIGATION

While we waited and wept and raged, the Pennsylvania State Police went about the sombre task of discovering who should be the target of our rage. Though we are by no means expert at criminal investigation, many hours scanning police files have given Kate and me some appreciation of the urgent tedium that is inherent in a real murder investigation, as opposed to the thrilling Hollywood caricature that takes an hour, minus commercials.

As soon as Andrew's body was found, the police initiated the painstaking steps required to collect evidence that could later be presented to a jury: seal off the scene, establish a log of every person who entered and left, photograph and collect every potentially relevant object at or near the scene, measure and record the precise location of each object, and systematically search the surrounding area for any physical evidence—especially the murder weapon.

Andrew's movements leading up to the killing were established through exhaustive interviews, beginning with everyone in the vicinity of Keystone State Park, all of Andrew's associates at Latrobe Area Hospital, and Kate and me. Each interview had the potential to initiate more interviews, as friends, family, and acquaintances reported other associates of Andrew, and thus did Shirley Turner's name come to the attention of police. Clark Simpson reported Andrew's Monday morning "psychotic bitch is on my doorstep" comment, leading police to contact Shirley by telephone at the clinic where she worked in Council Bluffs, Iowa.

FIRST SHIRLEY INTERVIEW

A little after 2 p.m. on Tuesday, November 6, 2001, Corporal Randall Gardner introduced himself, officially informed Shirley of Andrew's death, and commenced a detailed interview of this very important prospective witness and possible suspect.[1] But it took several minutes to get to the point because Shirley kept diverting the conversation into bizarre, irrelevant side topics: she thought that she was losing her Newfoundland accent and wondered if Gardner recognized it (he did not); she thought that the recording of telephone lines at the police station was much like that done at the telephone company; and, her home and cellphones had different area codes because one was in Council Bluffs, Iowa, and the other was in Omaha, Nebraska.

Gardner played along with these digressions to some extent, but always tried to pull the conversation back to Andrew, asking at one point, "When did you last talk to him?" Shirley's response was "Um…I think it was…Sunday." This lie, coming *before* she had been notified of Andrew's murder, would be a key point in the case against her.

A little over three minutes into the interview, Shirley finally asked what any innocent person would have been anxious to know at the outset: "Is this involving Andrew at all or…"

Gardner: "Yeah, I'm afraid it is."
Shirley: "Is he okay?"

Gardner: "No. No. I, I guess I have really bad news to tell
        you. I have to tell you that Andrew is dead."
Shirley: "Are you sure?"
Gardner: "Yes, ma'am, I am. I'm absolutely sure…"

The corporal offered her time to compose herself, but that wasn't necessary. Her voice became strained for a few moments—she seemed flustered—but she recovered and was able to carry on with the interview in a few seconds. He elicited several key statements from Shirley in the remainder of the telephone call.

She was romantically involved with Andrew in a long distance relationship. "We loved each other…we do date other people…we didn't really have a commitment…He did tell me that he had a date that Saturday when I left, and, uh…you know, I…"

Gardner interjected, "You didn't really need to hear that, right?"

"Exactly…we're not supposed to ask and we're not supposed to tell what the other person's doing."

Shirley recounted the rest of her story as follows:

On October 20, Shirley was in Latrobe for Karl and Marci's wedding, after which she went home to Council Bluffs. Friday, October 26, she returned to Latrobe and stayed with Andrew for a week. Saturday, November 3, she returned to Iowa, her departure at the airport being the last time she saw Andrew. Shirley referred to that last week they shared together as "one of the better weeks that we've ever had."

Since Saturday, she had been in Council Bluffs and Omaha, had gone alone to the zoo on Sunday afternoon, and alone to a movie (*Riding In Cars With Boys*) on Sunday evening. After that, she picked up something from

McDonald's, or maybe it was Kentucky Fried Chicken, and went home to dinner, alone. Sunday, she declared, was the last time she talked to Andrew, once in the morning and again in the afternoon, by telephone.

On Monday, Shirley stated, she was home alone all day with a migraine headache, sleeping most of the day. She called her nurse in the morning to say that she wouldn't be in to work, that she was taking medication and unplugging the phone, and that if they needed to contact her they should leave a message on her cellphone. She called the nurse again at about 10:30 in the evening to report that she was feeling better and driving around and to inquire whether she had any patients scheduled for Tuesday.

Tuesday morning, she went to the car wash and the post office, bought gas, and reported to work for an 11:30 appointment with a patient. She drove a Toyota RAV4.

A long way into the interview, after all the information above had been covered, Shirley remarked, "So far you haven't asked any offensive questions." Gardner replied, "Well, I'm gonna," and soon launched into a critical phase of the interview.

Asked if she owned any guns, Shirley said that she did own "a small hand pistol…like a .22…it should be in a case… either in my closet or my bedroom. Or it's in the car."

She agreed to meet with the local Council Bluffs police, to give them a statement and to turn in her gun for ballistic examination.

Five hours after this first interview, Shirley telephoned Gardner to report that her gun was missing. The case, she said, was in her car, which was locked and had not been broken into, but the gun itself was missing. In the midst of this conversation, Sergeant Jerry Mann and Detective Robert Sellers of the

Council Bluffs Police Department arrived at her door. Gardner advised her to talk to them and they hung up the phone.

SECOND SHIRLEY INTERVIEW

Before commencing this face-to-face interview, Shirley was asked to sign a statement waiving her right to remain silent and to obtain legal counsel before talking to police—standard procedure based on the well known 1966 United States Supreme Court decision in *Miranda v. Arizona*. Shirley signed the waiver.[2]

Sergeant Mann then turned on a tape recorder and began the interview with the statement that he thought that she had *gone to* Pennsylvania on Saturday, November 3. Shirley corrected him and recounted her week-long trip to visit Andrew, ending with her *return from* Pennsylvania on Saturday.

Mann took a brief history of her relationship with Andrew, from their first meeting in about June 1999 to the present, and their plans for the future—Shirley had airline tickets for another four-day weekend visit to Latrobe at the end of November.

Then he got down to the first critical issue—means. On October 11, 2001, Shirley had obtained a permit to purchase a handgun. On October 16, she purchased a handgun "for protection," she said. Asked why she felt the need for protection, she said, "Yes. It's actually something that I've been intending to do, ever since I moved to the United States, a single woman, living alone. I have a couple of friends who have been encouraging me…one…even recommended what type of gun to get… And he also recommended I get a German shepherd, but I don't like dogs…"

She had taken three shooting lessons from an instructor at an Omaha pistol range called The Bullet Hole.

Asked if she had taken the gun with her to Latrobe on Friday, October 26, Shirley said, "No, I did not."

Asked where the gun was when she left Iowa on October 26, Shirley said, "It should have been in the case," and added a lot of confusing detail about a possible missed appointment with the instructor.

Mann asked, "Shirley, the question I have for you is this, what happened to the gun?" Shirley said, "I honestly don't know."

Mann offered to let her take a break, but she said, "No, I'm okay."

Shirley went on about what happened to the gun: "My best guess is I can't see somebody coming into my apartment and going into my closet and knowing it was in that case and just taking the gun, I mean I have other things here, you would think somebody would steal. That is what they wanted. So my best guess would be…must have been while it was in the car. And it has on occasion been in the car for a full day and maybe even overnight by accident. I always try and lock my car, I'm really good about that as well, so I really don't have, you know, an explanation."

They sparred a while longer, arriving at no satisfactory explanation for the missing gun (neither her apartment nor her car had been broken into), before Mann addressed the second critical issue—motive.

Asked if she knew of anyone who would want to harm Andrew, she said, "No, I don't." Mann specifically probed whether Shirley had heard of any neighbours or patients, or perhaps financial dealings that would point to someone who might wish to harm Andrew. She said, "Again, not that I'm aware of."

Did she know of anyone else who might be especially close to Andrew? Shirley replied that Andrew had told her about a clerk in radiology that he was interested in, and she guessed that he was probably attempting to make her "a little bit jealous because he was a little bit jealous over someone that I had been dating."

Mann asked Shirley about Andrew's colleagues and friends at Latrobe, rehashed some of her previous answers, and then turned the questioning over to Detective Sellers, who ratcheted up the pressure.

Sellers asked if she loved Andrew. She said, "Yes, I did."

"Did he love you back?"

"Yes, he did."

"Did you guys have any plans for future marriage or anything like that?"

Shirley said, "No...I guess we called it a special relationship...I didn't want another commitment, because I've been married and divorced twice. And I'm older than Andrew, I'm forty and he's twenty-eight."

"He's twenty-eight?"

"Yeah. He was honest, he said five or ten years from now he would, you know, like to meet the right woman, someone his age maybe or whatever."

Sellers asked, "Did he ever try to break off the relationship with you?"

Shirley said, "Not really," and rambled on about their occasional disagreements and their "mature" relationship and Andrew's "plans with this other woman."

Sellers asked if Shirley was jealous of the radiology clerk and she said, "I don't think so...the only thing that I didn't like was that he told me [about their planned date] the day that I was leaving." Shirley said that Andrew and she had discussed the radiology clerk over lunch at the airport on the Saturday she left Latrobe: "I heard that she was upset, because somebody had been saying things to her…I wanted to make sure that I didn't upset her, I didn't want to do that."

Sellers shifted from congeniality to civil confrontation:

Sellers: "…as detectives…one of the things we are trained in is body language. I'm getting the distinct feeling that you are not telling us everything you know…that you are not being totally truthful. Now I'm not saying necessarily that you killed Andrew, I'm not saying that. But…one of the things I'm getting the feeling about is the firearm. Do you know where the firearm is?"

Shirley: "No, I don't."

Sellers: "When you were talking about the firearm earlier, clearly I'm thinking you do know where it is now; is it possible, did you take it with you to Pennsylvania?"

Shirley: "No, I didn't."

Sellers: "I'm not saying you used it to harm him, but did you take it with you out there and leave it for him?"

Shirley: "No, I didn't."

Sellers: "[Is there] any way he could have gotten your weapon?"

Shirley: "I don't see how…"

Sellers: "If you didn't take it and he didn't come and get it, there is no way it would have been out there, is that right?"

Shirley: "Not that I'm aware of."

Sellers: "Once again, I'm getting the feeling you are not being truthful with me. Nobody is saying…"

Shirley: "I don't know how to say it any different."

As later evidence would demonstrate, Shirley was a very experienced liar and manipulator, so Sellers was not likely to break her story in a short interview, but he certainly tried.[3]

SHOOTING INSTRUCTOR

Immediately after Mann and Sellers terminated the interview and left Shirley's apartment, she called one of her few acquaintances in the Council Bluffs area, the handgun instructor. As he later reported to police, she was crying and "a bit incoherent," but managed to relate the basics of her story: a friend of hers in Pennsylvania had been killed, she could not find her gun, and "the police think I did it." The instructor had "a sick feeling" when she told him the gun was missing, and didn't want to get involved any further "just in case she had done it."[4]

Regarding Shirley's gun, he told police during his subsequent interview that it was a Phoenix Arms .22 calibre single action semi-automatic of poor quality, sometimes failing to feed properly and ejecting a live round onto the ground. In an attempt to correct the problem, Shirley had switched ammunition from American Eagle to CCI Stinger, which was "somewhat better but still malfunctioned."

The instructor had only spent a few hours with Shirley, teaching her the basic use and maintenance of her weapon and going for coffee once after class. He suspected that "she may have had the hots" for him, but he never dated students. He "appeared to be upset" at the possibility that he might have trained someone in the use of a weapon to commit a murder.

Shirley also told him that she "might have misspoken" to the police during their interview. He didn't ask what "misspoken" meant, and she didn't elaborate.

WHERE'S THE GUN?

The first variation on her gun's location came early the next morning, Wednesday, November 7, when Shirley, crying and distraught, called Corporal Gardner to report that she had not been truthful yesterday. She had not misplaced the gun and it was not stolen; she had given the gun to Andrew, she said. She added, "There was a lot [the police] didn't know about Andrew."

Shirley was well acquainted with Andrew's circle of medical school friends, having partied with them on numerous occasions. She considered them to be her friends, as well. Over the next few days, she telephoned several of these people to talk about Andrew's murder and, in the process, she related several more variations on the gun's location. On November 9, to Chad Burkhart, she reported that she and Andrew had gotten back together, and that she had last seen him on Monday (the day he was killed). Burkhart was absolutely certain she said Monday. He didn't ask her specifically *where* she saw Andrew on Monday, but he did ask about newspaper articles reporting that she had given Andrew a gun. She denied both reading the articles and giving Andrew a gun. (Note that this was *after* she told Gardner that she gave Andrew the gun.) She also said that she had an attorney who advised her not to talk to anyone. Fortunately for the progress of the investigation, the attorney may as well have advised spontaneous combustion to a block of ice.

About two days later—approximately November 11—she added two more details, telling Andrew Zohrab (another member of Andrew's medical school cohort) via telephone that she had taken a gun to the park and given it to Andrew on the Monday night he was killed.

So far, then, the essence of Shirley's statements had progressed from "I was home with a migraine when Andrew was shot, I never took my gun to Pennsylvania, and I will turn my gun over to police for ballistic examination" to "my gun is missing" to "I gave my gun to Andrew" to "I didn't give my gun to Andrew," and finally to "I took my gun to Pennsylvania and gave it to Andrew in the park the night he was killed." Why the changes?

In a later phone call to Zohrab, he asked her about media reports of contradictory statements concerning the gun. She replied, "Yes, I know. So, I lied, I know. Given the state I was in, anyone would feel uneasy, and it's only natural to perhaps lie in that state."

Zohrab asked her if she was in Pennsylvania for a week and flew home to Iowa and then drove back to Pennsylvania. She said,

> Yeah. Andrew called me and asked me to bring him the gun. He offered to buy me a plane ticket, but since a gun can't be taken on a plane I took it to him by car. I made the drive in twelve hours and got there in the morning, but didn't give him the gun right then. I saw him again at lunch and again that evening. He put the gun in a bag in the trunk of his car.

Despite extensive searches in the area around the parking lot, including Search and Rescue Team dives into the nearby lake, the gun was never found, and almost certainly never will be found. It could have been discarded anywhere between Latrobe and Council Bluffs, under any convenient body of water, or wrapped in paper and tossed into any available dumpster, which would put it in a landfill awaiting discovery by some future archeologist. Or, perhaps Shirley's latest story was the truth. Perhaps she gave Andrew the gun, he put it in his trunk, she drove away, and, before *he* could drive away, the actual killer appeared. This hypothetical killer struck up a conversation with Andrew, who, for some unknown reason, took the gun out of the trunk. The killer, again for some unknown reason, managed to take possession of the gun, shoot Andrew with it and disappear, taking the gun with him, and leaving Shirley in one hell of a spot.

CIRCUMSTANTIAL EVIDENCE

The case against Shirley Turner was almost entirely circumstantial, which garners little respect in popular culture, as if the
evidence isn't real. In fact, circumstantial evidence is *not*
absolutely conclusive; hence—popular mythology goes—the
prosecution can't prove guilt. Judi Petrush, the Assistant
District Attorney handling Shirley's case, explained circumstantial evidence to Kate and me using a simple example from
the Standard Civil Jury Instructions used in Pennsylvania: "You
are sitting in your windowless office on a winter day when an
associate enters with snowflakes clinging to his coat. Based on
the circumstantial evidence of snow on the coat, you draw the
quite sensible inference that it is snowing outside."

While there may be other explanations for snow on the
associate's coat (he stashed a snowball in the freezer from a
previous storm and is having a little fun at your expense?) you
are entitled to draw the simplest, most obvious conclusion
from the given evidence. But should someone be sentenced to
prison for life based on such evidence? Probably not, if there is
only one circumstance. But what if there are multiple circumstances and they all point to the same conclusion?
Fundamentally, it is a question of probabilities. More and
more circumstances imply a higher and higher probability,
until finally the conclusion must be accepted *beyond a reasonable doubt*, which is the legal standard for determination of
guilt in a criminal trial.

Vincent Bugliosi (famous for prosecuting the Charles
Manson family in the 1970s) used a rope metaphor to explain
circumstantial evidence to the jury in a double-murder case:

> Circumstantial evidence is not, as they [defense counsel]
> claim, like a chain. You could have a chain spanning the

Atlantic Ocean from Nova Scotia to Bordeaux, France, consisting of millions of links, and with one weak link that chain is broken.

Circumstantial evidence, to the contrary, is like a rope. And each fact is a strand of that rope. And as the prosecution piles one fact upon another we add strands and we add strength to that rope. If one strand breaks— and I'm not conceding for a moment that any strand has broken in this case—but if one strand does break, the rope is not broken. The strength of the rope is barely diminished. Why? Because there are so many other strands of almost steel-like strength that the rope is still more than strong enough to bind these two defendants to justice. That's what circumstantial evidence is all about.[5]

ANDREW WANTED OUT

Kate and I never pried into Andrew's love life and he did not volunteer much information to us. However, during the months leading up to his murder, he dropped several very strong hints that his relationship with Shirley was over and that he was quite happy to see the end of it. Hints like, "I don't expect you'll be hearing much from Shirley anymore," and "Why is it that some women have to make such a big deal out of breaking up." On several occasions in the months leading up to his murder, Andrew mentioned how isolated Shirley was in Iowa, with very little social life and almost no opportunity to meet unattached men near her age. It is true that right up to the week before he was killed—October 26 to November 3— Andrew entertained Shirley at his home, or at least didn't turn her away. But she *nearly always* went to visit him; he only visited her once in Iowa, a long time before the murder.

On July 21, four months before the murder, Andrew was best man at his friend Matt's wedding. At breakfast on the wedding day, Matt overheard Andrew's side of five or six harassing telephone calls from Shirley, who was upset at not being invited to join Andrew. His anger grew with each call, until he finally exploded, "What is your fucking problem!" and hung up on her. He then turned off his cellphone to avoid further interruptions, but when he later turned it back on, Shirley had left over 30 angry messages in his voice mailbox.

The last time Kate and I visited Andrew in Pennsylvania, the weekend of October 20, Shirley was his date for a wedding in which he was once again the best man. As a child, Andrew had a habit of blinking under stressful situations and Kate noticed that he was often blinking during the wedding festivities.

Around October 23, two weeks before the murder, Andrew told medical-school friend Ken Eckhert that he and Shirley had broken up because he was "losing interest in the long-distance relationship" and it was "going downhill."

On Monday, November 5, the day he was killed, Andrew told Clark Simpson that he "had broken up with [Shirley] over the weekend," and that he was going to meet her after work to "send her on her way."

That makes at least five people (Matt, Kate, Ken, Clark, and me) who reported to police that Andrew wanted out of the relationship, whereas Shirley told several different people several different stories on their status: he had never really tried to end it, they had broken up at her instigation, and they had gotten back together. Definitely circumstantial and definitely not conclusive, but there is no reasonable doubt that Andrew was dumping Shirley, providing a possible motive and thereby increasing the probability that she killed him.

BABY CONFLICT

Andrew's ex-fiancée, Heather Arnold, became acquainted with Shirley during the 1999–2000 school year—Heather's first and Andrew's fourth at MUN MED. During the last few weeks before the murder, Shirley called Heather several times seeking friendly female advice. She claimed to be pregnant with Andrew's baby and complained that he "wanted her to have an abortion and he was becoming cold, mean, and verbally abusive towards her."[6] Some time later, she told Heather that a miscarriage had obviated the need for an abortion. Shirley's overall credibility was close to zero but, if this story were true, Andrew's "cold, mean" determination not to be the father of her baby could certainly provide a motive for murder.

FAULTY WEAPON

Shirley's gun had an occasional malfunction that kicked out unspent shell casings. An unspent casing was found next to Andrew's body. Obviously lots of guns besides Shirley's exhibited the same faulty behaviour, but it was another circumstance adding to the growing probability that her gun was the murder weapon.

LIAR, LIAR

Two years before the murder, one of Shirley's residency supervisors at the medical school wrote her a negative evaluation, igniting a flurry of hostility: yelling, crying, and accusations of unfair treatment. In an exceptional display of lying acumen, Shirley declared that all of her previous evaluations had been above average and that no other medical supervisor had ever had a problem with her performance. Both statements were easy to check and both statements were false, but she had no trouble arguing them forcefully to her supervisor's face. After this unpleasant encounter, the wary physician adopted a policy of never again speaking with Shirley alone, feeling that he might need third party confirmation if she ever carried out her threats to lodge a formal complaint against him. With two decades of teaching experience behind him, that was a first for this teaching physician. This episode does not provide any additional circumstances directly implicating Shirley in Andrew's murder, but it casts her self-serving statements in further doubt by showing that she was a practised, though not very polished, liar and manipulator.

POSSIBLE BURGLAR

Andrew spent his first year after medical school in a surgery residency in Syracuse, New York, before switching into family practice medicine and moving to Latrobe, Pennsylvania. On the morning of May 29, 2001, Andrew left his Syracuse apartment and went to work. Shirley had been visiting with him for several days, but was returning home to Iowa a couple of hours later. She left his door unlocked while going back and forth to pack for the return trip and forgot to lock it on her final exit (she later said). Andrew reported a burglary to local police that evening. Missing items included his laptop computer, Palm Pilot, several DVDs and CDs, and the Zippo lighter I had given him as a memento of my stupid youthful habit. The investigating officer told Andrew that, although nothing would likely ever be proven, Shirley was the most likely culprit. Andrew didn't believe it, since she earned a lot more money than he did. In hindsight, we can now infer that the theft was probably not about money; it was about spying—getting access to his email address book and Palm Pilot contact list, probably to ensure that he wasn't secretly seeing another woman.

JEALOUSY

During her interview with police, Shirley claimed that she and Andrew had a "mature, open" relationship; one in which they both dated other people and there was little or no jealousy. Specifically asked if she was jealous of a radiology clerk Andrew was trying to date, Shirley replied, "I don't think so...." However, the clerk was able to identify Shirley's voice (especially her distinctive Newfoundland accent) as the one that left ten or eleven messages on her answering machine about ten days before the murder. In the most manipulative of these, Shirley said, "This message is for ———. From another employee of Latrobe Hospital...Ask Doctor Bagby about the beautiful blond lady doc he's been seen with. He's already hurt a number of people here. Take care. Bye."[7] While she liked to portray herself as mature, Shirley was in fact consumed by the basest of human emotions: jealousy.

NO FREE DUMPING

A concerned citizen contacted police three weeks after the murder, having seen Shirley's name in the media. In 1999, he reported, he owned a company near Philadelphia and had in his employ a Canadian citizen who was involved in a *Fatal Attraction*-like relationship with Shirley Turner. She had "left around 15–20 harassing and threatening voice mail messages at the company," and local police had become involved at one point.[8] Investigators contacted these local police and the employee to get the full story.[9]

The Canadian man met Shirley in St. John's in 1994; they dated on and off until August 1996, when he ended the relationship and moved to Port au Basque, on the other side of the island of Newfoundland. Then Shirley "started with the phone calls," many of them, usually late at night, at one time whispering, "You will die," he told police. "When I first broke up...she displayed this weird psycho behaviour. Like a stalking behaviour, like she wasn't going to be dumped. I tried to break it off with her three or four times. She wouldn't take no for an answer." She also appeared at his doorstep with no warning on several occasions, even though she lived ten hours away by car.

He moved to the Philadelphia area in 1998 to work. Shirley continued her pursuit and they started occasional dating again. After a while, he again broke it off, telling her by phone "not to bother coming down [she was still living in Newfoundland]. I didn't want to face her because she showed violence in the past. She hit me once...in the face."

On April 7, 1999, after flying down to Philadelphia from Newfoundland, renting a car, and stalking her ex-boyfriend's residence for two days, Shirley bought some roses, sleeping pills, anti-nausea medication, a can of potato chips, and a bottle of Pepsi. Behind his apartment building, she used the Pepsi to wash down the potato chips and the drugs. Then she started the climb to his third floor apartment. On the way up, she repeatedly punched the stairs in front of her, cutting her knuckles and leaving a trail of blood and rose petals on the steps behind her and in the hallway outside his apartment. The man and his roommate came home from work to find Shirley sitting on the steps, writing letters to him and to the roommate's girl-friend, who was also an acquaintance of Shirley's and was inside the apartment at the time. The handwriting was progressively worse as the drugs took affect, but the gist of her letter to the woman was, "I never wanted to hurt you...I forgive you. I hope God forgives you, too. I am not evil, just sick...I really do wish you all the best." There was no indication of the woman's actions that supposedly warranted Shirley's forgiveness.

To her ex-boyfriend, Shirley wrote:

I know you don't want to see me or talk to me ever again. Believe me all I wanted was closure. To say goodbye in person. I'm sorry if I hurt you in any way...I thought you would always be my friend. How could you be so cruel and uncaring...Maybe I am "evil" like [the roommate] said. But you know I'm not. Everybody does stupid things when they're angry and hurt. Take care and have a great life. This is getting harder to write. Love always, Shirley

P.S.) I think I'm going to pass out soon. Could you please take back my rental car...I still have you on my life insurance...Please when you get the money split 3 ways for my kids...I want to be cremated...Why couldn't you meet me...I'll be...

The rest was completely illegible, as were some sections throughout both letters.

It's fairly certain that Shirley took at least some medication that evening, but not enough to actually put her life in danger. Ambulance and police were called, and she was conscious enough to provide her date of birth and to understand the officer's explanation of her options: she could be taken to either the police station or the hospital. She chose hospital, and was released the next day, flying back to Newfoundland and never bothering him again. He was luckier than Andrew.

CELLPHONE RECORDS

Even with all this information at hand, police would still have had no definite means to place Shirley in Latrobe at the time of the killing. Airline records placed her in Council Bluffs, Iowa, on Saturday afternoon and witnesses placed her there again on Tuesday morning; in between, there was no independent confirmation of her whereabouts. To determine that, a search warrant was obtained for Shirley's cellphone records, requesting not only the calls that were made but the location of her phone at the time of each call. While telephone companies could quickly provide a list of calls to and from a particular cellphone, the *location of the phone* could only be determined by a search of cell tower databases—a process that had to be performed manually and took many days to complete.

On November 21, Shirley's cellphone records were delivered to police and they contained no surprises. They showed that she had used her phone three times on Sunday evening as she drove towards Latrobe: twice in the vicinity of Chicago, checking voice mail, and once from somewhere near South Bend, Indiana, talking to Andrew for eleven minutes.

Shirley's call to her nurse on Monday morning, in which she claimed to be home in bed with a migraine headache, proved to have originated from the Pittsburgh area. The Monday evening call to her nurse, to see if she had any Tuesday patients on the schedule, originated near Cleveland, Ohio, on her way back to Iowa. The final call of her return trip—a quick check with her clinic on Tuesday morning—originated near Stuart, Iowa, about seventy miles east of Council Bluffs.

Her cellphone records placed Shirley in the vicinity of Latrobe on Monday, November 5. Two additional circumstances strongly indicate that she was in Andrew's apartment on that day. First, after putting her on the plane on Saturday, November 3, he had bought a box of Trojan condoms at the RiteAid drugstore in Latrobe. A search of Shirley's Council Bluffs apartment after the murder turned up an empty box of Trojan condoms stamped with lot number 04214. Police investigators later found a package of condoms on the RiteAid shelf bearing the same lot number. Second, examination of Andrew's laptop computer revealed that it was used on Monday at around 9:50 a.m. to access Shirley's password-protected email account. She had bid on eBay to purchase a Barbie doll for her younger daughter and, while waiting around to shoot Andrew after he got off work, she went online and confirmed that hers was the high bid.

With this confirmation of Shirley's presence in the Latrobe area at the time of the killing, plus her resentment over Andrew's terminating the relationship, plus her jealousy of another woman, plus her conveniently missing gun, police could now seek an arrest warrant with a reasonable expectation of success.

CHAPTER 6
ESCAPE

Once she had been officially informed of Andrew's murder on Tuesday, November 6, Shirley, ostensibly distraught over this tragedy, took a leave of absence from work and consulted a physician, who prescribed a sedative. She also consulted an attorney, Julianne Herzog, of Omaha, Nebraska. Herzog did her job, shielding Shirley from additional direct questioning by police and offering instead to respond in writing to any written questions the police cared to submit. Shirley was, Herzog said, psychologically very fragile and unable to endure the stress of another face-to-face interview with police.

In the immediate aftermath of Andrew's murder, his extensive network of medical school friends spent hours on the phone consoling each other and hashing over what little was known about their cohort's killing. One of these friends, Carol Ross, upon learning of the murder called the medical school student affairs officer, Vera Griffin, and expressed her snap judgment that Shirley did it: "Another man rejected her and she wasn't going to take it." Apparently, Carol later talked with Shirley by telephone and reversed her opinion. On Saturday, November 10, she flew from her home in Sioux Falls, South Dakota to Council Bluffs, in answer to Shirley's desperate plea for emotional comfort. In a November 23 telephone interview with Trooper McElfresh, Carol stated, "No one can convince me that Shirley did it…her state of mind does not appear to be that of someone who just killed someone." In her righteous zeal to protect her friend against this horribly unjust accusation, Carol—a psychiatry resident—offered to provide formal psychiatric counselling, with a proviso that Shirley pay her twenty dollars (to make it official) so that their communications would be privileged and she could not later be forced to testify against her "client."

At a Sunday, November 11, meeting in Herzog's home, Carol and the lawyer wanted Shirley "to go to Canada to be with family and lifelong friends for a couple of weeks for the emotional support available to her there. Dr. Turner did not want to go but the lawyer and I [Carol Ross] managed to convince her."[1] Carol helped the supposedly reluctant Shirley purchase a roundtrip ticket and pack a bag, and then took her to the Omaha airport for a flight to Toronto early the next morning, November 12, one week after the murder. She was scheduled to return to Omaha on November 30.

Shirley's reluctance to leave for Canada is perhaps belied by her placing a hold on her mail at the local Council Bluffs post office on Friday, November 9, two days before the Herzog/Ross meeting.

Although both Herzog and Ross were able to state in their affidavits that Shirley did not flee and only went to Canada for emotional support, she never again set foot in the United States. By pure coincidence, her eighteen-year-old son suffered a serious injury in an automobile accident on the day she arrived in Canada, providing a convenient excuse to prolong her stay well beyond her supposed November 30 return date.

ARREST WARRANT

With the November 21 arrival of the cellphone records, which placed Shirley in Pennsylvania at the time of the murder, police had enough evidence to seek an arrest warrant. But with her out of the country, a warrant would only initiate an extradition request to Canada, which promised to be a long and tedious process stretching over perhaps several years. Better to try and lure Shirley back into the States and issue a warrant while she was in the country. Unless she was totally stupid, this tactic was doomed to fail; but facing the daunting prospect of extradition, it was worth a little additional delay to make an attempt. Kate and I were to play a gut-wrenching role in this nearly hopeless ploy.

We lived at the house on Tacoma Street in Latrobe from November 7 to November 21, nominally waiting for police to release Andrew's apartment and car; but more importantly, aching to know who the killer was—who should be the target of our rage. Andrew's property was released to us on November 16 and over the next two days we packed his things, shedding a bucket of tears in the process. God*damn* it! *Andrew* should be going through *our* things after *we* die, not the other way around! Most of his furniture and clothing we turned over to Jan Mills for donation to Goodwill, but there was a lot left over that we wanted to keep, partly because it was useful but mostly because it had been Andrew's. Kate very specifically kept his lab coats with his name sewn over the breast pocket. Movers loaded the bulk of these "keepers" and we retained a few boxes of critical papers and precious mementos with us, hoping they could be squeezed into his car for the drive to California.

On November 20, with the cellphone records still not available, with Shirley already in Canada, and with no definite arrest in sight, we decided to head home. The rest of the day was mostly devoted to farewell visits with our new friends, lots more hugs and tears, and another long talk with police followed by another long, sad night.

Up the next morning with heavy hearts. Andrew had found heaven in Latrobe. He loved the intimate patient interaction of a family practice doctor, his great group of colleagues, and the small-town atmosphere. But now his ashes were locked in the trunk of his car as we made a last stop at the bank to close out his accounts. While the manager was verifying our identities and ensuring that we were indeed entitled to Andrew's money, my cell phone rang and I stepped a little away from the desk to take the call. Trooper McElfresh had Shirley's cellphone records and they confirmed that she had been in Pennsylvania at the time Andrew was shot—she was the probable killer. Kate watched my face anxiously, but I couldn't say anything out loud with the bank manager listening, so I just smiled slightly at her and nodded. McElfresh and I agreed that Kate and I should still head home, but we would keep in touch and return to Pennsylvania in a heartbeat if they made an arrest.

Now I had a definite face to put above the throat that slowly gave way to my thumbs. Once outside the bank and mostly hidden from public view in Andrew's car, we both lost it completely in what was a common pattern, almost an emotional division of labour. Kate was reduced to helpless sobbing: "I want my Andrew! I want him back in the world!" I was reduced to impotent rage: "You fucking bitch! You goddamned motherfucking bitch!"

It seems ridiculous as I write this, but over the next two thousand miles we would discover that driving—like showering, shaving, and dressing—can be done in relative safety while crying. Not tear-blinded uncontrollable sobbing, and not with other traffic nearby, but you can cry softly on a straight, lonely interstate. And you can quickly push it aside and be in complete control if another vehicle comes near.

We made St. Louis the next day, in plenty of time for Thanksgiving dinner with my family. There didn't seem much to be thankful for, but we ate and talked and even laughed a little. Andrew couldn't join us; he was still locked in the trunk of his car.

Andrew's grandmother (my mother) and his uncle Bob (my brother) had both died of lung cancer and donated their bodies to the Washington University Tyson Research Center for cancer research. Once finished with these research bodies, the university had them cremated and scattered in a nearby woodland park, just off Interstate 44, southwest of St. Louis. This was where we wanted to leave the Missouri share of Andrew—mingled with his grandmother and his uncle. Our niece and nephew, Rhonda and Glenn, had made the arrangements before our arrival.

Three days after Thanksgiving, our Missouri family and friends were gathered in a small clearing at Tyson Research Park. Kate and I stepped a little away from the group, slipped open the knot on a velvet bag, and each dug a hand into Andrew's dry grey ashes. While my heart was breaking, my head was somewhat functional, so I noticed that he wasn't a consistent size; part of him was chunks—presumably bone—while the rest ranged down to a fine powder. He slipped easily through our fingers when we opened our hands and waved them slowly back and forth over the fallen leaves covering the autumn earth. I had my arm around Kate's waist as she held the bag. Dig in and repeat, spilling our beautiful baby, our cheerful son, our determined young doctor, onto the cold ground. Kate sobbed, I seethed, and the family arrayed behind us could do nothing to relieve our agony or theirs. At one point Kate's knees started to give out. I suppose that rage triggers adrenaline, because I was able to pull her tight to my side and we finished emptying the bag.

At the end, Andrew was hardly visible as his ashes quickly filtered through the leaves and down to the earth below. Everyone came forward then to help spread bright red rose petals over the brown leaves. Nephew Glenn said a prayer and we all piled into the cars for the drive back to his church where he had arranged for a small memorial service.

We were anxious to get home, so we hugged everybody one more time and, the next morning, began the four-day drive from Missouri to California. The long uninterrupted hours on the road allowed us to review ad nauseam our contacts with Shirley: the endless telephone chatter, our first meeting at the backyard wedding reception, the Christmas visit with her three children, the emotional outburst over Newfie jokes, the indifference to thousands of lives lost on September 11. We could find no solid indication of what was to come, and always came back to the same two punch lines: "We knew she was strange, but we never thought *murder!*" and "Andrew knew her as well as anyone, but he didn't see it coming until he was looking at the gun!"

On the drive home we kept in daily contact with McElfresh, who was still holding off on requesting an arrest warrant in hopes that Shirley might attend a memorial service in California planned for December 8. In the middle of our second day on the road, we made a call to McElfresh and he asked if we could stomach a conversation with Shirley; could we bear to talk to her in an effort to get her back into the States? Damn right, we could! He warned us not to solicit statements from her, but only to ask if she would attend the service. If she talked of her own volition, that was fine, but we *must not* ask her anything related to the case.

Over dinner that night, November 27, at a coffee shop next door to our motel in Gallup, New Mexico, we determined that I would make the call. I would not accuse her. I would not argue with her. I would maintain a civil tone, take good notes, and, if the opportunity arose, offer gentle encouragement for her to attend Andrew's California memorial service. Perhaps she would need money for the airfare, or would want to speak at the service. We weren't hopeful, but if there were something we could do to entice her back into the States, we were prepared to do it.

Kate was in bed but wide awake and anxious as I sat down at the table with a notepad in front of me and psyched myself into a kind of battle mode: "If talking to this goddamned bitch has any chance of getting her back into the country, it's worth it, so just dial the fucking phone and get on with it!"

She answered. I tried to keep a neutral tone when I said, "Shirley," but it seemed to me that I sounded nearly as cold as I felt. She said, not cheerily but urgently, "David! I've been trying to get a hold of you!" Then she launched into a long dissertation on her travels and her troubles, with me scribbling notes as fast as my horrible handwriting would allow. Omitting insignificant or redundant details, she said that she was on sleeping pills and, though she remembered talking to Chad, couldn't remember what was said. (I thought she might be starting to build a cover for her ever-shifting stories: "I was zonked out most of the time; I might have said anything.") She didn't know if she should tell us right now…it might upset us, especially Kate…

I interrupted this stuttering introduction and told her, "I want to know everything."

She said, "That's just like Andrew," and told me she was six weeks pregnant and had probably conceived at Karl and Marci's wedding. In a pitiful tone, she added, "I wish Andrew was here to talk this over with."

We knew that she had shared a room with Andrew at the wedding reception hotel, the Mountain View Inn outside Latrobe, about a month before. But we also had some indication that she might be a compulsive liar, or at least a highly motivated one, given the trouble she was in. Hence, I neither believed nor disbelieved that she carried Andrew's baby. I could think of no reason for her to invent a pregnancy, but with no confirmation available, I muttered something neutral and let her go on.

She was concerned that her high stress and occasional alcohol use might affect the baby. In a pitiful tone, she whined, "Sometimes I can't believe Andrew's gone. I call his cellphone sometimes."

Because the press made her sound like a suspect, Shirley told me she had retained a lawyer, who advised her to get in her car and go to Canada. She hadn't wanted to, but then her son had the accident so she left her car and apartment and took a flight to Canada.

This last point would later prove to be a lie, since his accident occurred on November 12, the day after she made flight reservations from Omaha to Toronto. She was, in fact, already in Toronto at the time of the accident.

Shirley also said that Carol Ross was there for the interview with police. Another blatant lie, with no discernible motive; Ross was not present when Gardner interviewed Shirley by phone, nor was she present when Council Bluffs police interviewed her in person, and there were no further interviews of Shirley by police.

There was a lot of circumstantial evidence (including something mentioned in a newspaper article about gum and tissue paper found in Andrew's car). She told me, "The gum in the tissue paper is mine."

"If the police have a case," she said, "I wish they would arrest me so I can have my day in court."

She was sending a locket with Carol to the upcoming service in California. Her lawyer was adamant that she should stay in Canada.

There it was! Not surprisingly, she was not coming to California. I hadn't even mentioned the subject, but she cut me off at the knees. With no conceivable argument to counter her *adamant lawyer*, I choked down the bad news and let her spring wind down.

As in any Shirley conversation, she did the vast majority of the talking, leaving me free to take notes. I told her a few things, however: we would be home on Thursday or Friday and would call her again from there, and the police knew more than they were telling us, and that was fine with us—we just wanted them to find the son-of-a-bitch who did this.

As soon as we hung up the phone, while the conversation was still fresh in my mind, I expanded my scribbles into readable form. Kate had taken a sleeping pill and was already unconscious when I crawled in next to her and went straight to sleep. Dancing with the devil is exhausting.

I called McElfresh first thing the next morning and gave him the not-unexpected news, reading my entire set of notes to him over the phone. We hit the road again while he, with no further need to wait, prepared his application for an arrest warrant citing two offences under the Pennsylvania criminal code:

Section 2501. Criminal homicide

A person is guilty of criminal homicide if he intentionally, knowingly, recklessly or negligently causes the death of another human being.

Section 2502. Murder of the first degree

A criminal homicide constitutes murder of the first degree when it is committed by an intentional killing.

To-wit:

Defendant Shirley Jane Turner did intentionally and knowingly cause the death of Andrew David Bagby. Bagby's death was a result of several gunshot wounds with a .22 calibre firearm. Bagby was shot several times, twice in the head, once in the chest and twice in the rectal area. Bagby also received a blunt trauma to the back of the head.

This formal legal description of our baby's horrific end was accompanied by a three-page summary, an Affidavit of Probable Cause, of the case against Shirley. Later that day District Justice Mark Bilik signed the warrant and Shirley was officially a fugitive from justice in the Commonwealth of Pennsylvania. As we would soon discover, that was only the first of many, many steps in the cumbersome extradition process between the United States and Canada—two friendly neighbouring countries that share a great deal of common culture, including similar systems for the removal of murdering monsters from the general population.

CHAPTER 7
LIMBO

Pennsylvania State Police announced the arrest warrant for Shirley Turner on November 29, 2001. By December 6, she had retained a Canadian attorney—Randy Piercey—with extensive experience in extradition, and she was therefore quite prepared to respond when the formal request for extradition reached Newfoundland on December 11.

At that time, Kate and I, and most of our friends and relatives, were almost completely ignorant of the process of extradition. Because it was so widely covered in the media, we knew something about the Charles Ng case, but saw few parallels between him and Shirley. He was charged with the murders of six men, three women, and two babies—plus kidnapping, rape, and torture—so the State of California obstinately refused to renounce its intention to put him to death. Canada had abolished the death penalty and was extremely hesitant to extradite a fugitive to face possible execution, so it took six years and a trip to the Supreme Court of Canada before Ng was finally returned to the United States in 1991. Shirley, on the other hand, was charged with one murder motivated by her lover's rejection and the death penalty—under Pennsylvania law—could not be imposed in her case.

We naively hoped to see her returned in a few weeks, maybe several months at the most.

BAIL RELEASE

How can they let a probable murderer walk around free!?

That was our incredulous response upon reading the online newspaper story from St. John's: "...The Royal Newfoundland Constabulary received the warrant for Turner's arrest Wednesday [December 12, 2001] and notified her lawyer Randy Piercey. He then arranged for his client to appear before Newfoundland Supreme Court Justice David Russell who released Turner."[1] Obviously, we had a great deal to learn about the criminal justice system in general, and about extradition and bail in particular.

We have since had an opportunity to examine the court transcript and other court documents related to Shirley's bail release. The transcript clearly shows that Crown Prosecutor Mike Madden, representing the United States, and Shirley's lawyer, Randy Piercey, entered the courtroom with an agreement in place. There was no confrontation over *whether* she would be free on bail, nor did the opposing attorneys do public battle over the *conditions* of her release: she was to surrender her passports, remain in the province of Newfoundland, post $75,000 in sureties, sign in once each week at the local police station, possess no weapons, and avoid contact with a specific list of people related to the case, including us.

A surety, we later learned, is a person who promises to pay if the accused fails to appear in court; no actual money changes hands when the surety signs on the dotted line. The original surety amount, $100,000, was crossed out and replaced with $75,000. Two of Shirley's friends each signed for $5,000. The remaining $65,000 was promised by Shirley's psychiatrist, Dr.

John Doucet, in what we thought must surely constitute a violation of his professional ethics.

PSYCHIATRIST/SURETY

Sometime in 1997 or 1998, during her fourth year of medical school, Shirley had undergone a two-month psychiatry rotation, sometimes working with staff psychiatrist Dr. John Doucet. Four years later and two weeks after Andrew's murder, on November 20, 2001, Doucet saw Shirley as a patient for the first time and "elicited a history, which was consistent with what we call an 'Adjustment Disorder' with features of anxiety and depression." Shirley laid out for Dr. Doucet the stressors in her life: her boyfriend's murder, her son's serious automobile accident and subsequent hospitalization, and a positive pregnancy test. Doucet would later report that Shirley "felt a terrible sense of helplessness and hopelessness and loss of control and inability to be of significant help to her boyfriend Andrew, the police, and Andrew's family…She complained of severe emotional distress, crying spells, poor sleep and appetite, distressing dreams, and having difficulty focusing and concentrating. Her past history revealed episodes of depression and anxiety…"[2]

Late on the morning of December 12, Shirley called Dr. Doucet at his office and requested that he come down to the courthouse because she was about to be arrested for the murder of her boyfriend, Andrew Bagby. Doucet went to the courthouse and, late that afternoon, signed a $65,000 surety for his patient Shirley Turner, who was then released pending a hearing on the request for her extradition to the United States.

ANXIETY

Shirley's bail release generated a wave of anxiety among Andrew's medical school classmates, many of whom had personally witnessed her emotional instability and confrontational personality. Chad Burkhart, whom Shirley had called four days after the murder, lived in Ontario. In a telephone conversation a month after the murder, Chad clearly expressed his anxiety to me: "Dave, she's a ferry ride away from me and my family."

Five days after her arrival in Canada, at 1:30 in the morning on November 17, Shirley appeared on the doorstep of Heather Arnold, Andrew's ex-fiancée. (Shirley had telephoned Heather on November 7 to tell her of Andrew's murder.) By this time, Heather knew that Shirley was the prime suspect, so she was understandably frightened out of her wits; whatever maniacal hatred might have driven Shirley to kill Andrew could spill over onto Andrew's ex-fiancée. Heather planted herself squarely in the doorway, preventing Shirley's entry into the house. Shirley prattled away for nearly an hour, professing her innocence and proclaiming, "You could have killed him just as easily as I could." (At the request of Pennsylvania police, the Health Care Corporation of St. John's verified that Heather had been working in St. John's on November 5 and 6, 2001.)

COMPULSION

Kate and I had already determined that, if someone were charged with Andrew's murder, we would attend a trial in Pennsylvania; we had a nearly obsessive compulsion (probably not in a clinical sense) to understand exactly how and why our baby had died. We imagined a scenario in which a jury reached a verdict of "not guilty" without our understanding *why*. Media reports would provide only a rough approximation of the evidence presented to the jury, if indeed a publication ban didn't preclude all media discussion of the evidence. The only relief for our compulsion was to see for ourselves exactly what the jury saw. But now there was a possibility that Shirley might never even face a jury. Again, if that were the outcome, we must understand *why*, and the only path to understanding was first-hand observation of the extradition process.

There was also the baby that may or may not be real. Shirley seemed capable of making up stories on a moment's notice so we had no assurance that she was even pregnant. If she was pregnant, we had no assurance that it was Andrew's child. And if it was his child, she might not carry it to term. However, if she did eventually deliver Andrew's baby and end up in prison, Kate definitely wanted to raise the child as our own. I was initially ambivalent.

From my journal on December 15, 2001: "Kate wants to raise the baby. I can live with that."

Her attitude never wavered and mine quickly came into alignment with hers. Andrew's child, if there were one, would be the end of our line, the last of our DNA. Plus, with Daddy murdered and Mommy in prison, Baby would be starting life in a very deep pit. We, too, were in a pit, so maybe the three of us could help each other climb out.

Just as Reverend Batchelder had done in Latrobe, Canon Linda Taylor's December 8 memorial service homily provided a significant insight into the painful loss of our beloved Andrew: "…It is not supposed to happen this way…in some far, far distant time, some other priest is supposed to be looking down the years of Andrew's life…" Given that nobody could bring Andrew back, it mattered a great deal to Kate and me that the church was filled with hundreds of friends and family, all trying, through a blur of hugs and tears, to help us (and themselves) integrate this atrocity into our souls.

Shirley Turner did not attend the California memorial service. Her only ally from the medical school group, Carol

Ross, came in her stead, and joined the crowd at our house later that evening. After several hours of food, drink, tears, laughter, and plenty of Andrew stories, Heather played a videotape of the November 20 memorial service in Newfoundland. Carol sat next to Kate on the sofa, holding her and consoling her as we watched this distant tribute to Andrew, which included Heather's jazz band performing several touching songs and a reading of Dylan Thomas' "Do Not Go Gentle into That Good Night." At the end, the camera panned over the departing crowd and Shirley was clearly visible for a few seconds. Kate lost it: "You murderer!" she screamed. "How can you have the audacity to show up at Andrew's service!" I quickly ushered her outside, where we fell against the garage door and, to paraphrase Thomas, "raged against the *killing* of the light."

WHAT TO DO?

Two pressing issues: when would the Canadian extradition hearing take place; and, if it wasn't soon, should we go back to work while we waited? We pondered these questions throughout a ten-day visit with Kate's brothers in England.

Upnor is a small village on the north bank of the River Medway, perhaps a mile from the village of Frindsbury, where Kate grew up. Upnor's Anglican church is, for England, a relatively new structure built of red brick less than two hundred years ago. (Frindsbury Church is over nine hundred years old.) If you enter the Upnor churchyard through the heavy metal gate from the street and take the path around to the left, the first two gravesites along the back bear the names of Kate's maternal grandparents. Grandma and Granddad Dalley were interred intact, as was the custom of their day. Kate's parents, first her dad and then her mum, were cremated and their ashes returned to the earth above Grandma Dalley. The morning of

December 19 was very cold but clear and bright when Andrew joined his English ancestors. A small hole, not very deep; a third of a grown man's ashes doesn't take up much space.

Had Kate's parents (or my mother) still been alive and standing with us beside Andrew's grave, would this disaster have killed them? It nearly killed Kate. Her meltdowns were excruciating and a terrible fright to me. "I don't think I can go on" and "I want my baby" she moaned over and over, on dozens of occasions. All I could do was hold her and wait and hope she came back to me. I asked her to carry on at least through the trial, since her testimony may be significant in stopping the monster that did this to Andrew. Once, when she was trapped in a cycle of uncontrollable sobbing, it hurt both of us so much that I offered to kill her, to end her misery. She settled down and said, "If I want out, I'll do it myself." I would not have tried to stop her, nor would I have called 911 to bring her back.

I hardly cried any longer. Was my love for Andrew less than Kate's or just different? When I couldn't sleep for thinking of him, I usually went to the kitchen for something to eat, whereas Kate usually cried for a while and then took a sleeping pill. I suspect there is something nearly mystical that happens when a mother looks into the eyes of her baby as he feeds at her breast. The nipple, lips, and tongue are very sensitive, so the physical-emotional tie must be a wonderful thrill. Kate had that connection with Andrew. I didn't.

On December 20, I woke up way too early and wrote this in my journal: "My pop-psych on Shirley: She has failed twice to maintain a life-long connection with a man, she has very little connection with her three children (who live with their fathers), she is a failure as a physician, she has no real friends, and Andrew told her it was over—really finished. That was the last straw. If she had any character, she would have killed her-self. Instead, she killed the one who crystallized her failure."

Throughout this long period of limbo, Kate and I scrupu-lously avoided contact with the press, with two exceptions. In late January, a freelance Newfoundland reporter named Danette Dooley contacted us by email, asking if we would agree to an interview for an article she wanted to write about Andrew's scholarship fund in Latrobe. After checking her repu-tation with the Royal Newfoundland Constabulary, we agreed to the interview and emailed her our phone number. When she called, she was true to her word and stuck to the subject of Andrew's scholarship. We talked about Andrew's great experi-ences in medical school and his path to the Latrobe family practice residency. Part way through the interview, I asked, "Are you recording this?" Danette said, "Yes." I said, "Good. You'll get the quotes right." And she did. The article was very touching and perfectly accurate. Danette would become a good friend over the coming months.

Our second contact with the press was not so pleasant. On February 5, the day Shirley publicly announced her pregnancy to the press in St. John's, a *Pittsburgh Tribune-Review* newspa-per reporter, Richard Gazarik, called our home and Kate answered the phone. Gazarik asked, "Did you know that Dr. Turner was pregnant?" Kate was caught off guard and didn't respond at first. Gazarik quickly added, "I know you do. The DA told me that you were contacted by CBC. What do you think of the defense lawyer saying the whole of 2002 will be taken up with extradition? Do you believe him?"

Kate said, "If that is what he said, I suppose so. I have never been through this terrible thing before," and hung up the phone. In his article the following day, the reporter mis-interpreted Kate's simple comment in three significant ways, the most annoying being an implication that she had given a full interview. We never spoke to the press again for a year and a half.

Partly for the cash flow and partly to keep our sanity, Kate and I both went back to our jobs on January 2, 2002. We remained employed until early June, except for two trips to Newfoundland for extradition court dates and custody battle preparations.

CHAPTER 8
TWO FRONTS

A courtroom is a war zone where enemies confront each other in a bloodless battle using only the weapons of information, principles, and logic instead of fists, knives, and guns. Kate and I had no official role in the battle to extradite Shirley to Pennsylvania, but the intensity of our despair at Andrew's loss and our hatred for his probable killer gave us a feeling of desperate spectators on a hill overlooking the carnage of an actual battleground.

Custody of our possible grandchild, however, was a very different matter. We were combatants who could not allow despair and hatred to interfere with the practical necessity for a reasoned assault on the enemy and a prudent defense against her possible counter-attacks. The prize was a good start in life for our only living progeny and a very good reason to carry on living ourselves.

At the outset of these two wars, we were ignorant observers on one front and ignorant warriors on the other.

EXTRADITION

In 1999 the Parliament of Canada passed new legislation in an attempt to streamline a very slow and cumbersome extradition process—one in which fugitives had often spent many years in

Canada before their return to the United States, if they were returned at all. Under the old act, an accused could force a virtual practice trial of the case in Canada, calling witnesses and challenging evidence to a standard normally reserved only for an actual trial in the jurisdiction of the crime.

To this non-lawyer, the speedy new extradition process still seemed quite cumbersome, with six major decision points following receipt of an extradition request from another country (referred to as the "requesting state"—in Shirley's case, the United States):

1. Authority to Proceed: The federal Minister of Justice must issue an Authority to Proceed with an extradition hearing.

2. Committal Order: Once an Authority to Proceed is in place, a provincial court (in Shirley's case, the Supreme Court of the Province of Newfoundland and Labrador) must hold an extradition hearing to determine if there is sufficient evidence to send the fugitive back to the requesting state. If so, the court issues an order committing the fugitive into custody. The fugitive may appeal this order to the provincial Court of Appeal.

3. Surrender Order: Once a Committal Order is in place, the Minister of Justice must issue an order to surrender the fugitive to the requesting state. The fugitive may appeal this order, as well, to the provincial Court of Appeal.

4. Committal Order Denial: The provincial Court of Appeal must deny the fugitive's appeal of the Committal Order. The fugitive may appeal this denial to the Supreme Court of Canada.

5.	Surrender Order Denial: The provincial Court of Appeal must deny the fugitive's appeal of the Surrender Order. The fugitive may appeal this denial, as well, to the Supreme Court of Canada.

6.	Supreme Court Denial: The Supreme Court of Canada must deny both Committal Order and Surrender Order appeals.

Kate and I missed only two extradition court dates, very quick ones that did not justify roundtrip airfare from California to Newfoundland. The first, a documentation status check, took place on February 15, 2002. The transcript of that hearing indicates that Crown Prosecutor Mike Madden informed the court that the official request for extradition had been received from the United States. The Minister of Justice then had thirty days in which to issue an Authority to Proceed (ATP), so the matter was adjourned until March 11, by which date either the ATP would be issued or the matter would be dropped.

The presiding judge at that hearing, Newfoundland and Labrador Provincial Supreme Court Chief Justice Derek Green, expressed some concern that this delay "must be frustrating for her [Shirley]," and encouraged Madden and the Minister to move "as quickly as possible so that this matter is not kept in limbo and [Shirley] is not kept in suspended animation until decisions are made for her future." The transcript contained no mention of Andrew's suspended animation and lost future.

CUSTODY

Madden informed Kate and me by email of the March 11 extradition court date and also kindly referred us to a Newfoundland law firm, Rose and Brazil, with expertise in

family law. Over the following week, we contacted the junior
partner Jackie Brazil (rhymes with "frazzle") by telephone and
arranged to meet with her and the senior partner, Linda Rose,
on Sunday afternoon, March 10, at their offices in St. John's.

Atlantic Place, the modern office building in which Rose
and Brazil leased space, was virtually deserted when we met
with Linda and Jackie. After filling them in on the background
between Andrew and Shirley, we received a brief introduction
to Newfoundland custody law and its possible application to
our case.

Since the baby would not be recognized in law as a person
until it was born, there was probably no legal manoeuvre we
could make until that time. More important than the legal status of the baby was our fear that, if Shirley learned our
intentions, she may harm the baby in utero, just to spite us. I
think it was Jackie who made the sobering observation that
"whatever we do here, she may still harm that child, before or
after delivery!"

As soon as the baby was born, Jackie, who would be handling our case, would file two applications for us with the
Unified Family Court (UFC): one for a DNA test and one for custody, if the DNA test results proved the baby was Andrew's.
Shirley may *herself* submit an application for DNA testing, in
order to establish Andrew's paternity to back up a claim on his
estate for child support.

We would need to be living in St. John's when the baby was
born, and we would need to stay there for the duration of the
custody battle, since our physical presence would be the
strongest possible indicator of sincerity in our custody request.
With the baby's estimated delivery date sometime in July, this
fixed the date of our contemplated move to Newfoundland at
no later than June.

Custody law explicitly provided only for the rights of living fathers, but the welfare of the child was the law's primary concern, so we had a reasonable chance of success.

This all seemed fairly sensible to Kate and me, except for the possibility of paying Shirley even a penny from Andrew's estate. We would happily provide anything the baby needed, but the prospect of handing money directly to Shirley filled us with disgust. We put the issue aside, to be fought later if Shirley made a formal application for child support.

We had no way of knowing if someone from Shirley's family might be seeking custody of the baby, and we discussed the possibility of a battle with a foe as yet unknown. I said, "We don't know Shirley's relatives. They might make perfectly good parents, and we should be prepared for them to have a role in the baby's life." Linda replied, "That attitude puts you over the top. Very few people are that reasonable." Long before this meeting, we had decided that Shirley was the only monster in this story. Everyone else, especially her children, was an innocent victim.

With the basic custody battle plan in place, we turned our attention to tomorrow's extradition hearing. Kate and I had no experience with courtrooms or the media, so we had asked if Jackie could accompany us to the hearing and, if the press bugged us, speak to them on our behalf. This was a very bad idea, she informed us, because Shirley's lawyer Randy Piercey would know immediately that we were planning to seek custody—Rose and Brazil being well-known for their family law practice.

Still, we needed handholding for our first exposure to court and media, so Jackie arranged to have John Ennis, a well-known St. John's criminal lawyer, join us for the end of our meeting and accompany us to the courthouse the following day. We explained our situation and arranged to meet with

John the next morning at his office, which was only a short walk from the courthouse.

Exhausted, we dragged ourselves back to the hotel, where we enjoyed a leisurely dinner in the hotel restaurant, served by a pleasant young waiter. Afterwards, up in our room, we got a call from Heather and Matt inviting us to join them for dinner. We weren't hungry, but went back down to the dining room to keep them company while they ate. The pleasant waiter was amused to see us again and said, "Back so soon?" Then he said to Heather, "Aren't you Heather?" She hesitated, then replied, "Yes." To Kate and me, he said, "You must be the Bagbys." We were all stumped as to how he knew us, but I told him, "That's not public information until after the hearing tomorrow." He apologized for intruding and we completed the introductions. His name was Mark Lombard and his wife, Jennifer, was one of Andrew's medical school classmates. She had helped organize his memorial service and put together his memory box. Over the coming months, Jen and Mark would become good friends.

CHAPTER 9
THE ENEMY

The following morning, well in advance of the ten o'clock court hearing, John Ennis led Kate and me from his office up Duckworth Street to the imposing old stone courthouse. Throughout the short walk and up the steps and into the heavy main door, my gut was tight with pre-fight tension and I scanned the streets and the small crowd in search of the enemy. Inside, there was a large foyer with a Sheriff's desk to the right and open space to the left. There were more people milling around than John expected, and he guessed that they were prospective jurors waiting to be called for another case. He and Kate went to the left wall of the foyer to check posted court-room assignments while I stood just inside the main door and scanned faces until Shirley appeared.

From about ten feet apart, we saw each other at the same time. Through hard eye contact, I felt as if we could both read the primitive animal emotions of the other: my rage, her fear. I'm certain she knew that, were we not embedded in this complex civilization, one of us would very soon be dead. Probably it would be her, since I weighed half again as much as she and males tend to be stronger than females. If she were a trained fighter (I'm not) or had a hidden weapon (I didn't), then I, like my son before me, might instead be lying dead at her feet.

My strangler image had grown much clearer since first appearing to me in Latrobe four months before. Now, in my imagination, I straddled Shirley's torso, my knees widespread for maximum stability, and gripped her throat firmly in both hands while she tried to pry my fingers loose. Failing that, she switched to clawing at my face. Her arms were too short, so she abandoned my face and scratched deep gashes into my forearms in a vain, desperate attempt to distract me with pain. She expended most of her remaining energy trying to buck me off by arching her back, but I was too heavy and she was losing strength from lack of oxygen. Through this struggle, the initial fear in her eyes morphed into panic, then to hatred, back and forth a few times, and finally to nothing. The eyes were still open, but lifeless. She was gone, but I was not joyous. I was not even happy, nor contented. I felt only relief at being rid of this abomination that plagued my consciousness.

There was only time for a quick flash of this barbaric fantasy before Shirley turned and disappeared down a hallway.

John, Kate, and I regrouped and found the designated courtroom, number six. It was a small room, with the judge's bench on a raised dais at the front. Below that was a table for the court clerk, then a long table with several goosenecked microphones where the opposing attorneys stood to address the court, then a small bench enclosed by rails (the docket) on which an accused would normally sit, and finally three long benches for public seating. Along the left wall was a row of chairs, nominally for the media. We sat on the middle public bench, with me on the right, then Kate with my left arm around her shoulders, then John. On the other end of our bench sat a lady we didn't recognize.

We had been seated for several minutes when Shirley came into the room and took a seat in one of the chairs to our left. She managed a few sweeping glances over the scene, trying to take a look at us without being obvious about it. I stared directly at her for long stretches, my mind flashing an image of her bent over Andrew administering the execution shot to the back of his head.

Two television cameramen moved quietly around the room recording Shirley, her defence attorney Randy Piercey, the Crown Prosecutor Mike Madden, and finally Kate and me. In our culture, it is considered rude to stare directly at another person for any extended period of time, but reporters must overcome such niceties if they wish to get their stories. One of them dropped to one knee on the floor next to me with a television camera perched on his shoulder and the lens steadily gazing at my face for several minutes. To express my discomfort at such an intrusive appraisal, I considered putting my hand over the lens, which would not have even required the full extension of my arm. Uncertainty won out and I sat motionless, looking straight ahead, waiting for the lens to go away, which it finally did.

The clerk said, "All rise." Chief Justice Green came into the courtroom and took his seat on the bench. Madden rose to his microphone and told the court that the Authority to Proceed with an extradition hearing had been received from the Minister of Justice, along with the Case Record for Prosecution—an eight-page summary from the Americans of their case against Shirley. These two documents had been forwarded to Piercey, who had not yet had time to review them with his client and had requested a two-week delay. Madden had agreed. Judge Green emphasized, for the record, that the delay was at the request of the defence. The matter was set over until March 25 at ten o'clock, at which time a date would be set for the actual extradition hearing. The clerk said, "All rise." The judge left the courtroom.

We stepped into the hallway and introduced ourselves to Madden. He seemed too formal, somewhat aloof, as he briefly described the extradition process and advised us, "The law is slow." Then he speculated on some possible upcoming issues. The actual extradition hearing was estimated to take about a day, but Piercey might raise various issues that could delay the process. For example, the defence may ask to postpone the whole process until after the baby is born, to alleviate stress on his client. Or, he may ask to have the whole process aborted because the United States had not provided assurance that the death penalty would not be imposed, or because a life sentence in Pennsylvania may be somewhat more than a life sentence in Canada.

Madden abruptly broke off our conversation when the press appeared down the hall. He obviously did not want to be seen conferring with us, for reasons we could not fathom at the time. Since then, we have come to understand that, because we were not his clients (he represented the United States of America), he needed to keep his distance from us in order to maintain both his objectivity and his *appearance* of objectivity.

Outside the courthouse, Kate and I went down the street a short distance while John Ennis spoke for us to the media. He explained that we were in St. John's "just…to make sure their son is not forgotten about through all of this." On the tricky question of our possible interest in the baby, he hit it just right: "The baby is not even with us yet, but they certainly are concerned about the welfare of that child, as we all should be."

The courthouse sits on the edge of a steep hill between Duckworth and Water Streets, with a long stairway alongside the building connecting the two streets. While we waited for John to finish with the reporters, I glanced down the steps and saw Jackie coming up from Water Street to join us for a quick debriefing at John's office. With the slightest of cloak-and-dagger headshakes, she reminded me not to acknowledge her, providing the only comic relief from the tension of sitting in the same room with Andrew's probable killer.

After the debriefing, Kate and I returned to the hotel where I called Westmoreland County, Pennsylvania, District Attorney John Peck to ask about the possibility of a death penalty. He told me that, under Pennsylvania law, the death penalty could not be imposed unless there was at least one aggravating circumstance: multiple murders, torture, or killing a police officer. Since none of these applied to Shirley's case, the death penalty was not an option. Also, he said, the sections of the Pennsylvania Criminal Code defining these circumstances had been included in the documents sent to Canada.

At five o'clock we met with Jackie and Linda for another debriefing. All agreed that they should get started on our custody application, as it seemed almost certain that the baby would be born in St. John's. The biggest news was that Piercey had called John Ennis to ask if his client had anything to fear from us. John had scoffed at the suggestion and told Piercey that we were decent people and his client was safe. My hard stare in the courthouse foyer had not been planned for effect; rather, it had been a spontaneous reflection of my genuine hatred. I took some satisfaction, however, in the knowledge that she was experiencing a small taste of the fear that Andrew must have felt staring into a gun barrel for the last few seconds of his life.

Later that evening we telephoned Danette Dooley, the free-lance reporter who had written such a good article about Andrew's scholarship fund, and invited her to join us in the hotel dining room. She turned out to be the unknown lady on the other end of our courtroom bench at the hearing earlier in the day. Over dinner, we compared observations. Danette had written a great many human interest articles for local papers over the years, but had a particular interest in crime-related stories. Hence, while this was Kate's and my first day ever in a criminal courtroom, she had loads of experience observing the dramatics of criminal law confrontations. She thought Shirley seemed far too self-assured, as if she expected to get away with it. Most people in her situation would surely display at least a hint of anxiety or agitation. Except for her avoidance of direct eye contact with Kate and me, however, she was the perfect picture of cool. She might just as well have been attending a lecture on the proper pruning of roses.

Jen Lombard was out of town so Mark (the pleasant, insightful waiter in the hotel dining room) offered us the loan of her car. We accepted, and he brought it to the hotel early the next morning. We used it to visit the medical school and meet some of Andrew's old friends, professors and office staff, many of whom were upset by Shirley's frequent visits to the office. But they were afraid to treat her with anything but courtesy.

In the afternoon we dropped in on Rana Mercer, who, with her husband Greg and baby Aaron, had accompanied Shirley on her visit with us in California in September 2001. Rana reported that Shirley had called her a few weeks after returning to Newfoundland and said of Andrew's murder, "You don't think I had anything to do with it!" Rana had terminated the conversation as quickly and politely as possible, and then called Greg, who asked his lawyer to ask Piercey to advise Shirley not to contact the Mercers again.

Early the next morning Mark drove us to the airport for our flight back to California, where we returned to work-and-wait mode. Since the March 25 hearing was only to set a date for the extradition hearing—it was a "hearing hearing"—we saved our money and stayed in California. The three-page transcript shows that we made a wise choice. Justice David Orsborn would speak with Chief Justice Green, who would assign the case to a judge, who would then meet with Madden and Piercey prior to an estimated two-and-a-half-day hearing commencing at ten o'clock Monday morning, May 27.

CHAPTER 10
NITS

CUSTODY

An overnight flight brought us back to St. John's on Saturday, May 25, two days before the scheduled extradition hearing. We rented a car and moved into Greg and Rana's spare bedroom. At two o'clock Sunday afternoon we had our second meeting with Jackie in her office at Atlantic Place. Her law clerk, Cindy Starkes, had researched and prepared a draft of the custody documents, which Jackie would submit to the court for us as soon as the baby was born. Kate and I reviewed them for accuracy only, since we had no idea in advance exactly what they should contain.

Two affidavits stated our situation in very precise language. Briefly: we were Andrew's parents, he had been murdered, Shirley had been charged with his killing, she was pregnant and claimed him as the father, we intended to confirm that claim and to provide a stable home for our grandchild, and we preferred to raise him in California but were willing to relocate to Newfoundland if that were found to be in the child's best interest.

An application referenced the affidavits and asked the court for an order that we be granted "sole physical and legal custody and primary care" of the child; or, failing that, "reasonable and ample access" to the child.

As in our first meeting with Jackie in March, this all seemed very sensible and straightforward. There was nothing more to do about custody until the baby was born.

EXTRADITION

John Ennis would once again hold our hands on the first day of the extradition hearing and also speak for us to the press, so we met again at his office and walked the short distance to the courthouse on Monday morning.[1]

Shirley seemed very much at home in the courtroom, pouring water for Randy Piercey and adjusting the window blinds for everyone's comfort. She was also very large with child and missed no opportunity to display her condition to the most sympathetic advantage, straining to ease herself into a chair and lovingly stroking her tummy. To any viewer, it must've been clear how much she loved the dear little soul developing in her womb and how difficult it was to maintain her composure in the face of this terrible miscarriage of justice. But, she was determined to show, she was a trooper. She would stoically bear her burden. She would survive.

Chief Justice Green had assigned the case to himself. He opened the proceedings by having the clerk read into the record the Authority to Proceed (ATP), a very simple document: "The Minister of Justice authorizes the Attorney General of Canada to proceed before the Supreme Court of Newfoundland and Labrador to seek an order for the committal of Shirley Jane Turner who is being sought for prosecution by the United States of America. The Canadian offence which corresponds to the alleged conduct is: Culpable homicide contrary to section 229(a) of the Criminal Code."

Judge Green then asked a critical question: "Do you have any objection to the sufficiency of the form [of the ATP], Mr. Piercey?"

"No, my lord."

This simple exchange over a seemingly simple paragraph would prove critical in later stages of the battle.

Piercey asked for a ban on publication of the content of the hearing. Madden had no objection, but Glenn Deir of the CBC asked for a delay in imposing the ban to allow the legal staff of the broadcaster time to argue the point. I thought, "Shit! How long will that take?" To our great relief, the judge declined Deir's request, citing "a specific requirement [under the Extradition Act] that the court deal with the matter by way of an early date and to sit outside of the normal term if necessary to ensure that that takes place." This seemed to portend a speedy process.

But things got messy in a hurry. Piercey had two technical issues he wished to bring before the court.

ADMISSIBILITY

First, he invoked a provision in the Extradition Act relating to where evidence was collected: "…evidence gathered in Canada must satisfy the rules of evidence under Canadian law in order to be admitted [at an extradition hearing]." The Case Record provided by Pennsylvania prosecutors contained evidence that may have been collected in Canada, so Piercey had a monkey wrench he could toss into the gears of justice.

Listening intently from the back of the courtroom, Kate and I could not follow precisely the arguments put forth by Piercey and Madden on this issue. They consumed most of Monday and Tuesday and included numerous references to the Extradition Act and Extradition Treaty, and to case law from previous extradition hearings. During the breaks on Monday,

John Ennis clarified the issues for us as much as he could, but we had only a cursory understanding at the time. We were constrained by court decorum to sit quietly and just grind our guts, fuming over this esoteric prattle about words on a piece of paper. To us, it was about our baby lying on the ground squirting blood from five holes in his body, probably put there by Shirley. We wanted to get on with the question of whether she actually did it, and we thought that question should be addressed *once*, and *soon*, in a Pennsylvania courtroom.

Since that day I have had ample opportunity to pore over the hearing transcript and attempt a layman's construction of the arguments put forward by the two attorneys. I offer here only the briefest summary (dedicated masochists are free to purchase the transcript from the records department at the Supreme Court of Newfoundland and Labrador).

According to the defence, most of the evidence in the Case Record was gathered in the United States. However, two witnesses—Heather Arnold and Andrew Zohrab—had been interviewed in both the United States (by Pennsylvania police over the telephone) and Canada (by Canadian police assisting the Pennsylvania police). Some of the Arnold/Zohrab evidence was hearsay ("Shirley called me and said, 'blah blah blah.'"), which did not satisfy Canadian rules of evidence and would therefore not be admissible. Judge Green could not determine which parts of the evidence were taken in which country without reviewing police notes. Hence, Piercey asked the judge to issue an order that Canadian police turn over their notes from the Arnold and Zohrab interviews. Later, if these notes indicated that the Arnold/Zohrab evidence was collected in Canada, Piercey would be arguing that Madden had to either call the witnesses to the stand (where Piercey could cross-examine them) or excise their evidence from the Case Record.

Madden submitted that, historically, Canada's extradition partners, especially European Union countries, had long complained about Canada's admissibility requirements and considered them to be "needless technicalities." The Parliament of Canadian responded in 1990, and again in 1999, with new extradition laws intended to expedite the process by requiring minimal compliance with the stringent rules that applied to Canadian domestic criminal law. The fugitive was not being denied the right to challenge admissibility of evidence; he or she could do that in the trial courts of the requesting state.

Piercey countered, pointing out that the new extradition laws had in fact expedited the process by waiving Canadian standards for evidence gathered *outside* Canada. If, however, foreign authorities come into "our country," they have to comply with "our laws" when they gather evidence. The Treaty said that extradition decisions "shall be made in accordance with the law of the requested state [Canada]. And the person whose extradition is sought shall have the right to use all remedies and recourses provided by such law." If the same evidence were gathered both in the United States and in Canada, as may be the case for Arnold and Zohrab, Madden would have the burden to demonstrate the admissibility of that evidence under Canadian law.

Judge Green suggested the possibility that, if the Arnold/Zohrab evidence wasn't critical to his case, Madden had the option of voluntarily removing it from the Case Record, to expedite the hearing.

FLIGHT

Piercey's second issue related to why Shirley went to Canada after Andrew's murder. The Case Record contained evidence that could be construed as indicating that Shirley had fled from the United States to Canada.

According to Piercey, Andrew Zohrab stated that Shirley told him "she would be leaving the United States permanently." David Bagby stated that Shirley told him "she was going to get in her vehicle and go to Canada," and that "she'd walked away from her belongings in Iowa." These two statements were included in the Case Record "as an indication of flight" that "can be seen as an indication of consciousness of guilt." To counter the indication of flight, Piercey had affidavits from Carol Ross and Julianne Herzog (Shirley's Iowa attorney) showing that *they* had encouraged Shirley to leave the United States and that she "had an intention to return to the United States." Piercey offered to withdraw the Ross/Herzog affidavits if Madden were "prepared to put on the record that the issue of flight is not of relevance."

Madden had no submissions on the issue of flight, but requested time to consult with his cohorts at the Department of Justice on Piercey's offer to withdraw the affidavits.

RESOLUTION

Day three of the hearing took only thirteen minutes of court time.

After consulting overnight with his cohorts, Madden concluded that Zohrab's and my evidence didn't conclusively prove flight, so he agreed that the judge should not consider that issue when assessing sufficiency of the evidence in the Case Record.

The Arnold/Zohrab evidence, however, was deemed to be significant, so Madden declined to withdraw it. Judge Green was not prepared to make a ruling on disclosure of the Arnold/Zohrab police notes at this time, so the hearing was set over until June 11. At that time, it was expected that three additional days of court calendar would be needed to complete the process.

Part of the debate over admissibility centred on the meaning of Section 32 of the Extradition Act, which seemed to differ between the French and English versions (every official document—and many unofficial documents—in Canada must be produced in both languages). In an effort to resolve this section's precise meaning, Judge Green invited Madden and Piercey to submit an English translation of the French version prior to reconvening on June 11. At that point, I exploded internally: "Now the bastards are going to debate words on a piece of paper in two languages! Andrew is still dead, goddamnit! The question is *Did Shirley do it?* And the answer to that question is not your business! It's the business of a Pennsylvania jury!"

OFFENSIVE

The two lawyers and the judge maintained an impersonal demeanour throughout most of the arguments. However, during a discussion of Judge Green's authority (or lack thereof) to order disclosure of Pennsylvania (as opposed to Canadian) police notes, Piercey indignantly proclaimed, "I find it somewhat offensive that they [Pennsylvania police] can come into our country and use our resources to attempt to extradite one of our citizens, but then are able to stand back and say, well now I don't have to comply with the orders of this court."

Kate and I had less part to play in this hearing than the water pitcher on the clerk's desk, but I would like to have shouted into the court record, "I find it offensive that Andrew's probable killer can run off to a foreign country and use their legal technicalities to evade answering the most important question: *Did she do it?*"

The snail's pace of this hearing removed any lingering doubt about where the baby would be born. In fact, it was beginning to look like the baby's babies might be born before Shirley was sent back to the States. And if she were sent back in our lifetime, Kate and I would probably be rolled into the courtroom in a couple of wheelchairs to listen to a new round of legal machinations in Pennsylvania.

The bright spot, however, was Madden's performance—a pleasant surprise to us. Before this hearing our impression of him had been less than stellar, but his response to Piercey's admissibility arguments seemed extensive and thorough to Kate and me.

Before going home to California we met with an immigration lawyer, John Mate, to explore our options in case we had to make a permanent move to Canada. Immigration seemed as messy as extradition—it's just about as hard to get into Canada voluntarily as it is to be taken out involuntarily. However, John's opinion was that, if we were eventually given custody but were required to keep the baby in Canada, permanent resident status would probably be a slam dunk. In the meantime, we could stay in Canada up to six months at a stretch on a visitor's visa. We still hoped that would be long enough to see Shirley board a plane for Pittsburgh.

CHAPTER 11
MOVE

We could only stay in California for a week and we had a lot to do. Kate took a three-month leave of absence from her job. I had to resign from mine because my company couldn't afford to hold my position open. My boss did promise, however, that if they had an opening when I returned, they would want me to fill it.

Our dear friends again took over the practical home duties—paying bills and tending the house and garden—as they had done back in November when we were first thrown into this nightmare. We set up an electronic path to retirement money to live on, stuffed four suitcases in preparation for a long stay up north, and went back to St. John's on Saturday, June 8, to be there for the extradition hearing three days later.

It took five minutes. Judge Green had received the French-to-English translations from Madden and Piercey but, because the admissibility issue "may well have some implications for not only this particular case but others that may follow," he was not "in a position to give [his] ruling this morning." Continued to July 30 and 31. Anything else? No, my lord. No, thank you, my lord. All rise. Court adjourned.

Diane Rowsell of Victims Services (part of Newfoundland's department of justice) had accompanied us to court for this hearing. When the delay was announced we kept our composure (never let the enemy see you cry) until we were safely inside Diane's office, next door to the courthouse. There, the familiar division of emotional labour kicked in: Kate sobbed and I exploded, screaming some guttural protest that would have gotten me arrested two minutes earlier and planting a violent kick on Diane's open file cabinet drawer. She was naturally alarmed at this outburst and made appropriate soothing sounds. What else could she do? What else could I do? Or Kate? Nothing. Helpless sobbing. Impotent rage.

NEWFOUNDLAND HOSPITALITY

Mark and Jen, who were away on vacation the first three weeks we were in Newfoundland, left the keys to their house and cars with Heather and Matt and a note on the kitchen table inviting us to make ourselves at home. Sweet kids. We moved in, opened a bank account, bought a laptop computer for emailing family and friends, and prepared to wait as long as the battles might take.

Several of Andrew's medical school classmates were in town for a wedding, and they included us in the festivities: a barbecue and an overnight stay at their cabin outside Bay Roberts. Ken (the groom), Andrew, Anthony, Chad, and Jim had bought the cabin for peanuts early in medical school and fixed it up as a retreat from their rigorous studies. Four of the five owners were there, along with Ken's fiancée, Sherri-Lynn, and several others of their family and friends.

We weren't good company. We were a couple of serious downers nearly every waking hour. But all these fine young people kept including us in their lives and we loved them for it, while simultaneously hating Shirley for putting us there in Andrew's stead.

SHIRLEY GOSSIP

At Ken and Sherri-Lynn's wedding reception, we picked up some gossip originating from Shirley. She had recently been visiting old acquaintances at the medical school, playing the role of innocent, and prattling away, as usual.

Shirley had said that the baby was a boy, whom she would name Zachary Andrew Turner. His due date was July 13 and Carol Ross would be in town to help her through the delivery. If she went to prison, she claimed we would not get her baby because we had lied about her. Carol Ross would like to adopt Zachary, but was too busy with her own career to take care of a baby. Hence, he would probably end up in foster care. There would be no DNA paternity testing unless she was forced into it. If she went to jail while Zachary was still very young, she would keep him with her in order to breastfeed.

This all came to us second-hand, but we had no reason to doubt that Shirley had actually said these things. If she had, we could draw some insights. She was acknowledging the possibility of actually being extradited, tried, and convicted, and she seemed to be making a stab at rational planning for that eventuality. Of course, we didn't agree with her particular plans, but at least she was planning. We thought that was a good sign. There probably wasn't anyone from her family offering to take care of the child, so we would have a better chance of taking him home to California once she was in prison. Her choice of foster care over Kate and me gave some indication of the level of hatred she held for us. Kate had a theory that was probably right: Shirley saw us as the *perfect* family she never had, and was never going to have, and she resented it enough to kill someone. She would probably view DNA testing as an insult: "Of course Andrew was my only lover. I'm no slut!"

OUR CONTINUING LEGAL EDUCATION

At about 1:30 a.m. August 5, 2001, approximately 130 miles off the coast of Massachusetts, a Russian ship named *Virgo* ran over a small American fishing trawler named *Starbound*. Three of the four fishermen were fast asleep and went down with the boat. One miraculously survived and was picked up by the Coast Guard. The *Virgo* steamed on to Newfoundland, where Canadian and American authorities began an investigation of the incident. Eventually, the captain, first officer, and one crewman of the *Virgo* were charged in Massachusetts with manslaughter, and extradition proceedings got underway in St. John's. Randy Piercey represented one of the Russians, while Mike Madden was the Crown Prosecutor, acting on behalf of the United States. With no jobs and no regular commitments, Kate and I had too much time on our hands and took ourselves once again to the back of a courtroom. We wanted to understand as much as possible about extradition, and particularly to see the lawyers in action again, especially Piercey—know thy enemy.

We sat through most of a week's testimony by one witness, Captain Clement Murphy, a steamship inspector who had been sent to look over the *Virgo* after it docked in Newfoundland. Madden led Murphy through an account of his inspection, and then the defence lawyers, one by one, nibbled at his testimony and his inspection report, trying to demonstrate that he had illegally conducted his inspection as a ruse to gather evidence against their clients. As in Shirley's case, we thought this was a silly waste of time. The real question was *Did they do the crime*? And that question, we thought, should be addressed *once*, and *soon*, in a Massachusetts courtroom. (Lest the reader infer that I am a nationalistic bigot, I believe that a fugitive charged with committing a crime in Canada should be dealt with once, and soon, in a Canadian courtroom.)

Unfortunately, by Friday's adjournment, they had not finished with Murphy and we still had not seen Piercey on his feet, which had been our primary goal in sitting through this tedious nitpicking. But we gained a little more insight into courtroom proceedings, which served to thicken our cynical skins in preparation for the long road ahead.

CHAPTER 12
HAPPY BIRTHDAY

While waiting for the birth of our grandson we had frequent talks with Jackie Brazil, trying to cover all angles to ensure the baby's future.

CHILD, YOUTH AND FAMILY SERVICES

Jackie met with Child, Youth and Family Services (CYFS) Regional Director Elizabeth Day on June 17, 2002—several weeks before the baby's anticipated delivery date—to express Kate's and my concern for the baby's safety if he were left in Shirley's care. We primarily based that concern, Jackie told Day, on Shirley's probable guilt in the murder of our son and the emotional instability that would be implied by such guilt. We also suspected that she had not been a full-time parent to her other three children, and that she had displayed periods of instability during her tenure at medical school. We hoped that CYFS would thoroughly investigate these allegations as part of their decision-making process in dealing with Shirley.

Jackie asked Day if we would be considered as caregivers if Shirley were incarcerated. Without acknowledging that Shirley was even a client of CYFS, Day replied that relatives were always given consideration in placement decisions.

Before ending the meeting, Jackie asked that Shirley not be informed of our intent to apply for custody of the baby. Again, Day did not confirm that her department had any dealings with Shirley, due to client confidentiality rights and because there was no protective intervention being contemplated at that time.

This meeting was a calculated gamble on our part. If Day considered it her duty to inform her client—if indeed Shirley was her client—of our concerns for the baby's safety, Shirley's reaction might be the sort of rage that had cost Andrew his life.

While the standard for conviction in a criminal court was "beyond a reasonable doubt," the standard for CYFS removal of a child from a potentially dangerous situation was much lower. Our hope was that someone in Day's organization would be prodded into examining the record on Shirley's extradition case, which was available at the courthouse. If they read the detailed charges against Shirley, they might, we hoped, take the prudent step of removing the child from the care of an accused murderer until a jury could render a verdict.

BACKUP PARENTS

If Shirley went to prison and we got custody of the baby, we might die before he reached maturity; at his birth I would be fifty-six, Kate sixty-one. This might be a factor against us in a custody battle, so we asked four younger couples—relatives and friends—if they would act as backup parents. Each couple wrote a letter describing their family and career situations and agreeing to take over care of our grandson if we both died before he reached maturity. These letters reached us in late June and early July, in time for Zachary's birth and the upcoming court battle. If there was in fact a court battle, all four couples had agreed to fly to Newfoundland and appear in Family Court to be examined by Jackie and cross-examined by Shirley's attorney.

POLICE CLEARANCE

Kate, Jackie, and I considered the possibility that Shirley might try to impugn our character if we got into an all-out custody war over Zachary. The best defence against such an attack is good references, which we obtained in abundance from our friends. Also, most police departments will perform, on request, for a fee, a routine check of their files on any citizen who wants one. The result is a certificate stating that the named citizen has no police record in their jurisdiction. Kate and I each obtained one of these certificates from the Sunnyvale Police Department just before leaving California for Newfoundland.

FINAL PREP

On July 11, two days before Zachary was due, we met with Jackie for a final pre-battle conference. She offered us an out: "You can go home now and no one would think any less of you." We practically sang our response *en duet*: "That's not an option. We're here for the long haul. We must have some influence in the baby's life."

Jackie raised the possibility that Carol Ross might, with Shirley's written permission, take the baby out of our reach. To head off that tactic, she proposed that we submit, in addition to our custody and DNA testing applications, an application asking the court to order that Shirley not allow Zachary to be removed from St. John's. We agreed, and all three applications were signed the following day. Then we could do no more until our grandson was born.

TENNIS BALL TEST

If you repeatedly toss a tennis ball to a dog, he will quickly learn to catch it in his mouth. If you then toss two tennis balls, he will be confused and miss them both. We were about to face a tennis ball test.

On Thursday, July 18, 2002, we learned via the hospital grapevine that Shirley had been admitted to the maternity floor but was not in the delivery room, indicating that her doctor would probably induce labour.

That afternoon we also learned that a postponement of the extradition hearing was being contemplated. I called Mike Madden, who said there was to be a meeting of the lawyers in Judge Green's chambers at 9:45 the next morning, and that he would press for a new date in early September.

The hospital grapevine delivered the good news early Friday morning: Zachary had been born late Thursday night by Caesarean section. Shirley was on the maternity floor and the baby was in the routine nursery. We finally had a grandson. He was healthy, but he was nursing at the breast of a woman who was probably an emotionally unstable killer. Welcome to the world, kid!

In the courthouse waiting room, Madden came out to speak with us after meeting with Judge Green and John Kelly, who was standing in for his partner, Randy Piercey. Madden took one look at Kate and said, "Mrs. Bagby, you look awful! Shouldn't you see a doctor?"

She did look awful: pale, with heavy sacs under her eyes. Always within a second or two of tears, on the slightest provocation. Never still, squirming in her seat or shifting from one foot to the other. Constantly churning the horror of it through her mind: "How can my Andrew be dead! Murdered! How can this bitch be having his baby! Kill him and have his baby! How can I go on living?!" If breathing were voluntary, we both would have died the day we heard of Andrew's murder. The rest of life's normal functions—eating, showering, brushing our teeth, exercising, even making love—had been mostly done through force of habit. But as long as we were alive, we focused on two simple goals: get the bitch and get the baby. All we could do to help get the bitch was show our faces in court, hoping to keep Andrew's humanity alive in the eyes of the judge. To get the baby, we had prepared as thoroughly as possible and the action was about to begin.

"It's not physical," I told him.

His concern was genuine. "It looks as if she could do with some sleep and a doctor could help with that."

Kate replied, "I have sleeping medication if I want to take it."

Madden got back to business and told us that the extradition hearing was postponed because Judge Green had not completed his decision on disclosure of the Arnold/Zohrab police notes. The judge, he said, had promised to do so by September 2 and had rescheduled the hearing for September 19 and 20.

The judge, Madden continued, had also commented on the birth of Shirley's baby and presumed that the grandparents would now show an interest. Madden, who knew of our intention to apply for custody, had quite properly kept his mouth shut. Kelly had said that they expected papers any day.

Danette Dooley was waiting for us in the hallway and had a quick exchange with Madden after he left us. He told her, "The Bagbys are devastated." Dooley replied, "What did you expect?" It seemed to us that he grasped, for the first time, the effect of all this delay on a murder victim's family. "The law is slow," he had told us months before. It damn sure was.

Danette accompanied us to the hospital, where we hoped to get a peek at our new grandson. Mary Dray from the medical school Student Affairs office helped us locate Shirley and

Zachary's room, but the door was closed. A nurse informed us that Shirley was not accepting visitors. Kate cried and set a gift on the counter for the baby. I thought, "He's five feet away, right through that wall, and you can't see him! But this is not a time for the rage. Keep cool. If you blow up, she'll use it against you in Family Court."

Walking back down the hall to leave, a nursing supervisor hurried after us and apologized, but she could not allow us to see the baby without Shirley's permission. Painful, but we understood that she was bound by these normally reasonable rules.

CHAPTER 13
ACCESS

Jackie had lots of news when we met at her office late in the afternoon of Zachary's first full day breathing air. She had filed our applications and the non-removal order had been granted immediately; Shirley couldn't send Zachary away. Jackie had called Piercey's partner, John Kelly, who said that Shirley wasn't upset by our custody application. In fact, Kelly reported, she seemed almost pleased that we had shown an interest.

Shirley already had a Legal Aid attorney (similar to a Public Defender in the States), Mike Newton, to help her with the custody battle. Jackie had met with Newton, who saw no problem with our request for DNA testing. In fact, Newton said that he would have requested it if we hadn't. Jackie told Newton that we were anxious to see the baby and he said that something could probably be worked out.

Jackie had learned that Shirley's daughter from her second marriage had been the subject of a Family Court fight three months ago. The girl had come to St. John's for a short visit with Shirley, but had not returned to her father. Shirley's second husband had retained a lawyer and tried to have his daughter sent back to him, but had to give up the fight when his limited money ran out. So now an accused murderer had custody of *two* children: a twelve-year-old and an infant.

Four days later, Newton called Jackie to say that Shirley had changed her tune. Things *couldn't* be worked out. She claimed to fear for the child's life. If we were to see the baby, we would have to be searched beforehand and supervised throughout the visits. Jackie told us, "She's just trying to wind you up."

Shirley also claimed that we had harassed and threatened her in the presence of a nurse. Jackie asked for the identity of the nurse, so that a subpoena could be issued. The fight promised to be a dirty one. Are there any clean court fights? Are there any clean fights?

"Legal Aid attorneys are overworked and underpaid." Everybody said so. Mike Newton was no exception. He had a very busy court schedule and Jackie had a tough time tracking him down to discuss a possible agreement on our visiting the baby. She had arranged a court date on August 6 for something called "case management," which, in this context, meant the two parties would be trying to reach agreement rather than all-out fighting. She was leaving messages for him every day, seeking a negotiation meeting. If he didn't respond, it would look bad for his client at the August 6 hearing.

Newton did eventually respond. Shirley was balking at our visits with the baby because of her extradition bail condition, requiring her to keep away from Andrew's family. She wanted to talk to Piercey before agreeing to visits.

On July 30, Judge Seamus O'Regan presided over a one-minute *pro forma* hearing to officially postpone the extradition hearing until September 19 at 10 a.m. Afterward, Madden told us that the Arnold/Zohrab evidence might be dropped from the record, in which case Judge Green would not have to make the disclosure decision and things could move ahead sooner. He also said that Piercey had relayed Shirley's concern about violating her no-contact provision. Madden had told him, "Jesus Christ! Just go into a room at the back and leave the baby with the Bagbys and a third party." This made sense to us, but Madden said he had no objection to Shirley being in the room with us while we visited the baby. That, we thought, would be hard to stomach. As he walked away, he said, "She's half-cracked."

When we later recounted all this to Jackie, she did not like the idea of us sitting in the same room with Andrew's probable killer during our Zachary visits. That would be far too traumatic for us, she feared, and she was probably right. But we were prepared to eat a very large shit sandwich to get time with our baby's baby.

On August 1, Shirley had a new Legal Aid lawyer, Cynthia Janes. Jackie had telephoned Cynthia, who would be away for a two-week trial in Corner Brook and thus wanted a postponement of the August 6 Family Court date. Cynthia also suggested that Shirley would be more likely to agree to access if we had not applied for custody. Jackie suggested that Cynthia carefully review the file before they talked further. She wanted Cynthia to understand her client thoroughly before entering into serious negotiations.

The next day, Cynthia called Jackie. She wanted to keep the August 6 court date and would send another lawyer from her office to cover for her. They had filed no affidavits, but Shirley claimed to have "reasons" for wanting us searched. Cynthia would not elaborate on these reasons, but wanted us to withdraw our custody application and agree to Shirley having "interim sole custody." This term denoted a legal status, which, had we agreed to it then, Shirley could later use against us: *If you thought I was an unfit mother, why did you agree to my having interim sole custody?*

FAMILY COURT

Our first day in Family Court, August 6, 2002, began with Kate and me moving into one conference room while Shirley occupied another. Our lawyers met somewhere in between to negotiate: my client wants *this*, your client wants *that*, maybe both would settle for *the other*. Then Jackie and Mary Boulous, who was standing in for Cynthia, would split up and present *the other* to their clients, get their new positions, and return to the negotiation. After perhaps half a dozen rounds of this, we nearly had agreement on our access to Zachary.

If we could not reach agreement, we would go to full battle mode, which would take perhaps several months and place the outcome entirely in the hands of a judge, in addition to aggravating our emotionally unstable opponent. If, however, we could agree on a set of conditions that were acceptable to both sides, then the judge would likely order both sides to abide by those agreed conditions. This was called a Consent Order, and it was the only kind of order the judge could issue in a case-management hearing.

If either side refused to reach agreement and forced full battle mode, they ran the risk of having a judge eventually rule entirely for the other side. For us, that meant the possibility of having no access to Zachary until the extradition hearing ran its course. For Shirley, the risk was that a judge might take Zachary away from her and put him in our care. Both extremes were very unlikely, but it was safer to agree now on something we could live with, rather than risk losing all in a protracted war. And, just as important, we could avoid further antagonizing Shirley—she held the hostage.

Judge Robert Wells took the bench at Unified Family Court for a nice friendly case management hearing. The courtroom was smaller than the ones we had seen at Supreme Court Trial Division, where the extradition hearings were held, because there was no need for spectator seating. Family court sessions were "in camera" (closed to the public) so that the contestants' faces and stories wouldn't be exposed to media exploitation.

The clerk had a small table off to the side. A long bench with two widely separated podiums faced the judge. There was a row of chairs for contestants across the back wall, in the centre of which was the courtroom door, providing a natural dividing line between the opposing sides. Kate and I sat to the left of the door, Shirley to the right.

Jackie stood at the podium in front of us and presented our position on access to Zachary. We wanted two one-hour visits per week with the baby at UFC and no direct contact with Shirley, who would wait in a separate room (Shirley agreed to that).

Shirley's attorney, Mary Boulous—standing in for Cynthia Janes—stood behind the other podium and stated her client's position. Shirley wanted one one-hour visit per week, supervision of the visits by a professional access worker, for which we agreed to pay; a body and bag search of Kate and me prior to each visit, to which we agreed; and taxi service for Shirley and Zachary between her home and the court, for which we agreed to pay.

Up to that point the only contentious issue was one versus two weekly visits. Boulous argued that it was quite a strain on Shirley, only a few weeks after a Caesarean delivery, to pack up the baby for an extra visit with us.

Jackie, with our concurrence, offered to have the access supervisor, at our expense, assist her in preparing Zachary for the taxi rides.

At one point Judge Wells asked, "Why all of this difficulty…is this the criminal case in the U.S.?"

Jackie, again with our concurrence, didn't want it on record that we thought Shirley had murdered our son, so she just said, "Yes, my lord."

The judge said, "I take it the difficulties are arising because of strong feelings on both sides…usually these things can be worked out."

Kate and I wanted to ask, "How do you suggest we work out this little difficulty? Go out to dinner, share a bottle of excellent Cabernet, swap stories about our good times with Andrew, and then perhaps move in together?"

Jackie had no choice but to hide her incredulity: "Well, my lord, it's not your typical case…but at this stage my clients are desperate to see their grandson."

Judge Wells was leaning towards one visit per week to start, with more later if things went well. They moved on to other issues.

Boulous complained that Shirley's mother, who lived across the island in Corner Brook, had not seen Zachary because of the non-removal order restricting the baby to St. John's. She asked the judge to extend the non-removal order to cover all of Newfoundland, so that Shirley could take the baby to Corner Brook.

Jackie explained our fear that, without the non-removal order, Shirley might send Zachary out of our reach. She also pointed out an inconsistency in Boulous' argument: preparing the baby to visit Corner Brook would be at least as physically demanding as preparing for a second weekly visit with us.

Boulous pointed out that Shirley had another child at home who would not be coming with her to the court during our visits. With all her family on the west coast, she was "here by herself." There was no one to look after her twelve-year-old daughter during the visits. Jackie offered to speak to her clients about funding a babysitter for the twelve-year-old.

Boulous asked the court for an order giving Shirley interim sole custody of Zachary. Jackie countered that, while that issue may come up later, it had no bearing on our attempt to get access to the baby. She suggested that the issue had been "placed on the table to make this more difficult for my clients." She went on to list all the conditions we were willing to accept in order to see Zachary and noted that there were "constantly new hurdles being placed in our path."

When she referred to the supervision and bag and body searches, Judge Wells said, "... this troubles me, I mean, are they [the Bagbys] criminals?"

Jackie replied, "No they're not, my lord."

"I don't understand it."

"They're people who have had a very difficult..."

Boulous interrupted: "My lord, there is an issue...I have a copy of a sworn affidavit from a doctor who has indicated that Ms. Bagby...has threatened to kill my client."

Jackie objected strenuously and the two lawyers shouted over each other until the judge took control. He tried to smooth things over: "The only way that any kind of relationship with the child is going to be fruitful and worthwhile is if there's a bit of give and take on both sides." He suggested that we start with one hour per week and "see how that works out...let other issues go to the background for the moment." The only alternative, he suggested, was to "make your various applications and come and fight it out. That would be very sad."

The judge's suggestion was close to our objective: postpone the expansion of non-removal and the interim sole custody issues until a later date and get us some time with Zachary, starting *now*. We would have preferred two weekly visits, unless, of course, Shirley miraculously agreed to leave the baby with us full-time and report to the Greensburg Barracks of the Pennsylvania State Police. That wasn't likely, so two visits was our best hope and one was what we got.

In a calmer atmosphere, Jackie told the judge, "I don't appreciate standing here today and being blindsided with such an inflammatory…allegation." The reason for the allegation, she submitted, was to throw up "another hurdle" in our path to see the baby.

Boulous still did not produce the affidavit, but instead went back to the non-removal issue. Shirley was "not agreeable to access" until she could take the baby to see her family on the west coast.

Normally a judge would not make any orders during a case management hearing, but Judge Wells told Boulous,

> If I were to be making an order today…I wouldn't lift [the non-removal order]…If I were being asked to make an order today, and that could only be done by consent [between Shirley and us], I would only order one thing and that would be one-hour per week under the conditions that have been suggested, leaving other things to possibly calm a little and be reviewed again in probably a month.

We took a break and met Jackie in our conference room. She was pissed! At first, Kate thought Jackie was angry with her, but Boulous was Jackie's target. Boulous, she explained, was way out of line to introduce an accusation into the court record without warning and without providing the supporting affidavit. This warning and affidavit would normally have been provided to the judge and the opposing attorney by noon of the day before a hearing.

Jackie would be hounding Shirley's attorney mercilessly until the affidavit was submitted to the court or the charge was withdrawn, in writing, on the record. If they did produce the affidavit, Jackie would demand to cross-examine its signatory, whom we guessed must be Carol Ross. And if Kate had in fact said something threatening against Shirley, who would blame her?

From Kate's journal, August 6, 2002: "Strange that I should have an affidavit against me when I could not kill her—rather kill myself. If asked, I shall have to respond that I might have said it but cannot remember—probably distraught at my great loss—a son murdered and his killer free."

The out-of-court negotiations continued. Kate and I finally accepted one visit per week and agreed to allow Shirley to visit the west coast of Newfoundland, provided her trips did not interfere with our scheduled access visits.

Back in the courtroom, the final agreement was read into the record and we were set to see our baby's baby in three days.[1]

CHILD, YOUTH AND FAMILY SERVICES

After Zachary was born and we filed for custody and Shirley took the baby home from the hospital, CYFS officials recognized Shirley's increased stress level and provided extra home support services: family counselling, a breastfeeding support group, bus passes, and advocacy for social assistance money. Arrangements were set in motion to place Zachary in short-term foster care if Judge Green ordered Shirley to jail. A prospective foster family was identified and assessed, in consultation with Shirley. CYFS never contacted us regarding these arrangements, and never removed Zachary from Shirley's care.

CHAPTER 14
ZACHARY

Kate and I were in a strange zone as the sheriff's deputy led us down the hall to the visiting room at Unified Family Court. Zachary lay in an infant carrier on the sofa, with the access supervisor sitting next to him. We didn't actually notice her, as we were overcome with the sight of Andrew's last living legacy. We knelt before him like two Magi at the manger and let the wonder of it wash over us. Every grandparent must know that complex mix of feelings: joy, hope, pride, reverence. Is it rooted in the selfish satisfaction of knowing part of us will live on Earth beyond our own lifetimes?

He was beautiful! Well-proportioned, with reddish-blond hair and Andrew's nose. His head tilted a little to the right because he had lain that way in utero. In time, if he were frequently put down on the left side for sleeping, his neck would slowly straighten out.

After a lot of ooing and cooing, Kate finally picked him up and I turned to get the camera. Then I noticed the supervisor. She softly greeted us, "Hello, I'm Maureen."

"Pleased to meet you," I said and took out my camera.

For the remainder of the hour, we passed him back and forth for cuddles, chatted with Maureen, took a lot of pictures, and spoke to Zachary in a mixture of baby babble and real words, mostly about his wonderful daddy.

He slept through the whole thing. Several times his eyes flitted open—they were dark blue, like Andrew's—and we thought we might get a proper introduction, but he always went right back to sleep.

Near the hour mark, I said to Maureen, "This is when we leave without a scene, right?" She softly said, "I'm afraid so."

She gave us some photographs of Zachary from Shirley. We left some diapers. The deputy knocked on the door. We packed our things and were led out to the parking lot. Thankfully, we never saw Shirley that day.

What a high to see him! What a low to leave him.

PETTY BICKERING

Back at home we had a call from Vera Griffin, who worked with Mary Dray in the Student Affairs office at the medical school. Shirley had written a letter of complaint against us, claiming that we had been trying to see Zachary at the hospital just three hours after he was born. Vera had been asked to check this claim and to find out if Heather Arnold had informed us of his birth. Shirley was obviously trying to get Heather into trouble for breaching her medical privacy, presumably by looking at her chart on the hospital computer.

Shirley couldn't prove either charge, and we couldn't disprove them. Zachary was born just before midnight and we were definitely asleep at 3 a.m. the following morning. Furthermore, Heather did not tell us of his arrival; it was common knowledge around the hospital. In fact, it was common knowledge all over St. John's. Even Judge Green knew about it at his 10 a.m. meeting with Madden and Kelly. Zachary was, after all, the famous baby of an infamous mother.

Jackie took us to dinner at The Hungry Fisherman to celebrate our first visit with Zachary. We naturally discussed Shirley's complaint and marvelled once again at her sense of proportion: *If you're going to complain that I shot your son to death, I'll complain that your friend looked at my medical records without permission!* Jackie reiterated what we already knew: "She is pure evil! We must never underestimate her!"

BONDING

After that first wonderful visit, they got better and better. Zachary was awake more often than not and thoroughly enjoyed waving his arms and legs and smiling and chatting with his Nan and Pop. I spent twenty minutes of one visit lying on the sofa with him sitting on my tummy considering, and commenting on, my suggestions for his possible future career.

Shirley sent studio photos of Zachary to us. We sent our photos of Zachary to her, and also to our family and friends. They, in turn, sent lots of lovely outfits and toys for the baby. Some of these we passed to Shirley and some we hoarded just for visits. At one visit, Shirley sent his baby book so that we could fill in our side of his family tree. The insanity of this situation—little notes and civilities passed back and forth between us and Andrew's murderer—was not lost on us, but we were so overjoyed at having time with our grandson that we wilfully ignored the horror and focused on the immediate pleasure.

If Zachary fussed, Kate tried to calm him with her brand of stand-up rocking cuddles. If that didn't work, Maureen took him to Shirley for a breast and then brought him back to us for a burp. If he fell asleep, whoever happened to be holding him lucked into some extra cuddle time. I spent over half of one visit slouching on the sofa with Zachary asleep on my chest, his head pressed against my cheek. Good times—the best in nearly a year.

THE MISSING AFFIDAVIT

Jackie tore into Shirley's custody lawyer, Cynthia Janes, about the surprise unfiled affidavit alleging that Kate had threatened Shirley. Cynthia asked if we knew who signed it. Jackie said, "My clients can think of only one MD to whom they have spoken who is also in contact with Shirley and that is Carol Ross." Cynthia confirmed that it was indeed Ross. Jackie said that the accusation was now on the record at Family Court and would have to be acted upon. Cynthia promised to listen to the tape in which Boulous raised the issue. They left it at that for the moment.

Days later, in a courtroom hallway chat, Kate told Madden about the affidavit, but Piercey had already shown it to him. Madden said that he had been in a very bad mood that day and raved at Piercey: "You're usually a nice, reasonable guy, but this is ridiculous! Here's a woman who, *if* she said it, was one month out from having her son, her only son, murdered! It's an understandable statement! And, Mrs. Bagby has been here six months and no harm has come to Turner. If you try to file such a ridiculous affidavit, I'll fight it!"

In early September Kate spent a week in California officially retiring from her job and putting our household into storage, with a lot of help from our friends. Virgil, our friend across the street, agreed to find a renter for the house and manage the property for us.

We tried to reschedule the Zachary visit so that Kate wouldn't miss it, but Shirley couldn't accommodate us because of a meeting with her lawyer. That was the only time either of us missed a visit, but Kate wrote a note that I read to Zachary in her absence. In addition to the usual bag of diapers, I took some baby formula, at Shirley's request, relayed to us through the visit supervisor, Maureen Kendall. Shirley planned to put Zachary on one bottle per day, in preparation for her possible incarceration after the September 19 extradition hearing.

CHAPTER 15

EXTRADITION HEARING

At 10:16 a.m. on September 19, 2002, Judge Green took the bench and reminded everyone about the publication ban in effect for Shirley Turner's extradition hearing.[1]

He then announced that Dr. Turner had delivered a baby who was in the courthouse, under the care of another individual (Maureen, our visit supervisor), and may have to be fed periodically. Appropriate breaks would be taken.

Regarding Mr. Piercey's application for disclosure of Canadian police notes, that was now a moot point. The United States had provided a Supplemental Case Record, which contained the information the defence had requested.

Judge Green asked, "So you're satisfied…that I should not give my ruling [on disclosure] and that we can proceed…with the main extradition hearing. Is that right?"

"Yes," Piercey replied.

"Hallelujah!" I sang to myself.

HEATHER ARNOLD

Madden had no submissions beyond the Case Record and the Supplemental Case Record. Piercey had one witness, Heather Arnold, who was called to the stand and sworn in.

Piercey read out part of Heather's statement to police as it was summarized in both the original and supplemental records: "Ms. Arnold will testify that Shirley Turner had told her that she drove to Pennsylvania with her .22 calibre pistol to discuss the miscarriage with Dr. Bagby."

Piercey said, "I read that to mean [in what I heard as an exaggerated mock belligerent tone] 'I'm taking my gun down to discuss this with Dr. Bagby'. Was that the way you meant these words to come out?"

Heather replied, "No, what I'm pretty sure I told them… was that she was going to take the gun down to him because he wanted to borrow it…[and] within the same conversation but…definitely [not] in the same sentence that she said she was going…to be consoled…about the miscarriage."

He reiterated that the two issues—taking the gun to Andrew and discussing the miscarriage—were not related. Heather agreed.

Piercey turned the witness over to Madden, who asked, "Is there anything [in either the Case Record or its supplement] that you would like to change, amend…disagree with or think was misinterpreted, other than what we've already heard here today?"

"No." Heather was excused from the stand.

THE CASE

Madden stepped to his microphone and summarized the purpose of an extradition hearing and the role of its judge, using a quote from case law:

> The purpose of an extradition hearing is not to determine the guilt or innocence of the fugitive. It is merely an inquiry to determine whether there is sufficient evidence to warrant sending the fugitive to the demanding State so

that he may stand trial...The...extradition judge is not required to weigh the evidence or to decide the credibility of witnesses; his duty is to determine if the evidence would justify the committal of the fugitive for trial if the alleged crime had been committed in Canada.

[The fugitive can] point out weaknesses or deficiencies in the evidence of the demanding State...[and] present arguments as to why he should not be extradited.... [However] the full determination of the fugitive's rights will take place in the courts of the demanding country. It is a basic assumption of extradition proceedings that the fugitive will receive a fair and just trial in the demanding State.

Embedded in Madden's summary was the key test that a judge should apply in making an extradition decision: "[To] determine if the evidence would justify the committal of the fugitive for trial if the alleged crime had been committed in Canada."

He then presented a synopsis of the evidence with the goal of persuading Judge Green that, had the crime been committed in Canada, Shirley Turner would be committed for trial. He touched on the discovery of Dr. Bagby's body, the gunshot wounds and blunt trauma, the unspent shell, Dr. Turner's early morning appearance at Andrew's door, her jealousy, her shifting stories on where she was and where her gun was, and the damning cellphone records placing her in Pennsylvania. On he plowed, systematically hitting every significant point, finishing with motive: "One of the oldest motives in the book; that being jealousy, and...revenge on a man who she believed was breaking up with her at a time when she, herself, was particularly vulnerable, believing perhaps that she was carrying his baby."

It took Madden about forty-five minutes to march through the evidence. When it was over Kate and I were drained. We had picked up most pieces of the story over the many months since Andrew's murder, but hearing them all put together brought the horror of Andrew's last few months and minutes into sharp focus. Our baby must have been a miserable wretch from the strain of trying to disentangle himself from this emotional octopus.

CHAPTER 16
MORE NITS

After lunch, Piercey had two issues for Judge Green's consideration: the validity of the Authority to Proceed and the treatment of circumstantial evidence at an extradition hearing.[1]

AUTHORITY TO PROCEED

"My first argument this afternoon is that there is no valid authority to proceed before the Court in this case...these proceedings have been invalid since at least March the 12th, 2002... [my client] should be discharged."

Piercey's argument for this monstrous miscarriage of justice went like this: Dr. Turner was arrested in Canada on December 12, 2001. Through a combination of time requirements in the Extradition Treaty and the Extradition Act, an Authority to Proceed must be issued within ninety days of arrest; that is, by March 12, 2002. The "purported" Authority to Proceed supplied to the court was issued within the ninety-day limit, but only specified the offence as, "Culpable homicide, contrary to Section 229(*a*) of the Criminal Code."

This section defines culpable homicide under Canadian law as, "where the person who causes the death of a human being" and has two subsections: "i) means to cause his death, or

ii) means to cause him bodily harm that he knows is likely to cause his death, and is reckless whether death ensues or not."

Because the Authority to Proceed failed to specify subsection (i) or (ii), Piercey argued, it was a nullity thereby effectively requiring the judge to do the prosecution's job by selecting one of the two subsections. Furthermore, while amending an Authority to Proceed is allowed under the Extradition Act, it has to be done "on a timely basis."

Piercey stated that it was far too late to amend the Authority to Proceed on a timely basis. Therefore, Dr. Turner should be discharged and no future Authority to Proceed on this charge should be allowed.

Kate and I wondered if Piercey could endorse such an argument if he had kissed the cold dead forehead of his own murdered child.

POOR SHIRLEY

Piercey went on to complain about the hardships to which his client had been subjected due to delays caused by the Crown: "They've delayed Dr. Turner from June until September…by refusing to give us something that clearly now they acknowledge we were entitled to have."

He was referring to the information that was provided in the Supplemental Case Record. In a later court hearing, Judge Green would make it very clear that the United States provided that information, not because they thought Piercey was entitled to have it, but to expedite the process and that Piercey understood that motivation when he accepted the new information.

The defence attorney continued: "Dr. Turner has…undergone the birth of a child while under arrest." Though free on bail, she was still considered in law to be "under arrest." Piercey further argued that "she's a doctor—that career is held up

because, to a great extent, she's here under an invalid Authority
to Proceed....

"If your lordship accepts that this is an invalid Authority to
Proceed and...you grant [the Crown time to make] an amendment...it's just further delay, delay which is fully attributable,
again, to the Crown."

MADDEN'S RESPONSE

Crown attorney Madden's responses to Piercey's Authority to
Proceed arguments are best summarized using two cases he
quoted: "[T]he classification of murder is irrelevant in the
extradition context. [The extradition judge is only required to
determine] whether the conduct of the fugitive...had it
occurred in Canada, [would] constitute any Canadian crime,"
and "[Canada's] only responsibility is to satisfy ourselves that
the conduct alleged is specified or described in the
[Extradition] Treaty, and that [it] is punishable in Canada."

Judge Green noted that both these cases fell under the previous Extradition Act, and he and Madden sparred for a while
over the relationship between the old and new extradition laws
and between an extradition hearing and a domestic indictment.
Green asked Madden, "Would a charge under domestic law that
Mike Madden committed culpable homicide...be a sufficient
charge [in a domestic case]?"

Madden replied, "We're not...dealing with domestic
law.... [to say that the Authority to Proceed] now has to follow
along with what would appear in [a domestic indictment
would be] importing into the extradition law standards which
have previously only existed in relation to domestic law."

Just in case the judge ruled against him on the validity of
the current Authority to Proceed, Madden referred to another
extradition case (*Thailand Kingdom v. Karas*) in which the

"extradition judge...permitted an amendment to the Authority to Proceed."

In short, Madden's position was that the original Authority to Proceed was valid, but if Judge Green ruled that it was not, it was at least amendable.

DEFENCE RESPONSIBILITY?

During Piercey's submissions, Judge Green asked, "If [the Authority to Proceed] is a nullity, what responsibility is there on Dr. Turner's part to challenge it as a nullity, before we get to the stage we're at now?"

Piercey thought that issue should be raised at a second extradition hearing, if the judge quashed the current Authority to Proceed and allowed the Crown to file an amended one.

The judge said, "So that would be the equivalent...in a domestic case [of if a] person charged with murder says nothing, leaves the Indictment [as] a nullity because it doesn't properly describe the offence, goes through a trial, hears all the evidence, and at the end of the Crown case, gets up and says this is a nullity?"

"And I would think that's permissible, my lord," Piercey replied.

After a break, Judge Green read back to Piercey from the May 27 extradition transcript, in which the Authority to Proceed was read into the record: "And then I said: 'Do you have any objection to the sufficiency of the form, Mr. Piercey?' And the answer was no. I'm just wondering whether that was the time to address the sufficiency of the form of the indictment and to raise the point that you're making now. Did you not concede it at that point?"

Piercey replied, "I don't think it would [be fatal to my argument] to bring it to your lordship's attention now because if it's void, it's void. And me saying well, it's fine, would not impact upon that."

CIRCUMSTANTIAL EVIDENCE

Piercey's argument on circumstantial evidence was based on the strength of the evidence and on the test an extradition judge should apply to that evidence: *could a properly instructed jury convict based on this evidence?* With circumstantial evidence, however, the judge's task is more complicated than with direct evidence. He or she must "engage in a limited weighing of the evidence [to determine whether guilt] may be reasonably inferred from the circumstantial evidence." If there are other reasonable explanations for the circumstantial evidence besides guilt, the judge should deny extradition and save the bother of a trial. Piercey argued that the circumstantial case against Shirley was weak, primarily because there were other reasonable explanations for the evidence and that Dr. Turner should, therefore, be discharged.

Compared to his argument on ATP validity, this was much more difficult to follow from the back of the courtroom without a law degree. I had a vague notion, confirmed by a later study of the transcript, that Piercey's position relegated all significant decision-making to the judge, leaving juries with practically nothing to do.

Before countering Madden's arguments, Piercey raised an issue that the Crown had not even addressed. The defence submitted that the autopsy report, which was not introduced into evidence, indicated the time of death was 11 p.m., when Dr. Turner was "a fair distance from Latrobe." I have read the autopsy report several times, very carefully, and found no reference to time of death. Furthermore, I submit that if time of death estimates were accurate and the autopsy report had stated 11 p.m., that would have ended the case against Shirley, since her cellphone records placed her at least three hours away, near Cleveland, at 11:26 p.m. Eastern Standard Time.

Turning to the arguments actually submitted by Madden, Piercey countered that, while Dr. Turner may have been angry with Dr. Bagby, and while that may supply a motive, "it's not to the strength or to the degree of proof that my friend [Mr. Madden] would have you believe."

About Shirley's car at the crime scene, Piercey said, "An SUV of unknown colour" was seen in the park, and "Dr. Turner... owns a RAV4 SUV," but "it's one more circumstance" that "doesn't prove anything," and "it's not enough to take them [the Crown] over the hurdle they have to meet."

Regarding the murder weapon, Piercey said "I don't know if a .22 calibre gun is a pistol or a rifle; I'm pretty sure it's not a shotgun... We know... that Dr. Turner had a .22 calibre weapon that ejected live ammunition. I think the Crown could've supported their case further if they had said there's ten people in the United States with .22 calibre weapons. We don't know if this is a common, everyday weapon in the United States, and we don't know if .22 calibre weapons regularly eject."

"David Bagby... spoke to Shirley Turner on November 27 [and he says that she stated] the gun and the tissue paper were hers." Piercey said. He didn't think this would assist Judge Green in making his decision.

Regarding "the strange calls that [the radiology clerk that Andrew had intended to date] says she got around Halloween," and the calls to her phone from Dr. Turner's phone number, Piercey pointed out, "we don't know if the two coincide."

Mr. Piercey summarized: "So if we look at the most nefarious [interpretation] for the Crown: Dr. Bagby was breaking up with Dr. Turner; Dr. Turner was in Latrobe on the day he was killed…Dr. Turner had a .22 calibre gun that sometimes ejected live ammunition, that's the kind of gun that Dr. Bagby was killed with. [If it were] those three things…alone we would probably not be here. It's the fourth one I think they're relying on…the contradictory statements."

OTHER REASONABLE EXPLANATIONS

Piercey submitted that Shirley's guilt could not be inferred because there were other reasonable explanations for the circumstantial evidence presented by Madden. In particular, Piercey stated, regarding "these contradictions or lies, or whatever you want to call them…the other reasonable explanation that comes to my mind is distress and distraught, finding out not only that Dr. Bagby is dead, but now the police are essentially alleging it's you."

Shirley lied to Corporal Gardner *before* he told her that Andrew was dead. By the way, I did not notice the significance of the timing of Shirley's first lie until I was nearly finished writing this book. I believe this demonstrates why courts should be very hesitant to pre-empt the trial process since it is during trial preparation that the two parties really dig in to the minute details and discover this type of small but significant connection.

Judge Green asked Piercey, "Isn't that indirectly…applying a reasonable doubt standard at the Preliminary [Inquiry]?… [Other] reasonable explanations…could be put to a jury.… [If] you apply that sort of standard at the Preliminary Inquiry, you're getting ahead of yourself, aren't you?"

"I guess," Piercey responded, "what the [Supreme] Court is saying here, my lord, is if…there are other reasonable explanations…you can't commit [the accused for trial] because why bother?"

The judge reiterated: "If you're applying that at the Preliminary, you're effectively applying the same standard that you would ask a jury to [apply]."

MADDEN'S RESPONSE

Madden acknowledged that many features of this case were circumstantial, but disagreed with Piercey's assessment of their significance: "[They showed something] a little more serious than what Mr. Piercey [conceded]... we not only have Dr. Turner in Pennsylvania with Dr. Bagby on the date in question, November 5, with a gun, with a motive, we also have her in the park... she was the last to see Bagby in the park. And of course we know that the body of Dr. Bagby was found in the park and that he didn't show up for his 7:30 meeting with his friend."

He also acknowledged an extradition judge's duty to perform some weighing of evidence, quoting the Crown from *Giacinto Arcuri v. the Supreme Court of Canada*: "The preliminary inquiry judge must, while giving full recognition to the right of the jury to draw justifiable inferences of fact and assess credibility, consider whether the evidence taken as a whole could reasonably support a verdict of guilty."

Madden continued: "In the present case [however] there is an inference that this killing was done according to a plan. There was the long drive [from Iowa to Pennsylvania]... having just left [Pennsylvania] on November 3 a drive was felt necessary when a phone call would probably have done just as well. The gun was taken on this drive.... The meeting was arranged in a park as opposed to an apartment or a house or a restaurant... obviously the gun was brought there for a reason but the reason was not [to] pass it over to Dr. Bagby."

RESOLUTION

There was no resolution of the two issues Piercey had raised. He had managed to insert another step in the process, since Judge Green now had to rule on whether the Authority to Proceed was valid. If he ruled that it was not, he would also have to rule on whether it was amendable. And finally, Judge Green noted, "If I rule that the Authority to Proceed is deficient and it is not amendable, [that] might be the end of it."

This would mean, of course, that Shirley could hide in Canada for the rest of her days while Andrew's ashes continued their steady dispersal into the soil of Missouri, England, and California. And, perhaps worse, Zachary would grow up under the influence of an emotionally unstable killer who had never learned to handle rejection. And, perhaps worst of all, some other man (or Zachary himself) might someday reject her and become another victim of her wrath.

Judge Green: "Well this is an unusual twist because…I certainly started out this morning assuming that I would be hearing final arguments…and then be charged with [determining] whether or not Dr. Turner should be committed.… [Instead] I should set another date for the delivery of my judgment on…the sufficiency of the [Authority to Proceed and then] give both parties an opportunity to make a further submission to me.… This will delay the matter somewhat for which I think we all ought to be concerned because…the Extradition Act does contemplate that these matters be dealt with expeditiously and in as efficient and timely way as possible, but by the same token, justice must be done in relation to the issues and arguments that are presented.…I'm going to suggest that we set this matter for Friday, October the 18th…at 10 a.m."

Piercey had gained an extra month on the streets for his client.

Presumably for the benefit of Kate and myself, as well as Shirley's family and friends who were present in the courtroom, the judge added, "I know there are other people in the court who are interested in the outcome of this case and all I can say to them is that these matters sometimes take longer than may be initially anticipated. My overriding concern is to make sure that every matter that is properly raised in front of me is fully and properly dealt with and...I hope that [these interested persons] will understand the [delays]."

This policy was later explained to us as "appeal proofing." Judge Green had to treat any issue raised by either side in a serious manner, review the arguments and the law, and deliver a well-reasoned ruling. Otherwise, an appeals court could overrule his decision and drag the whole thing out even longer.

Through most of this hearing I distracted myself from pain and rage by taking careful notes and by staring holes in the back of Piercey's head. Kate suffered a few minor breakdowns at Piercey's most outrageous submissions, but kept enough composure to avoid ejection from the courtroom. Even after it was over and we had left the courthouse, we did not suffer the usual complete meltdown. We had come to expect the worst, so reality had a harder time breaking through our shell.

CHAPTER 17
ANOTHER HOUR

In the weeks surrounding the September 19 extradition hearing, Jackie and Cynthia carried on a running negotiation for their clients. Our main thrust was to get more time with Zachary, but the two lawyers also traded barbs on the other big issues: Shirley was angry that we learned about Zachary's birth so quickly, and we were angry that Kate's alleged death threat had been snuck into the court record without an affidavit. Shirley wanted to crucify Heather Arnold; we wanted to crucify Carol Ross. In the end, nobody got new holes in their hands. Both issues withered; Shirley's because she presumably determined that she couldn't hurt Heather and ours because we wanted to keep the peace. The substance of the debate remained: we wanted more time each week with our grandson. Shirley objected. See you in court.

More time with Zachary, preferably full-time access to Zachary, would have been a great comfort to Kate and me. That, however, was considered irrelevant, and rightly so; family law is supposed to be primarily concerned with the best interests of the child, not the need for comfort of the child's grandparents. Toward that end, we wanted a close relationship with Zachary so that, if Shirley went to jail and we took custody, he would be very comfortable with us.

We wanted an end to the body and bag searches, which we described in our affidavit as "degrading and unnecessary." The sheriffs routinely apologized for the intrusion, but they had to do a thorough job and we understood. In fact, since we were always on a high going in to see Zachary, these searches occasionally provided some amusement. Usually an officer just poked around in our bags and waved an airport wand over our outstretched arms and legs. On one occasion, however, the wand was too sensitive and Kate had to show her underwear to a female officer to demonstrate that she had no concealed weapons. On a separate visit, the wand failed entirely and we had to be patted down—Kate by a female officer, me by a male. No man, except an examining physician, has ever touched that high up my inner thigh. It was only a fleeting relationship. I don't remember his name and didn't get his phone number.

We also wanted off-site visits, so that we could show off our grandson to our many new friends at church and the medical school. We also wanted access supervision to continue, although we preferred to maintain the perception that it was at Shirley's insistence. In addition to being a kind and gentle soul, easy to talk to and easy to like, Maureen Kendall provided us a very practical benefit: she could give third party testimony to counter any charges of misbehaviour that Shirley might dream up and her written access reports absolutely radiated our love for Zachary. It was Jackie who put this in perspective for us, clarifying how Maureen's supervision would work to our strategic advantage.

Shirley didn't want us to have more visitation time. She said that we often kept him too long after he became upset so that he was distraught when we sent him back, he had a great deal of colic, bottle-feeding made him vomit, and "an additional visit would be burdensome" because she was very busy caring for her younger daughter and looking for a job.

She didn't want off-site visits because we might tuck him under an arm and run. If our friends wished to see Zachary, she said, they could always visit him at her home—they need only call first to arrange a time.

Throughout the custody battle, including these negotiations, Kate and I carefully avoided stating on the record that we believed Shirley killed Andrew. Our court applications and affidavits only referred to her as "charged with murder in the death of our son." This was a strategic decision based on a desire to avoid antagonizing Shirley and to minimize open hostilities between us, in hopes of spending more time with Zachary so that his eventual transition to our care would be as smooth as possible. But we were pretty damned sure that she did it and so were our friends. Hence, while they very much wanted to see Zachary, they were not about to go knocking at the door of an accused murderer.

On September 24, these negotiations culminated in another session at Unified Family Court. As before, Kate and I were in one room, Shirley was in another, and the lawyers met somewhere in between. Cynthia relayed Shirley's "distraught when we sent him back" accusation to Jackie, who brought it to us. We were all three struck by the feebleness of this attempt to manipulate the situation to her advantage. She obviously had not considered that the visit supervisor, Maureen, was being implicitly charged with failing her obligation to Zachary. By chance, Maureen happened to be in the courthouse working with another case at the time, so Jackie and Cynthia went together to confront her.

Nobody needs a warm, cuddly lawyer and, as Maureen later told us, we didn't have one. In a very direct, abrupt manner—we were running out of time to get a consent order that day—Jackie cut straight to the point: "Shirley says the Bagbys hold on to

Zachary too long after he's upset so that when she gets him back, he's often distraught. Is that true?" Maureen absolutely denied it, pointing out that Zachary's best interest was her primary job and she did her job diligently. Thus, that silly issue was easily laid to rest and we went back to negotiating.

After a few hours Shirley agreed to a couple of concessions: we could not take Zachary off-site but we could walk him around the grounds at Unified Family Court, and the sheriff need not conduct a body and bag search prior to our visits. We feared she might also spontaneously concede that supervision was unnecessary, but the subject never came up so we retained our third party oversight by default.

On the main point, however, there could be no agreement; Shirley adamantly refused to consider additional access time. At the end of the day, the agreed-to changes were written into a new Consent Order and a date was set for all-out war over one more hour per week with our grandson.

CHAPTER 18
ATP RULING

Madden called us on October 17, at Judge Green's request, to say that the hearing scheduled for the following day was delayed four days.[1] The judge had offered Madden and Piercey a quick verbal decision, or they could wait and get the written form on October 22. They chose to wait, which meant we had to wait, too. Kate raged and cried. I went stoic: a slight variation on the same old story.

Kate called her brother David in England. He and his wife, Mary, had been rocks for her, telephoning several times each week since Andrew's murder. In the roughest times, they spoke twice a day. This time, sensing Kate's hyperanxiety, he asked if we couldn't give it up and go home to California: "You have made new friends there, but they are not your old friends. Newfoundland is not for you. You love each other. Isn't that enough?"

"No. We cannot walk away from Zachary," Kate told him.

Softly, David asked, "Why not? Andrew would want you to be happy."

"Yes. That means not leaving Zachary."

Later, Kate asked me, "Is being together enough?"

"No. We need Zachary."

David and Mary never again wavered in their support for our mission to take care of our grandson.

Kate called Jackie to report this new delay and to vent. Jackie warned her to be careful where she expressed her despair, lest she be considered unfit for full-time care of a baby. Kate found it galling being told how she should feel, even by family and friends who meant well.

On October 22, Judge Green announced his decision on the Authority to Proceed and distributed his written reasons supporting that decision, from which I have extracted the key points.

Regarding the timing of Piercey's objection to the Authority to Proceed, Judge Green ruled that, even though Piercey had unequivocally accepted "the sufficiency of the Authority to Proceed at the commencement of the hearing," the judge was "nevertheless prepared to consider" the defence's arguments.

As for the general content of an Authority to Proceed, Judge Green ruled that the key issue was that "fair notice of the accusation against him" be given to the accused, that this was available to Shirley in the Case Record, and that it "cannot be reasonably suggested that...Dr. Turner...could not know the case [to which] she must respond."

With respect to Piercey's submission that the Authority to Proceed should have specified either subsection (i) or (ii) of the Criminal Code, Judge Green ruled that these two subsections distinguish the accused's state of mind at the time of the offence (whether he meant to cause *death*, or to cause *bodily harm* that he knew was likely to cause death), and that state of mind was not even relevant to a domestic indictment, so would definitely not be relevant to an extradition proceeding. He pointed out that, even at trial for a domestic offence, jurors do not necessarily have to agree on the accused's state of mind, they need only agree that he was in *one* of the two states of mind.

Another Hallelujah!

Another month had been wasted answering a trivial question of wording, but at least the judge got the right answer. Then he offered the parties a last opportunity to make further submissions on whether Shirley should be committed for extradition.

Madden reiterated his position: "We don't have anything to add."

Piercey requested more time to review the day's written decision to determine whether he had additional submissions.

Madden asked that, to prevent further delay, "any further submissions...be done in writing beforehand so that we would be in a position to argue them on the next court date."

Judge Green set the next court date for November 14. If Piercey had further submissions, he would get them to Madden and the judge during the week *before* that date, which would then be taken up in arguments over these new submissions. If Piercey had nothing further to add, Judge Green would issue his Committal Order decision on that date. If he got it right again, Shirley might finally be locked up and we might finally have the chance to look after our grandson full-time. More importantly, we'd be able to breathe a lot easier knowing that Zachary wasn't at the mercy of an emotional time bomb.

CHAPTER 19
COOPERATION

Since our arrival in Newfoundland on June 8, we had shame-lessly crashed with any friend who had a spare bed. Jen and Mark had put us up for several weeks, then Heather and Matt, and finally Daniele Wiseman. She had been a year ahead of Andrew's medical school class, stayed in St. John's for a radiol-ogy residency, and loaned us her house and car while she was away for seven weeks.

But we needed our own place soon, in case our "family" once again grew to three on November 14. There were very few newspaper ads for furnished apartments. We were literally cry-ing in our beer one evening with Jen and Mark, Jen's sister Kim, and Kim's husband Graham when Graham suggested that we look for an unfurnished apartment and offered to lend us a kitchen table and chairs. He also knew where we could borrow a sofa, and we quickly had loan offers of a bed, television, desk, and lamps—Newfoundland hospitality at its best. With the scope of our search thus dramatically enlarged, we started look-ing in earnest. Most landlords were skeptical, for good reason: we were foreigners, with no income, and no idea how long we needed the apartment. But we soon found a second floor unfur-nished place in a hundred-year-old building on LeMarchant

Road. After a dozen trips to the store for miscellaneous house-wares, plus some care packages from family and friends, we had a home for ourselves and a baby, indefinitely if necessary.

In the weeks since Kate and I first met Zachary, our contributions to his care steadily increased. Starting with a bag of diapers, we had added clothes and toys, a cheap portable CD player and some baby music, and finally a crib and mattress. All but the crib and mattress were passed to Shirley, via Maureen, at our regular visits. Maureen, in turn, brought us thank-you cards and gifts from Shirley. Bizarre! Swapping cordial notes with Andrew's probable killer.

From Kate's journal, late October: "It is a schizophrenic world—trying to be nice for the sake of our dear baby."

In the midst of all this superficial cooperation, we still had to prepare for the upcoming Family Court battle. Neither side had altered its position on more time with Zachary, so we had to sharpen our spears. On Monday, October 28, three days before the scheduled hearing, we occupied our familiar chairs in Jackie's office. She was conducting a mock examination of her clients on the witness stand. Kate went first. Where did she live? What was her relationship with Shirley? Why did she want more time with Zachary? Kate would be a good witness, Jackie said. Her answers were thorough and logical, but they also came from the heart.

My mock examination never took place because the telephone interrupted our preparations. Kate and I sat mute while Jackie listened to the caller for several minutes. After she hung up the phone, she floored us: "That was Cynthia. Shirley has had a change of heart. If she goes to jail on the fourteenth, she wants you to take care of Zachary until she can get bail." We were conditionally overjoyed! From one hour per week to full-time with our baby was far more than we had hoped for.

Our baby. We thought of him as our baby. It seemed very likely that Shirley would eventually be sent to Pennsylvania, tried and convicted, and nobody else had made a move to get Zachary if that were to happen. The DNA testing process was underway, but everyone who saw a picture of Andrew said the result was a forgone conclusion: Zachary was Andrew's child. If the DNA proved otherwise, we would be in big trouble because we already loved him, literally, like a grandson.

But first, of course, Judge Green had to lock her up on November 14.

SECOND CONSENT ORDER

Over the next few days, through Jackie and Cynthia, we hammered out the conditions of a second Consent Order. We would have two one-hour visits per week with Zachary, on Wednesdays and Fridays, at Shirley's apartment, supervised by Maureen. Both parties would be flexible about the schedule, missed visits would be rescheduled, and there would be no direct contact between Shirley and us.

This last condition was essential in order to maintain Shirley's compliance with her extradition recognizance order, which prohibited her from contacting Andrew's family. Its implementation was a little tricky and had to be spelled out in the Consent Order. First, we borrowed two cellphones from Jen Lombard's sister, Kim. We kept one and gave the other to Maureen. On a visit day, we would send a taxi to take Maureen to Shirley's apartment on Pleasant Street. Maureen would give her cellphone to Shirley, who would disappear, leaving Maureen in charge of Zachary. Maureen would call us on the other cell phone to say that Shirley was gone. We would go to Pleasant Street, visit with Zachary for an hour, and leave. Maureen would call Shirley to say that we were gone. Shirley would return home and give her cellphone back to Maureen, who would take a taxi home, leaving Shirley back in charge of Zachary.

Shirley asked for one final condition, to which we had no objection. Her younger daughter would be allowed to join us, if she wished, for the last fifteen minutes of each visit.

Jackie and her law partner, Linda Rose, advised against visiting with Zachary in Shirley's home. They feared that she might take the opportunity to harm—perhaps kill—us, as well as Zachary. Kate and I worked through the possibilities and decided to go against our lawyers' advice. If Shirley wanted to kill only Zachary, she had all but two hours a week in which to do it. If she wanted to kill Kate and me, that would be all right. We weren't happy souls anyway, and the murder would hopefully trigger Shirley's incarceration. Even if a murder charge in far off Pennsylvania didn't make her look dangerous, surely a double killing on their own turf would convince Canadian authorities to finally lock her up. Then Zachary would be safe and we would have no more pain. Unfortunately, we would also have no more influence in his life, so we didn't really want that outcome to this little experiment.

From my journal, October 30, 2002: "We also considered means to stop her killing us: don't sit together, keep one of us near the door, look over the room for defensive positions and weapons. All very 'James Bond,' but it seemed to make sense at the time. It occurred to us that if Andrew had thought more like that, maybe he would be alive today."

In Unified Family Court on October 31, Jackie and Cynthia presented the agreed-on conditions to the judge, who congratulated the parties on their successful negotiation. Kate took the opportunity to surreptitiously observe Shirley.

From her journal: "When she came in to have the agreement read, her right leg was always on the move, and she was crying—wiping her hand over her nose and eyes. I felt a deep sadness. Why did it have to get to this, why oh why? Poor darling Zachary, what obstacles to overcome."

A year and a day after Shirley killed Andrew, their son, in the arms of Maureen, greeted us at the door to Shirley's clean, comfortable little Pleasant Street apartment. He was wide awake and hungry. I gave him a bottle, Kate fed him some cereal, and we laid him on a blanket on the floor. He waved his arms and legs, chattered away, turned over back-to-front, did a few mini pushups, and made himself generally adorable.

We forgot all about the James Bond-like precautions, but it didn't matter. Shirley did not burst in through the back door and shoot us. Maureen oversaw the whole operation and then called Shirley after we left. We did not hide behind a tree and jump out and strangle her as she walked up to her front door. It was another great visit with our baby.

Her younger daughter came in for the last part of our second visit at Shirley's apartment. Kate and I each gave her a little hug and we made small talk about her school activities and Zachary's adorable habits. Somewhere in the conversation I unfortunately mentioned Greg and Rana's baby, Aaron, who was well known to her and Shirley from their pre-murder friendship.

Several hours later, Rana called our house in some distress. Shirley's younger daughter had reported my Aaron comment to her mother, who promptly decided that she had a born-again friendship with Rana, and promptly called to ask if Rana would like to see Zachary. Rana was stunned—their lawyer had formally asked Shirley not to contact them—but managed to make innocuous conversation for several minutes before telling Shirley, "I don't think it would be a good idea for me to see you right now."

Rana's worst fear was that Shirley might show up on her doorstep, with her daughter and Zachary in tow, for a friendly visit. I asked what she would do if that happened. She proposed to say something like, "I don't think it's a good idea for you to be here." And then she would close and lock the door and call the police.

THIRD CONSENT ORDER

As soon as the agreement was in place for these Pleasant Street visits, Jackie and Cynthia started to work on another agreement to cover Shirley's possible incarceration on November 14. Like the previous Consent Orders, this one took some strange twists. In its final form, we agreed that, if Shirley were remanded into custody by Judge Green, we would assume primary care of Zachary.

If Shirley were placed at the Women's Prison in Clarenville, about two hours west of St. John's, we would take Zachary on a weekly trip to visit her. We would drive up one morning, visit as much as the prison regulations allowed, spend the night in a hotel, visit as much as allowed the next day, and then drive back to St. John's.

During the rest of the week, when we weren't in Clarenville, we would accept one daily collect phone call from Shirley, lasting no more than ten minutes, to discuss only issues pertaining to Zachary. Either party would be free to record the conversation.

Her younger daughter and son would be allowed to visit with Zachary at our home every second day, except when we took him to Clarenville.

If Shirley were released on bail, we would return Zachary to her care.

I could not imagine sitting in the same room with Shirley, or talking with her on the phone on a regular basis, but Kate was sure that she could do it for Zachary's sake. I decided that I could, too, but feared an overwhelming temptation to tell her exactly what she ought to do—go to Pennsylvania and put an end to this farce.

On November 14, Kate and I met with Jackie and Cynthia in the courthouse waiting room to sign this agreement. Then we went into the courtroom to hear Judge Green's decision on Shirley's Committal Order.

CHAPTER 20
JAIL

Judge Green subjected everyone in the room to an additional twenty minutes of high anxiety before finally announcing his decision.[1] He began by marching through the legal criteria behind the decision, beginning with the four elements that must be in place to support a charge of murder. First, the fact of death: there was sufficient evidence that Dr. Bagby was dead. Second, the cause of death: there was sufficient evidence that Dr. Bagby died of gunshot wounds. Third, the mental state (intent) of the person who inflicted the gunshot wounds: there was sufficient evidence that the person who inflicted the gunshot wounds intended to cause Dr. Bagby's death. Fourth, the identity of the person who inflicted the gunshot wounds.

This last element was the crux of the case: was there sufficient evidence that Dr. Turner was the person who inflicted the gunshot wounds?

The judge very briefly summarized the circumstantial evidence placing Dr. Turner in the parking lot with her gun, with a motive to kill, at the time of Dr. Bagby's death. He then summarized Piercey's arguments that the circumstantial evidence was "really all too flimsy," and that Dr. Turner's inconsistencies and contradictions may be explained by her being confused and distraught over hearing of Dr. Bagby's death and being accused of causing it.

Even Jackie, with ten years' experience at the bar, later told us that she was about ready to leap to her feet and shout, "Are you going to lock her up or not?!"

Speaking directly to Shirley, the judge finally got to the point: "I am satisfied that [the] evidence taken together creates a web of circumstances that, if unanswered, could lead a properly instructed jury acting reasonably to draw the inference that you were the person who caused the death of Dr. Andrew Bagby....I therefore have come to the conclusion, I'm sorry to say, that Shirley Jane Turner should be committed to be held in custody to await a decision of the Minister as to whether she should be surrendered to the United States for trial."

After a lengthy discussion of legal housekeeping details, the judge addressed an issue that was technically outside of his domain, but demonstrated a normal humanitarian concern:

Judge Green: The final thing I would say...has nothing to do with my formal legal duties but...about Dr. Bagby's child. I just want to assure myself that arrangements have been made to care for this child...Can you help me here, Mr. Piercey?

Piercey: Yes, I certainly can, my lord. I notice, though, the reporters got their pens out when you said Dr. Bagby's child.

Judge Green: Did I? I'm very sorry.

Piercey: I think you meant Dr. Turner's child.

Judge Green: I meant Dr. Turner, of course....

Piercey: I'm not at liberty to discuss the arrangement, but the child is—

Judge Green: I don't want to know the details…but I want some assurance that the child is not to be abandoned or…

Piercey: No. My lord, my client is satisfied that the child is in good hands.

Nothing further. All rise. Exit judge.

Two Sheriff's deputies stepped forward, one on each side of Shirley, and placed handcuffs on her wrists and led her from the courtroom.

Although this was exactly the decision we had hoped for all these long months, it was not a joyous occasion. Kate and I had the same feeling: complete loss for everyone concerned. Andrew was gone, we were devastated, Shirley was miserable, hundreds of family and friends (hers and ours) were in agony, and nobody gained a goddamned thing! Not one winner in the whole mess!

BABY MAKES THREE

Even Zachary lost in the short term: babies need routine and his was shattered. We picked him up at Shirley's apartment, along with all his baby paraphernalia, and took him home to our apartment on LeMarchant Road. Kate invited his godmother, Penney, and younger half-sister to come along and see where he would be living. They joined us for a cup of tea and helped us put up Zachary's crib.

Kate took charge of him, but she wasn't his mother and this wasn't his house, so he loudly and continuously expressed his extreme displeasure to the world at large. Danette came by for a while and took a turn at rocking and cuddling him, but she wasn't his mother, either. Rana had the best luck in settling him down, perhaps because she had the most recent experience with her own baby, Aaron. After a little rest, however, he took up his complaint with gusto.

Most babies fall asleep in a moving vehicle, so we took him for a ride around St. John's. After twenty minutes he was still wailing at full strength so we gave up that tack and went home. I would have taken a turn walking him but Kate was reluctant to let go, so I went to bed leaving her strolling up and down the hallway singing baby songs. My personal favourite, which soon became Zachary's as well, was set to the tune of "Twinkle Twinkle Little Star." At random times, I expect to hear Kate singing this in my head for the rest of my days:

> Grandma loves you, yes she does.
> Granddad loves you, yes he does.
> Daddy loves you, yes he does.
> [break into sing-song]
> We all love you, all we can.
> Darling, darling little man.

While a shattered routine was tough on Zachary, he quickly settled into a new one. He usually woke up hungry between midnight and 2 a.m. Kate would wake me and then go back to sleep while I heated a bottle and changed his diaper. Then I sat myself down on the end of the sofa, supporting my right elbow on the armrest with Zachary cradled against my chest. He drank enthusiastically, while this soppy granddaddy gazed into his sweet little trusting face. He looked right back at me, without breaking off his sucking rhythm. With the bottle half gone I took the nipple out of his mouth and burped him, either sitting on my thigh or over my shoulder. Back in the cradle of my arm, he started back to work on the bottle, sometimes finishing it but often falling asleep before it was empty.

Then I would often sit and hold him for a while, watching his face and wondering what his daddy would have thought of him. Judi Petrush, the Pennsylvania Assistant District Attorney handling Shirley's case, had originally posed a theory that Shirley did not know she was pregnant when she killed Andrew. Had she known, she probably would not have killed him. Instead, she would have used the baby, and Kate's and my love for the baby, as a club to beat up Andrew for the rest of his life. This theory was at least partially confirmed when we later learned the date of Shirley's positive pregnancy test: November 19, 2001—two weeks after the murder.

Given the choice, Andrew may have accepted Zachary and tried to help Shirley with financial and emotional support. He probably never would have married her, but he may have sent money and spent as much time with his child as possible. Or maybe not. He may have rejected the baby outright, to Kate's and my disgust.

Andrew never had the opportunity to make a choice.

Zachary, of course, knew nothing of these musings. His tummy was full, he was warm and clean, and he got lots of loving cuddles, so he was happy.

I would slowly stand up and raise him a little higher so that I could glide my cheek across his forehead, soft and smooth— smoother even than his grandmother's belly had been twenty-nine years earlier, with his daddy inside. Then I would carry him to his crib and gently place him on his back and whisper, "Good night, sweet baby…my *God*, you are so *beautiful*."

He usually slept until about seven or eight in the morning. I took him to Kate for a cuddle in bed while I heated his bottle and made the tea. After breakfast, I crashed for another hour or so while grandma and grandson either took another nap or went to the living room to play.

Looking after our grandson full-time, Kate and I were happier than we had been since Andrew's murder. Zachary, in turn, was happy and content to be with us, and especially with Kate, his primary cuddler and nurturer. As a bonus, we were finally free to show him off to our new Newfoundland friends.

I'm not religious, but after Andrew's murder I started attending church with Kate. She felt close to Andrew during services, especially when she took communion, and I wanted to be close to her when she felt close to him. After our move to St. John's, Kate—with me in tow—tried several churches and settled on St. Michael and All Angels Anglican Church on LeMarchant Road, near our apartment. Its first attraction was the liturgy, which was conducted in song, very like Frindsbury Church where Kate grew up in England. It also had a warm, friendly congregation that made us feel immediately welcome. And most important, they quickly doted on Zachary, who revelled in the attention.

Jackie's partner, Linda Rose, and Linda's husband Bill were both serious chefs. Since one of Bill's specialties was roast turkey, Linda volunteered his services preparing an American Thanksgiving dinner for Kate and me and a group of our friends. It was the first time we took Zachary out for an evening and the first time some of the guests had seen him. He was somewhat awed by the crowd, and had a little cry when someone startled him with a loud, sharp laugh; but he soon settled into enjoying the adulation of his new friends as they passed him around for cuddles. After a scrumptious dinner everyone dispersed into the living room and Heather ended up holding Zachary as he fell asleep on her shoulder. I took a few pictures and then sat back to contemplate roads not taken.

Lots of our friends dropped in at our apartment to see Zachary and we took him to see some of Shirley's friends, as well. His godmother, Penney George, accompanied Shirley's daughter on one of her visits to our house. We were cordial but guarded around Shirley's family and friends, never discussing the criminal case and never, ever, badmouthing her. We had to assume her friends were potential conduits to the enemy's ear, and our goal was always the same: in case she later gets out on bail, we must maintain a civil relationship so that Zachary will see only peace and harmony among the adults in his life.

Shirley's daughter made regular reports to her mother on Zachary's new home, noting that Kate sometimes referred to him as "my baby," and that we had no pictures of his mother and father together in our apartment. Shirley complained to Kate about both issues during our telephone calls, suggesting that Kate should not be calling Zachary "her baby." Kate made no argument on that point, but told Shirley that we could not have a picture of her and Andrew together in our house.

CHILD, YOUTH AND FAMILY SERVICES

Information flowed our way, as well. Shirley's daughter told us that her father had contacted the Department of Social Services about her living arrangements once Shirley was in jail. A social worker, she said, had visited her and concluded that she was under the supervision of her twenty-year-old brother and that the arrangement was acceptable. We wondered if Social Services officials were aware that her father had tried in April to regain custody of his daughter through Family Court action.

Since Jackie's June 17 meeting with Elizabeth Day, we had often wondered why no one from CYFS contacted us. Now, with Zachary in our full-time care, CYFS's lack of interest seemed especially perplexing; not only had they left Zachary in the care of his probably dangerous mother, but they had allowed Shirley to determine on her own who would look after the baby while she was in jail. We knew that we were good people with Zachary's best interest at heart. For all CYFS knew, however, Kate and I might have been convicted child molesters in our home state of California. They never did a background check.

CHAPTER 21
ICE MODE

From Judge Green's courtroom, following his Order of Committal on November 14, Shirley was taken to the St. John's lockup, located in the courthouse basement. It was only a temporary jail, designed mainly to hold drunken rowdies from the George Street bars. From there, she would be transported the next day to the Women's Prison at Clarenville.

Just before six o'clock that evening, with Zachary wailing in the background, I accepted the first collect call from Shirley. She said, "I know I should only call tomorrow, but I just wanted to know Zachary's okay. I just talked to [my daughter]. She said she was at your house this afternoon with Zachary. That was very nice of you."

It felt like the call I had made to her from the motel in Gallup, New Mexico, nearly a year before: *ice mode*. Freeze emotions, tighten your gut, do the job.

I told her, "No problem. Zachary's fine."

She asked if we could bring Zachary to the lockup tomorrow, so that she could see him before going to Clarenville. I agreed. Peace and harmony.

ST. JOHN'S LOCKUP

At 10 a.m. the next day, November 15, Shirley called again to ask if we could quickly bring Zachary to the lockup, since she was allowed a visit right then, but probably not later. We agreed, dressed Zachary for the cold rainy weather, and twenty minutes later presented ourselves at the heavy side door of the big stone courthouse. A male officer let us in and led us down a short hallway to the main hall. Off that, there was a visiting room with windows on three sides. I asked if we could hand Zachary to Shirley and wait in the main hall. Another officer, a woman, said, "No. You have to stay in the room with the baby."

We took Zachary into the room. The female officer brought in Shirley and then left, closing the door behind her. I was a *glacier. Dear God! How was I not going to strangle this bitch?!*

Kate was cool. She managed to carry on a semi-normal conversation with Shirley about Zachary. What he liked to eat. How he was taking the bottle. His sleep patterns. But it wasn't really normal; Shirley was almost certainly a killer. But that didn't slow down her usual pattern—talk and talk, topped off by more talk.

After what seemed like a week, the officer came and took Shirley away. We wrapped up Zachary again and Kate carried him while I carried the diaper bag as we were led back to the big side door. Once outside, a complex mixture of pent-up hatred, rage, and despair congealed in my chest and forced its way into my throat, where it came out as a simultaneous shudder, groan, gasp, and quiet scream. Kate was holding Zachary, so she couldn't vent yet.

We took him across the street to Jackie's office. The receptionist let her know we were there, but she was on the phone with another client and we had to wait several minutes in the lobby. All the staff came out to see our beautiful grandson, who was something of a celebrity in the office. Jackie later told us that when she finally got off the phone and came out and rounded the corner and saw him sitting on Kate's lap, it was the most satisfying moment of her career.

Back at home, we had lunch, made formula, and played with Zachary when he wasn't napping. Shirley's daughter came straight to us from school, helped look after the baby, and stayed for dinner. Afterwards, she helped Kate prepare Zachary for bed. Once he was down, Kate delivered her to Shirley's Pleasant Street apartment, where her son would come to look after her.

COLLECT CALLS

The next day Shirley called collect from the Clarenville prison. According to the Consent Order, she was supposed to talk only about Zachary, but Kate was on the phone a long time listening to whatever came into Shirley's head, including complaints about the regimentation of prison life.

She had to go straight from her bed to breakfast without washing her face and brushing her teeth. Her hairbrush was taken away because it could be used to hide pills. Lip balm, lotions, and food could not be brought into the prison for fear of contamination. All photos were taken away, so she could not even look at Zachary's sweet face. She was initially fearful that we might take Zachary and run to California, but no longer.

Kate replied, "We certainly wouldn't do that."

"Thank you."

In fact, we had considered this option and rejected it. To make it work, we would have to sell all our assets, including the house and retirement funds, cut all ties to family and friends, and live a cash-only life—any paper trail would inevitably lead to capture. Ironically, if captured, we would find ourselves on the other side of a lengthy (one would hope) extradition from the United States to Canada on a charge of kidnapping. The most likely outcome would be a Canadian prison sentence for trying to save our grandson from his father's murderer. Zachary would probably end up in foster care. We would probably never see him again.

But even if we managed to avoid capture, Zachary would be entirely cut off from all family and friends—Shirley's and ours—and from any semblance of a normal life. He would grow up a modern Gypsy, with no anchor in his life but fugitive grandparents.

Shirley complained that she cried a lot because she missed Zachary and that as a mother Kate would understand. Kate did not point out to her that at least Shirley's son is still in the world.

She said that if she weren't out on bail in two weeks, her younger daughter would go live with her father on the west coast of Newfoundland.

Like all Shirley conversations, this one took far too long, but eventually wound down. Kate listened attentively right to the end. Do the job. Remain civil. Peace and harmony.

Shirley's daughter came by after school most days and played with Zachary. Sometimes she fed him a bottle or some cereal, or gave him a bath. Sometimes she tried to rock him to sleep in the evening, but it seldom worked for her, as it seldom worked for me. Kate was the only one who could consistently soothe him to sleep, as she was quickly becoming his *de facto* mother.

CLARENVILLE

Under the Family Court Consent Order, we were required to take Zachary to visit his mother once each week in prison. The first visit took place six days after Shirley was arrested. We left

St. John's early in the morning and drove the two hours to Clarenville and rang the bell at the gate to the Women's Correctional Centre. Once inside the building—a one-storey solid brick structure that could house twenty-two inmates but currently had only six—we found ourselves in a small lobby with several offices on one side and a heavy metal door on the other. The guards were polite, but thorough. While they searched Zachary's diaper and toy bags, and carefully felt his baby blanket for weapons and contraband, we hung up our coats and signed in. Then we were let in through the metal door to the visiting room. It was rectangular, about six-by-twelve feet, with our door on one end of a long wall. There was a table against the other long wall, with several chairs set around its three open sides. On the far short wall was another metal door, which was opened only after ours was closed and locked. I thought of a submarine decompression chamber.

Shirley came in, looking very pale and worn. A guard left the end door open, placed a chair in the doorway, and sat herself down. A handy position from which to pounce on me if I pounced on Shirley.

Kate handed Zachary to his mother, who cried and hugged him and kissed him and cooed over him for several minutes: "Oh, my baby. I have missed you so much. Mommy loves you so much." And so on.

Had I not known her, it would have been touching. But I did know her, and I was once again frozen—hardening myself was my only defence against explosion. Kate spread a blanket on the floor and Shirley sat down on it and held Zachary and together they played with his toys while she kept up the patter.

Kate and I sat on chairs at our end of the room and watched. The guard sat on her chair in the doorway on the other end, and watched. Kate, attempting to minimize communication without directly telling Shirley to shut up, lied, "During our visits at the courthouse, we always tried to block out Maureen and concentrate on Zachary, so please do the same. You don't need to entertain us."

Shirley played with Zachary and fed him cereal and a bottle and pattered throughout the visit, which was terminated when the guard took Shirley out and locked the end door. Then our door was opened and we packed up Zachary and went out and put on our coats and were let out through the gate to the parking lot. Walking to the car, Kate and I breathed freely for the first time in two hours, and told ourselves—prayed, really—that it would get easier.

We checked in at a motel and had lunch in the dining room, with Zachary conveniently asleep on a blanket on the floor. Then it was back to prison from two to four in the afternoon, and again from five-thirty to seven in the evening. Exhausted, we had a room-service dinner. Zachary had a bath and a bottle, and slept very well, from ten o'clock until six-thirty the next morning. Kate, on the other hand, heard his every noise and slept very little.

Back to prison for two hours the next morning and two more in the afternoon, and two days the following week, and each week after that, as agreed in the Consent Order. It did get easier. Sitting at our end of the visiting room the stream of patter blended into an amorphous blob of words.

According to Shirley, we were taking such good care of her precious baby. She now had Legal Aid for her extradition case and it was *so* different from a private attorney. The eldest of Shirley's two daughters was very angry at the legal system and advised her mother to call everyone she could think of to complain. Shirley had spoken with a human rights representative and told them that it wasn't for herself that she was concerned, but for her two children, Zachary and her younger daughter, who missed her so. The girl told her mother that we never said anything bad about her. Newspapers in the U.S. didn't respect the publication ban and published details about "the so-called case" against her. Her younger daughter didn't like talk of poop and pee and s-e-x at the dinner table. Shirley had talked to her about safe sex. Zachary was an accident, not a mistake. If she didn't get bail, her younger daughter would have to go live with her father, and that would make the child very unhappy, having to be away from Zachary. Some of her friends and family didn't agree with her letting us look after Zachary, because of our age, and other stuff, but she knew that we loved him. Shirley had stopped talking to Carol Ross—did not return her calls. If she didn't get bail, would we continue to take care of Zachary?

In answer to this last question, Kate said, "Of course."

Over the weeks I relaxed enough to read most of a history of Newfoundland—*As Near to Heaven by Sea*, by Kevin Major—and to take catnaps. I wasn't overtly rude during our Clarenville visits, just barely civil. Kate, too, always brought something to read, but allowed herself to be sucked into small talk with the prisoner. She was much closer to cordial than I was, bless her, and Shirley showed no outward signs of animosity towards either of us.

At the end of one visit, she looked directly at me and mewled, "Thank you for taking such good care of Zachary."

I deadpanned, "We're doing this for him and for Andrew."

On another occasion, she drew Kate into a discussion of Andrew's hair: was it curly when he was a child? Back in the motel room, I had a damned good cry over that, recalling that his hair was the only natural thing about him as he lay on the gurney, almost certainly put there by her hand.

DELUSION

When we weren't in Clarenville, we had our daily call from Shirley. Kate did nearly all the talking, but on one occasion, Shirley asked to speak with me. She said that she knew we couldn't talk about the criminal case, but her lawyer in Pennsylvania, Anthony Mariani, wanted to speak with us.

I called District Attorney John Peck. Peck was surprised at Mariani's involvement so early in the case, but saw no problem in my talking to him, so I called him.

Mariani said that, since we were cooperating so well with Shirley over Zachary's care, he wondered if we were interested in helping fund a private investigator to dig into Andrew's murder on Shirley's behalf. And, perhaps we would like to help with getting her released on bail.

I was stunned. I wanted to say, "Sure. Release her on bail at about 35,000 feet." Instead, I told him that I wasn't smart enough to answer that without talking to a lawyer. He thought that was wise, and would have recommended it to his own client.

When we told Jackie about this, she couldn't imagine what Mariani was up to, so gave him a call. They did a little verbal dancing, but Jackie learned nothing. We never discovered any hidden motive for this exchange, so we have to take it at face value. It seems likely that Shirley actually deluded herself into believing that our support for Zachary translated into support for her.

MERRY CHRISTMAS

On December 23, 2002, Dr. Charles T. Ladoulis of Paternity Testing Services unknowingly gave Kate and me a very nice Christmas present, in the form of a letter to Madame Justice Noonan of Unified Family Court. He had been tasked with comparing Zachary's DNA with that of his putative father, Andrew Bagby. On the first page of his report—the summary page—Dr. Ladoulis conservatively declared "the paternity of this man is not excluded." On the third page, after plodding through the technical jargon and mathematics, I found the key number: "Relative Chance of Paternity equals 99.9941 per cent."

With this report in hand, Judge Noonan issued a March 4, 2002, Consent Order declaring that "the late Dr. Andrew Bagby is the father of Zachary Andrew Turner."

APPEAL

Once Shirley was in jail, Piercey was no longer her extradition lawyer. She owed him a lot of money already and he could no longer accept the financial drain. Before resigning, however, he had filed a Notice of Appeal of Judge Green's Committal Order on two grounds: one, "The Learned Trial Judge erred in law by failing to quash the Authority to Proceed," and two, "The Learned Trial Judge erred in law by failing to properly apply the law as it relates to circumstantial evidence."[1]

Piercey had been replaced by a Legal Aid attorney, Derek Hogan, who had a "good technical point" to make with the Minister of Justice, but did not think there were grounds for an appeal of the Committal Order. He also thought Shirley would likely remain in custody pending the Minister's decision.

Jackie had spoken to Madden, who thought that, if there were no grounds for an appeal, Shirley would not be released on bail.

There were no guarantees in this, but it was tentatively wonderful news! All we had to do was keep marching to the Consent Order and maybe Zachary's future would finally be secure.

CHAPTER 22

BAIL APPLICATION

Two days after Christmas, in a regular daily telephone call, Shirley expressed some irritation that most of her incarceration may have been unnecessary. Kate and I later learned that she had written a six-page letter to Chief Justice Derek Green; and that Green's secretary, at his direction, had responded with advice on how she could get out of jail.

SHIRLEY'S LETTER TO JUDGE GREEN

Here are some key excerpts (the underlining is Shirley's):

December 20, 2002

Chief Justice Green:

I am writing to you to express a number of concerns I have regarding my extradition case.

As I write to you, I am still in custody.... That is my number one concern. My family (especially my children) and friends are absolutely devastated by this. I myself am finding this whole ordeal overwhelming and very stressful.

I have been incarcerated more than 30 days and it is very difficult to try to survive this.

Have my legal rights been violated?...On November 14, 2002 you advised me of my rights...to an appeal and a bond (bail) hearing pending an appeal. I strongly believe that both these rights have been denied me...Mr. Randy Piercey [told me I would be incarcerated]...a maximum of 10 days awaiting a bond hearing and an appeal. Randy assured me [that we had grounds for appeal]. Mr. Piercey informed me that he could not continue my case because I could not pay his bill. He said he could not do my appeal, but not to worry because he would have a competent legal aid lawyer take over my case. He also told me that if legal aid would allow him to continue for me he would (at legal aid rates).

I was very hurt...by Mr. Piercey's decision not to continue. Mr. Derek Hogan was assigned my case and Randy reassured me that he is one of the best with appeals....However...Mr. Derek Hogan has informed me (after reviewing your decisions) that the grounds for appeal that Mr. Piercey had filed were "frivolous" and had "no merit." I have tried to accept this and explain to my children and friends...

It is difficult to comprehend and/or explain....Are there arguable ground(s) for an appeal or not? Do I believe Randy Piercey or Derek Hogan? I have tried to understand [Piercey's] position & not be angry. But I do feel misled and betrayed. My family and friends are angry with him.

...I have 8 close friends in St. John's ready to be sureties for my bond....Some of my friends are attempting to find another private lawyer for me (pro bono)...I am considering asking for a new legal aid lawyer...

As you can see, I am "stuck between a rock and a hard place." I was not at all prepared for this & neither were my children. I appreciate your concern in the past for their well-being.

On Nov. 14, I was still breastfeeding my infant son, Zachary, and hoping to be able to continue after my release on bond (after a few days). He has adjusted to a bottle and his new caregivers. But I miss him desperately & he needs his mother who loves him so very much...his paternal grandparents, David and Kathleen Bagby...are prepared to take care of him as long as I need them to.... He is happy & doing well....My other children are <u>not</u> doing as well. My youngest daughter...is 12 years old and she...has agreed to go back to live with her father Dec. 24 because I am not home yet. She is <u>not</u> very happy about that. My older daughter...came home from Toronto for Christmas to see me and her new little brother, but she will <u>not</u> be able to see us together...

I am <u>not</u> asking for anything special for me or my children. If I have to wait here in Newfoundland, why can't I be home with my children? I would closely adhere to any conditions of my bond as I did in the past.

I am prepared to go to PA to try to clear my name & fight this awful charge against me, even though many people are convinced I will <u>not</u> get a "fair trial" there...I would like to have as much time as possible with my children, esp. Zachary <u>before</u> I am surrendered....I desperately wish to prove my innocence, but I do realize that may not be possible. I want to clear my name for me and esp. for my children. I pray every night for justice—for Andrew—for me—for Zachary—for the Bagbys. I am innocent and I will get through this. I have to. I still hope and pray that the person responsible is found.

[The following was on the back of the last sheet]

Sorry, but I'm locked in my cell & this is my last sheet of paper (it's 1 AM).

During my extradition hearing...I developed a great respect for you as a gentleman and a judge. You always treated me with courtesy and respect. I believe you were as fair as you could be given the "information" by the Crown. I also have a great respect for Mike Madden and I realize he was only doing his job. All 3 attorneys (incl. yourself) impressed me with their intelligence and competence. I never felt that my hearing was "a game" or that my life did not matter.

I appreciate your attention to this matter and your consideration, past and present. If you are able to answer any of my questions, please let me know as soon as possible. Thank You.

Yours sincerely,
Shirley J. Turner, M.D.

P.S.) I hope you can read my scribbles—no access to a typewriter or computer now.

P.P.S.) I have no idea when the Federal Minister will make his decision and/or how much longer I'll be here.

JUDGE GREEN'S SECRETARY'S RESPONSE

Here are some key excerpts:

December 20, 2002

Dear Dr. Turner:

Chief Justice Green has asked me to acknowledge receipt of your letter dated December 20, 2002.

Upon the filing of his judgment on November 14, Chief Justice Green ceased to have any legal authority, as the trial judge, with respect to your case. It is inappropriate, therefore, for him...to comment on the substantive matters raised in your letter, or to take any legal steps in relation to them.

However, in his capacity as Chief Justice responsible for the administration of the court, he wishes me to inform you that [your concerns] should be discussed further with [your] legal aid counsel....If you are not satisfied [you could ask for a different legal aid attorney]....Alternatively, [you could apply for bail yourself]...Chief Justice Green...can advise that, generally speaking, where an individual seeks to make a bail application without assistance of counsel, a greater latitude and informality of procedure is usually allowed by courts.

[Procedural details were then explained to Dr. Turner.]

Yours very truly,
Lorna J. Farewell
Judges' Secretary

Shirley told us about these letters and said that Judge Green was very sympathetic to her predicament because he had children of his own. When I read them (much later) I wondered if Judge Green was legally required to respond to Shirley's letter or could he have dropped it into the circular file and moved on? Could he have simply acknowledged receipt and left it at that? What compelled him to offer what seems to this layman like expert legal advice, or worse: encouragement?

BAIL APPLICATION

Shirley must have taken heart from Judge Green's reference to "greater latitude and informality of procedure." She sat right down and wrote her own bail application.

She summarized the history of her ordeal, beginning with her planned three-week trip to Canada "after [she] had received the news of the death of a very close friend," up to her incarceration after Judge Green's Committal Order.

Then, she itemized her perfect compliance with the conditions of her release on bail from December 12, 2001 to November 14, 2002—appear in court as needed, report weekly to the police, etc.

She professed her innocence and complained about the death penalty, wrongful convictions, and pre-trial publicity:

> The charge for which the United States of America seeks
> my extradition is first-degree murder and the
> Commonwealth of Pennsylvania can/may seek the death
> penalty for such an offense. I am innocent of this charge.
> I am innocent of any charge of murder.... The accusation
> and subsequent charge are horrible in and of themselves. I
> do not want to become another statistic in the legal records
> of an innocent person wrongfully convicted/sentenced. I

do not trust the U.S.A. justice system at all....The District
Attorney and or police...have supplied the media with
lots of information and "so-called evidence"...making it
highly improbable that I will receive a fair trial there.

Shirley reviewed her two grounds for appeal of the
Committal Order: The Authority to Proceed is a nullity and the
case is built entirely on flimsy circumstantial evidence. She
promised to obey any conditions of a subsequent release on bail
and proposed "to live with [her] good friends, Douglas and
Loraine Mercer...if released."

She wrote that she intended "to resume the physical care
and maternal nurturing of [her] son, Zachary, if released," and
that "This ha[d] been agreed to by the Bagbys in our consent
order and [that] Zachary w[ould] live with [her] at the Mercer's
until [she could] find employment and [her] own apartment."

She declared that she had applied for and received approval
for a full license in late October 2002. She wrote: "If released, I
will continue to seek locum work [short-term temporary
assignments] as a family physician in this Province," and noted
that she did not have a criminal record.

From Kate's journal on December 27: "I love Zachary so
much that in my mind he already belongs to David, our friends
and family, and myself....I wonder if I am strong enough to
accept parting with him."

CHAPTER 23
BAIL HEARING

On Wednesday morning, January 8, 2003, Maureen babysat Zachary while Kate and I went to watch Justice Gale Welsh preside over Shirley's bail hearing.[1] The Court of Appeals building had only one courtroom, smaller than those in the Supreme Court building next door. For observers, there was only one row of seats across the back, with no separation between spectators and the lawyers at their podiums—Madden to the left and Shirley to the right, representing herself. Andrew's supporters—Danette, Jackie, Kate, and I—took these back seats. Along the left side were several more spectator chairs, occupied by Shirley's supporters—her friend Loraine Mercer (who agreed to house Shirley upon release) and the two Anglican priests, Reverends Rowland and Parsons, who had baptized Zachary. Both Jackie and I later swore we could feel the hatred emanating from Loraine Mercer's eyes toward us, a reversal of my cold stare at Shirley back in March on our first trip to Newfoundland.

Two sheriff deputies led Shirley into the courtroom: a burly young man we didn't know and Kathleen, who had searched us prior to several Zachary visits at Family Court. They removed Shirley's handcuffs and shackles and flanked her in the seats to our right.

After the "All rise" and the "Who appears?" Judge Welsh announced a publication ban on details of the hearing, and then summarized the law covering bail during an appeal of an extradition Committal Order.

Section 20 of the Extradition Act says that "Section 679 of the Criminal Code applies with any modifications that the circumstances require…" Under Section 679(3), Shirley had the burden to show that: (a) her appeal was not frivolous, (b) if released, she would surrender herself as ordered and (c) her release would not place the public at risk.

Over the next two days, Shirley (representing herself), Madden, and Judge Welsh argued the application of these criteria to Shirley's case. I have extracted the essence of each party's arguments using the transcript, Shirley's application for bail, Madden's *factum* (written response to Shirley's application), and Judge Welsh's written decision.

(a) Frivolousness of Appeal

Judge Welsh and Mr. Madden engaged in a lengthy debate, not on whether Shirley's appeal was frivolous, but on whether the frivolousness of appeal criterion was applicable to Shirley's case.

According to Welsh, Section 20 of the Extradition Act says that "Section 679 of the Criminal Code applies *with any modifications that the circumstances require…*" (emphasis added). The Criminal Code states that Section 679(3)(*a*) applies "in case of an appeal…against conviction." Welsh said, "it seems to me that one of the circumstances is that Dr. Turner is not convicted of an offence… [hence,] she should be treated the same as if…she had been committed to stand trial after a preliminary inquiry [in a domestic criminal proceeding]." The judge continued, "The only consideration [in a domestic preliminary inquiry], because the presumption of innocence applies at this stage, would be the second and third elements of 679(3)."

According to Madden, "It is clear from the Extradition Act and from case law that a fugitive is not in the same position as an accused who has been ordered to stand trial [at a preliminary inquiry]." There is no requirement in the Criminal Code to lock up someone who is committed to stand trial at a preliminary inquiry. By contrast, the Extradition Act "states that a judge shall order the committal of the person into custody to await surrender. This is a mandatory requirement. There is no section of the Extradition Act which [empowers the judge] to reconsider the issue of [bail]."

A fugitive, he argued, is locked up at the end of an extradition hearing, in spite of the fact that he or she has not been convicted of an offence. If the absence of a conviction is irrelevant at that point, it should also be irrelevant when the fugitive later applies for release on bail. "To incorporate the notion of *never been convicted* [emphasis added] as a consideration on appeal of custody is...beginning to unravel the extradition process at the Court of Appeal level."

Tossing out the issue of frivolousness of appeal, Madden continued, "is not a modification but a re-writing of the explicit terms of Section 679(3) so as to enact fundamental changes to the substance of that provision." Hence, frivolousness of appeal should be considered in determining whether to release Ms. Turner on bail.

Madden linked the merits of Shirley's appeal with the merits of the case against her: "[T]he merits of the appeal are always relevant in the determination of the release [as would be] the strength of the case....Certainly if the...merits of the case [are] relevant...the merits of an appeal are relevant."

Judge Welsh said, "But the merits of this case have been considered....She was granted [bail] prior to the extradition hearing.... [The] last time the merits of the case were considered...it didn't result in Dr. Turner not receiving [bail] earlier."

The transcript of Shirley's initial bail hearing, on December 12, 2001, shows that the merits of the case against her were not considered in open court.

In a final general appeal to case law, Madden stated, "There have been no cases anywhere in Canada that I have been able to find...in which the court has ruled that an acceptable modification...would be to not consider the merits of the appeal."

RESOLUTION

Judge Welsh was not impressed. "Thank you, Mr. Madden, that was very helpful. Dr. Turner, I don't need to hear from you. Mr. Madden, I have carefully considered your submissions, they've been able submissions....But I'm going to make a determination right now on that particular issue....I am satisfied that the clause 'with any modification that the circumstances require'... must be interpreted to mean that [(a) frivolousness of appeal] would not apply in the context...of a Committal Order for extradition....The circumstances therefore require that the assessment of Dr. Turner's application for [bail] be limited to... (b) [she surrender herself as ordered] and (c) [her release would not place the public interest at risk]....This interpretation...is consistent with...the rights guaranteed under...the Charter, that is the right to be presumed innocent until proven guilty and the individual's right to have her liberty infringed only where and to the extent justified."

It took a day and a half to reach this conclusion. Since most of Madden's preparation had gone into the first criterion, which Judge Welsh had now declared moot, arguments on the second and third criteria went fairly quickly on the second day. The judge challenged Madden on only one minor point, whereas Shirley took an active role in these debates.

(b) Flight Risk

Madden argued that the risk of flight for Shirley had increased since her previous release on bail because the "risk of…a severe sentence…is greater at this stage [after the Committal Order] than it had been earlier." Contrary to Shirley's affidavit, the Case Record suggested reasons for Shirley's move to Canada that would be an indication of flight. Under the Criminal Code, Shirley had the burden to "show cause why [her] detention is not justified" for two reasons: she is not "ordinarily resident in Canada" and she is "charged with [a serious offence] (such as murder)."

Shirley countered that the risk of a severe sentence was the same after the Committal Order as it had been back in December 2001 when "I had two passports and I had the finances" to flee. Recalling that the extradition process consists of six steps, back in December 2001 the first step (Authority to Proceed) was still two months in the future. Shirley's ludicrous contention that the risk was the same then as it was after the Committal Order could only be true if (a) all requests for extradition resulted in the issuance of an Authority to Proceed, and (b) all Authorities to Proceed resulted in the issuance of a Committal Order.

She pointed out that, in addition to her own affidavit, she had corroborating affidavits from Carol Ross, Julianne Herzog, and her son showing that she did not flee to Canada. Madden did not press this issue, as he did not consider it to be of "any major significance" to the judge's decision.

Shirley also said that she had shown "good faith and relia-bility" by not fleeing when she still had her passports and money, and by her compliance with the previous release order. However, Shirley's "good faith and reliability" is only one possible explanation for her compliance with the previous release order. Another equally plausible explanation would be a desire to buy time until either the courts issued a "get-away-with-murder" pass or the risk of imprisonment becomes intolerable, forcing her to seek another exit from the legal system, at a time and place of her choosing.

She maintained that she didn't have a prior criminal record, had five family and friends who would sign as sureties for a total of $75,000, and, if released, she would swear to comply with the orders of the court.

When Madden raised the issue of why Shirley moved to Canada, implying that her affidavit was perhaps insincere, Judge Welsh turned for confirmation to Shirley:

> Judge Welsh: Now Dr. Turner...I'm assuming that you understand the seriousness with which the affidavit was prepared.
> Shirley: Yes, I do.
> Judge Welsh: And sworn to by you.
> Shirley: Yes.
> Judge Welsh: And that if I make an Order giving you [bail] you would not attempt to flee or hide or avoid subsequent judicial proceedings related to this matter.
> Shirley: Yes.
> Judge Welsh: Is that completely understood by you?
> Shirley: Yes, I completely understand that.

Kate and I wondered if an accused had ever responded, "Actually, milady, if I get the opportunity, you'll never see me again."

(c) Public Interest

According to Madden, "Contrary to what Ms. Turner has stated in her submissions, there appears to be an abundance of evidence substantiating the case…against Dr. Turner.…The charge…for which this fugitive has been ordered into custody [is] just about the most serious offence, [involving] extreme violence…"

According to Shirley, the case against her was "flimsy circumstantial evidence and there will be some new presentations given in the appeal on that." A promise of still more nits on appeal.

She continued, "There has never been any evidence given in court of any violent behaviour on my part or any psychological disorder." This contention raised what is probably the most perverse logical fallacy of this entire exercise. Because of the interpretation of "presumption of innocence" in Commonwealth legal culture, a "probable" premeditated murder in Shirley's past could not be used as an indication of possible risk in the future. (Note that "probable" is one of the two operative words in the legal standard for issuance of an arrest warrant; police must convince a judge that there are "reasonable and probable grounds" to believe the accused committed a crime.)

Madden had an opportunity at this point to introduce evidence of Shirley's phony suicide attempt on her lover's doorstep in 1999. That malicious charade may have indicated a psychological disorder, which may have induced the judge to consider Shirley's possible danger to the public. When Kate asked Madden about this incident prior to the hearing, he indicated that it had taken place three years before and would therefore not carry any weight in this bail hearing. On another occasion, however, he had noted that she was "effing nuts." He probably had that right, but didn't translate it into clean

English, take it into court, and make the formal argument that she was a potential danger to herself and/or others.

Shirley argued that the Newfoundland Medical Board had approved her "licence to practice medicine in this province [after] a thorough investigation of my medical competence and background....I think that has a lot to say about whether or not I'm a danger to anybody in the public." When pressed for details by Judge Welsh, Shirley admitted that her medical licence approval may have lapsed when she went to jail in November. She also noted that it took from January to October for the Medical Board to approve her request for a licence, a delay she attributed to "inaccuracies that were reported in the media about the case that had to be cleared, before I could have my licence."

RESOLUTION

There followed a lengthy discussion of the conditions for Shirley's release, which were essentially the same as in December of 2001. The only major glitch involved her recognizance order, which forbade her to contact Andrew's family, meaning Kate and me. On the understanding that Shirley and the Bagbys would find a solution to that problem that would be acceptable to Madden, Judge Welsh dropped the expected brick on my head: "[B]ased on the argument that I've heard, the affidavit evidence that was provided and any other relevant information, I'm satisfied that Dr. Turner should be granted [bail]."

During a short recess I called Kate with the bad news. She broke down, so I asked Danette to go help Kate cry. I had to stay and finalize some means by which to pass Zachary back and forth between his mother and his grandparents without violating Shirley's recognizance order. The details couldn't be settled that afternoon, so Shirley would have to spend one more night in jail.

Over the next two hours, working through Jackie and Cynthia, we reached agreement on a new Family Court Consent Order specifying that Kate and I would have a lot more time with Zachary and that we could take him away from Shirley's apartment, unsupervised. We would pick him up and drop him off, passing him through a third party so that there would be no direct contact between Shirley and us. Recalling the hard stare from Loraine Mercer, plus Shirley's comment to us that "Loraine can't get her head around you," we stipulated that neither Loraine nor her husband could be the third party. With this agreement in place, Shirley was taken back to jail while I drove home to Kate and Zachary, with Jackie beside me in the passenger seat.

FINAL DETAILS

The next morning Kate again stayed with Zachary while I went to court. Madden read the modified recognizance order into the record: "[N]o contact with David and Kathleen Bagby, except in accordance with any subsequent order of the Unified Family Court."

Judge Welsh thanked Madden "for a job well done" and court was adjourned. The sureties went down to the court-house and signed on the dotted line, agreeing to pay "Her Majesty the Queen" the following amounts if Shirley failed to appear: Loraine Mercer, $20,000; Philip Hefford, $20,000; James Thorne, $20,000; Turner J. Shears, $10,000; and Brian Madore, $5,000.

Some days after this hearing, Kate expressed her concern to Madden about the inability of at least two of the sureties to produce the money if Shirley later failed to appear in court. He advised Kate not to worry, because the State would go after them, even if it took ten years.

WRITTEN REASONS FOR DECISION

Many months later Kate and I carefully reviewed Judge Welsh's written reasons supporting her decision to release Shirley. Here are its key points:

> Dr. Turner provided an affidavit which amply supports the conclusion that she would comply with the order… the factors set out in the affidavit filed by Dr. Turner demonstrate a basis on which I would conclude that she will comply with a [bail] order.… The Crown had failed to establish that it was necessary to detain Turner in custody in the public interest, as her crime, while violent, was specific in nature.… Regarding the public safety issue, while the offence with which she is charged is a violent and serious one, it was not directed at the public at large.… Furthermore, Turner must be presumed innocent, in accordance with the Charter.… There is no indication of a psychological disorder that would give concern about potential harm to the public generally.

Whatever the legal rationale, Zachary was going back to his emotionally unstable mother.

BACK TO THE PIT

In the late afternoon, an elegant lady appeared at our door and introduced herself as the mother of a friend of Shirley. She had been nominated to pick up Zachary solely because she had a child's car seat for her granddaughter. We bore her no ill will, nor she us. I trundled Zachary's things out to her car. Kate zipped him into his snowsuit and carried him down the stairs. The lady waited patiently in the car as we stood on the porch and cuddled him and kissed him. Kate clung to him until I very deliberately removed him from her arms and placed him in the car seat and buckled the straps and kissed him again. Kate came over and kissed him again and I closed the car door. The elegant, innocent lady drove away and we dragged ourselves back up the stairs and into bed for another long, long night of despair.

CHAPTER 24
DÉTENTE

It was very difficult to get out of bed the next morning. There was no Zachary in the other room, there was no Andrew in Latrobe, and Shirley was once again free and back in control of our grandson's fate.

NORMAL

We did get up and do something useful: thoroughly clean the apartment. In the evening we met Jen for dinner; Mark was working, as usual, and couldn't join us.

From my journal, January 11, 2002:

Jen was her usual sweet, compassionate self. I can't recall what she said, or how she did it, but we always feel better just from being around her. Mark has the same effect, but he's not around as much as Jen, because of his sporadic work hours. I guess they're just stable, caring people, who are willing to be in our presence during our pain, or our laughter, or whatever we bring with us. And they remind us, with their stories of hockey and soccer and family and work, that normal life is still out there being lived by most people. And normal life is worth doing! We *must* get back

to it some day, and ensure that Zachary has a chance to
live that way.

After dinner, we escaped to a movie: *The Two Towers*, part
two of J.R.R. Tolkien's *Lord of the Rings* trilogy. It was a good
story, providing the escape we sought, but something more.
Near the end of the film, when Frodo feels that the burden of
the ring is overwhelming and he simply cannot continue the
struggle, Sam tries to convince him to hold on. Frodo asks,
"What are we holding onto, Sam?" "That there's some good in
this world, Mr. Frodo, and it's worth fighting for."

PEACE OFFERING

The next afternoon Jennifer, Shirley's upstairs neighbour at her
old apartment on Pleasant Street, called with a proposal from
Shirley. We needed to drop off some things for Zachary anyway
and we could have an unscheduled visit with him while Shirley
and some friends went to Subway for a sandwich. We eagerly
accepted and went off to see our little angel. Jennifer, holding
Zachary, met us at the door.

From my journal, January 12, 2003:

He was so sweet. He gave Kate a big smile and went to her
when she held out her arms. She held him while I brought
in the things from the car, and then we played with him
on the floor. His crawling movements seemed to have
improved in the short time he had been away from us,
and he was happy to play on his tummy most of the time.
He turned over with ease, both ways, and laughed a little
when Kate sang "The Itsy Bitsy Spider" to him. Then he
got hungry and inhaled most of a large bottle and all of a
small one. Then he slept in Kate's arms until Jennifer

arrived. We had nearly an hour of unexpected visit with the new center of the universe. Kate left a little thank-you note to Shirley on the coffee table.

As I backed out of the parking spot across the street from the house, someone waved to us from the entryway. I automatically waved back, thinking it was Jennifer. It wasn't Jennifer. It was Shirley. I had not seen her come down the street and go in the front door. Kate said, "That's Shirley!" and then we had a good laugh over the possibility that she might feel even more warm and cuddly with us now.

LORAINE MERCER

Three days later Jennifer called with another gift; we could babysit Zachary the next afternoon while Shirley moved out of Loraine Mercer's house and into her new apartment on O'Reilly Street. With that pleasant prospect in mind, we were settled in for the evening when the doorbell rang. I opened up to find Loraine Mercer on our porch. She handed me an envelope and said, "This is too personal and sincere to send in the mail, and if I've hurt you I'm dreadfully sorry." Then she hurried to her car and drove off, leaving me dumbstruck.

Negotiations for a new Consent Order were ongoing, with draft proposals flying back and forth between Shirley and us through Cynthia and Jackie, and the catalyst for Loraine's letter was the appearance of her name in one of these drafts. In order to avoid contact with Shirley, we had agreed to pass Zachary through a third party when we picked him up and dropped him off. We had stipulated, however, that this third party not be Loraine or her husband, and Shirley had shared these drafts with Loraine, who then wrote to us:

Dear Kate and David,

I must confront an issue that bothers me a great deal...that you want no contact with me....This leads me to believe that in some manner I have hurt you....I would never give you pain or hurt intentionally....I never wondered about Zachary while in your care. I believed that you would be parenting him as I would have parented my grandchildren if it were necessary.

On the few occasions I attended court sessions...I would look your way and hope you would sense my empathy...the fact that you came and stayed to be near Zachary showed your commitment. I know on the whole scene I would have done what you have done.

I admire you greatly yet felt that my greater ministry was to...support Shirley and I could not have sustained two relationships.

I have prayed that God will forgive me if I have harmed you emotionally or any other way...

Sincerely
In Confidence
Loraine Mercer

We reread this letter several times and decided that we must respond, but not before a new Consent Order was in effect. Our response would need to include Shirley's telling us that Loraine "could not get her head around the Bagbys" and had a hard time accepting our potential custody of Zachary. Her stern demeanour at the courthouse had also conveyed an impression of intractability. Furthermore, despite the compassionate tone of her letter, we had to maintain a healthy skepticism in case she shared our response with Shirley, who might fall off emotional balance again.

CONTACT

The following day Shirley and Brian Madore, her ex-landlord and current surety, came to pick up Zachary's crib. Shirley stayed in the car while Madore came upstairs to get the crib and to ask if we wanted to keep Zachary while they moved Shirley into her new apartment. Another proffered gift; another acceptance.

He was a happy soul, smiling and struggling to get down from Kate's arms. She set him on the living floor and we joined him, admiring his disjointed attempts to crawl. He so nearly had it that we hoped to witness his first success then and there. A couple of times he would draw both knees up together, raising his butt in the air, but he had not yet coordinated a pushup with his leg thrashing, so he only slid forward a few inches scraping his face on the carpet. Never mind; he had fun moving and we had fun watching him move.

Jennifer, acting as intermediary between Shirley and us, called several times trying to arrange Zachary's return to his mother, who was waiting at Loraine Mercer's house. There was no other third party available and we had to get him back soon, so we packed him into the car and drove over. I took him up to the house and rang the bell, expecting Loraine to answer. Shirley opened the door. We exchanged one-word greetings— "hello," "hi"—mine just civil, hers accompanied by a friendly smile. I handed over Zachary and left. Almost like a normal family, with the doting grandparents returning their precious charge to Mommy after a few hours of self-indulgent spoiling. Except that Mommy shot Daddy and Grandpa wanted to strangle Mommy.

Peace and harmony... *Focus, damn it!*...peace and harmony...peace and harmony...

NEW CONSENT ORDER

Negotiations were completed on a new Consent Order, which
was filed on January 30, 2003. It was a great improvement over
the conditions from before Shirley went to jail. We would have
six visits with Zachary every two weeks, including one
overnight, totalling thirty-seven hours, all unsupervised. We
would pick up and drop off Zachary at Shirley's apartment,
passing him through a third party so that there would be no
direct contact between us. The third party could not be Loraine
Mercer or her husband Douglas. (We would like to have withdrawn this condition, but Shirley might ask why and we didn't
want to tell her about Loraine's letter.)

There could be one ten-minute phone call per day to discuss only Zachary-related issues. We would be the first choice
for babysitting if Shirley found a job. Nobody would remove
Zachary from Newfoundland. We would deposit our passports
with Jackie, who would not give them back to us without first
informing Shirley. Nobody would provide pictures of Zachary
to the media. If Shirley went back to jail, we would again have
full-time care of Zachary and again accommodate visits with
his mother in prison.

This agreement formed the legal basis for the next half-year
of our relationship with Zachary and his mother. In its day-to-
day implementation, both parties went way beyond a strict
interpretation: we averaged far more visiting hours than called
for in the schedule, spoke with Shirley on the telephone far
more than ten minutes per day, and eventually spent a great
deal of time in her company, because we loved Zachary more
than we hated her.

RULES OF ENGAGEMENT

I have never been in an actual war, with bullets and bombs threatening to terminate my existence at any moment. It doesn't take much imagination, however, to see that decision making in such circumstances must be driven by two basic rules: first, survive; and second, kill the enemy. In our bloodless war, in which Kate and I found ourselves interacting with the enemy on a regular basis, we quickly formulated two simple rules of engagement.

Rule One: If Shirley Offers Time with Zachary, Take It

This rule—valid any time, any place, no questions, no exceptions—served not only our desperate need to be a part of Zachary's life, but the very practical function of ensuring that, once his mother was taken away, he would experience minimal trauma in the transition back to our full-time care.

The trappings, if not the spirit, of cooperation between Shirley and us grew rapidly, as did the contact. We looked after Zachary at her apartment so that she could make a quick trip to the local convenience store. We took Zachary out for a couple of hours while she had friends in for her birthday dinner. Passing him back and forth, we engaged in civil Zachary-centred chit-chat, and we occasionally met some of her friends.

Rule Two: Do Not Discuss Extradition with Shirley

If conversation edged close to a discussion of Andrew or the extradition case, Kate and I always clammed up, for fear of contaminating the case or becoming embroiled in a confrontation. Running errands one day, I ran into Shirley as she came out of Wal-Mart pushing Zachary in his stroller. She asked where Kate was and I almost said, "She's having a bad day." Our friends would have understood; they knew about Kate's occasional meltdowns. But I didn't want to give Shirley an opening to discuss anything personal, especially our despair at Andrew's murder, so I lied: "She's tired; taking a nap."

I squatted in front of Zachary and yammered at him while Shirley yammered at me. At one point he turned his head a certain way that showed off his blazing blue eyes in the sunlight. I said, "My God, your eyes are gorgeous!" and instantly feared that my comment might lead Shirley into talking about Andrew's reputedly gorgeous eyes. Fortunately she let it pass, only saying, "Yes, aren't they."

THIRD PARTY COUNSELLING

When we dropped off Zachary at her apartment one afternoon, Shirley asked us to come in and talk about a serious issue. We tensed up even more than usual, but took seats in the living room and listened. She proposed to have a social worker or psychologist sit down with the three of us and discuss Zachary's future in the event that his mother were sent to prison. Would it be good for him to visit his mother in prison as he got older? What and when should he be told about his parentage? How could we prepare him for some of the bad things he was likely to hear as he grew up; bad things about his grandparents as well as his mother? (We guessed that this was a reference to Carol Ross's ancient allegation that Kate had threatened to kill her, but we didn't ask what she meant by it.)

Kate and I just listened, and then I expressed some concern that we might be violating the current Consent Order by discussing this *sans* lawyers. Shirley said that she "put [her] trust in [our] good faith, and our common interest in Zachary, more than in the legal process of Consent Orders." We agreed in general that a meeting with a disinterested third party taking notes might be a good idea, and that we should ask Jackie and Cynthia to recommend the third party. The goal was to get these issues settled *before* Shirley was again taken into custody, so that we would not be hurried into a new consent order when the time came.

While we pondered these weighty issues Zachary crawled and squirmed his way around the floor and on and off our laps, distracting each of us in turn and keeping us marginally entertained. After a while I offered him a bottle, which he rejected in that brutally honest fashion of babies—puckered his mouth and yanked his head sideways as if I had tried to force feed him raw sewage. Kate offered him the same bottle a minute later and he took it. Fortunately, I had a thick skin; more accurately, I realized that babies have no guile, Kate was his favourite cuddler and bottle holder and he wasn't capable of lying about it.

In one of our daily telephone calls, nominally to discuss Zachary, Shirley complained to Kate about a television news story saying that she was $200,000 in debt, and that she had applied for government funding of a private attorney (preferably Randy Piercey) to represent her Committal Order appeal. A hearing would take place on February 18. Shirley considered that broadcast to be an invasion of her privacy.

PIERCEY

The February 18 hearing took place in the Court of Appeal, and was presided over by Justice Margaret Cameron. It spilled over into a second session, finishing on March 3, but the details are not worth a complete dissection here. Briefly, the issue before the court was whether Shirley should get a publicly funded lawyer to handle her extradition appeals. She had already appealed the Committal Order and, if the Minister of Justice issued a Surrender Order, she would appeal that as well.[1]

Three Legal Aid attorneys—Derek Hogan, Dennis McKay, and Newman Petten—thought Shirley's appeal of the Committal Order had no merit, so they had rejected her request for representation. Randy Piercey, however, was willing to represent Shirley's appeals if he could be paid for his efforts.

Judge Cameron determined that Shirley needed, and was entitled to, representation, even if only to argue that she needed representation. Hence, she ordered the Attorney General to fund Randy Piercey's representation of Shirley's appeals.

Kate and I didn't really care whether Shirley had an attorney, nor did we care who that attorney might be. We wanted whatever decision would move things along and this one seemed to further that goal. Obviously, Piercey already knew the case, so he wouldn't need weeks or months to get up to speed, which meant the court could hear the two appeals as soon as the Minister issued a Surrender Order... *if* he issued a Surrender Order.

At the outset of this hearing, during the "why-are-we-here" phase, Judge Cameron seemed to raise a curious eyebrow as she noted that "an assessment of whether this is a frivolous appeal...often that determination would have been made in the bail process, but in this case [Judge Welsh] chose to approach bail in a different way." We wondered if Welsh had blazed a new legal trail in deciding not to consider frivolousness of appeal.

Kate and I know that legal professionals can't slog through their entire workday in sombre contemplation of the seriousness of their duties. Like the anatomy student resting his Diet Pepsi on the cadaver's belly, they have to push the horror of their worst cases to the back of their minds and lighten up a little. However, to the observer with no legal standing, but with a heavy stake in the outcome, it's grating to hear light banter slip into the courtroom discussion. At one point, Judge Cameron started a sentence with "all of a sudden extradition seems to be the…" Madden finished it for her: "Flavour of the month." No cure for this. Just an observation.

CHURCH

Kate and I both played with Zachary as much as possible during our visits, but her connection to him was much stronger than mine; she did most of the feeding and bedtime cuddles. My closest moments were in the early mornings of his overnight visits. When he woke up and complained of his crib confinement, Kate usually slept in while I took him to the kitchen and strapped him into his high chair, which had some toys tied on a string and clipped to the edges of his tray. He amused himself with these while I explained the ancient art of making tea: "First, you fill the kettle, like this.…No, actually, first you take the lid off the kettle…can you say 'lid'? Then you push this handle up to turn on the water…" He divided his attention between gnawing on a toy and my thrilling narrative. If I said something especially clever he might break into a raucous display of approval, banging a rattle on the tray and shouting, "Ah, ah, ah, ah." I quickly learned his language and echoed back to him, "Ah, ah, ah, ah." Why not? It made as much sense as my tea dissertation and we came to understand each other perfectly.

If an overnight visit took place on a Saturday we nearly always took Zachary to the eleven o'clock service the next morning at St. Michael's Church, where we developed some great friends and Zachary became a favourite among the congregation. I contributed an article about him to the spring edition of the church newsletter:

Zachary loves church! Since he first saw the tall colourful windows in the rear semicircle, when he was only about three months old, he has enjoyed going back there early in the service and gazing up at the brightness. Now, at the ripe old age of eight months, he not only likes to look; he wants to touch and, if I could hold him up high enough, taste. He is completely enthralled. And for me, I love the way the blue and red diffused light bathes his eager little face.

When he gets too heavy, I put Zachary on the floor and let him roam. Before he crawled effectively, he was often content chewing on my bootlace for ten or fifteen minutes. Now he can't stay still that long and charges across the floor at his version of breakneck speed until he comes to a pew. Then he switches into vertical mode and struggles to a standing position. At first, a collection plate laid on the floor provided a distraction, but no more. How ya gonna keep 'em, down on the floor, once they have stood upright?

We always sit way in the back, so that if Zachary wants to comment on the proceedings, he won't disturb too many folks. For a long time, he only made a few little noises, trying out his newly discovered voice box with, "Ay, ay, ay, ay." Lately, he has added lots of variations, including a happy squeal that has steadily increased in both pitch and volume.

Though many have told us that it's not a problem, we no longer feel comfortable allowing Zachary to compete with Father Chris for congregational attention, so I have taken him upstairs to play in the kids' room. There, he has discovered not only a new set of toys to explore, but other small people to wonder about. If he could speak, I'm sure he would ask with great indignation, "How come Ryan can move so fast on his two legs, and I'm stuck down here crawling along looking at the carpet?!"

I always take Zachary back to the service before Holy Communion, so that Kate can take him up to the altar for a blessing. That is a most precious moment for Kate, as it is the time she feels closest to Zachary's father, Andrew.

After the service, we nearly always head down to the hall for a cup of coffee and some goodies and a chat with our new Newfoundland friends. This also allows Zachary to bathe in the love and affection of a good portion of the St. Michael's congregation. And of course he eats it up. You can't spoil a child with too much love. Our dear friends at St. Michael's have certainly taken Kate and me under their collective wing, and since Zachary has been attending services with us, these lovely people have helped us to smother him in Christian love. For Zachary, and for these wonderful new friends, we are truly thankful.

SNIPPETS

Thursday, February 13–15, 2003: Three Overnights

In a normal grandparent relationship we might have felt put upon by the randomness of Shirley's requests for babysitting service, but we loved it and she took frequent advantage of that. At one stretch, we had Zachary three nights running—Shirley had a headache on Thursday night, wanted to hit the George Street bars with her friends on Friday, and Saturday was a scheduled overnight. To us, a big deal!

Wednesday, February 19, 2003: Doctor Visit

We picked up Shirley and Zachary and drove them to see Dr. Marie O'Dea for his six-month injection. He was a dream, moaning for only a few seconds after the needle punctured his thigh. Then the doctor presented her otoscope as a distraction and he thought that was so cool he forgot about his thigh and set about gnawing on the scope's shiny metal casing.

Saturday, February 22, 2003: Music

Heather Arnold, who has a wonderful singing voice, was determined that Zachary would grow up with music in his life and she knew he wouldn't get it from Kate or me. Towards her goal, she and Matt, who plays cello, gave him an elaborate music box for Christmas. Still lacking accurate finger control, he banged away on the various knobs and switches with his open hand in a raking motion, but he did it with purpose. He soon learned that a certain switch yielded a certain song, and banged on his favourites over and over again, the intensity of concentration worthy of an assault on the intricacies of particle physics.

Sunday, February 23, 2003: Tuna Casserole

From my journal:

> After church we went to lunch at Shirley's house. I think Andrew would understand and approve, but there is nagging doubt about that. "You sat down on Shirley's sofa and enjoyed her tuna casserole, eh? Went back for seconds? Pretty good stuff, eh? Did she tell you about the last time she saw me? She tell you I tried to reason my way out of it? Or did she tell you I tried begging? What did you talk about over tuna casserole?"

If Kate's right and you are observing this, Andrew, you must know that Zachary is the most important person on the planet to us now, because he is the last of you. I would eat a bucket of worms for him, or for you, so I can surely have tuna casserole with your killer if it helps ensure a good life for Zachary.

Monday, February 24, 2003: Baby Pool

We enrolled Zachary for sessions in the baby pool at the Aquarena—an indoor swimming complex—and usually chauffeured him and Shirley to and from these sessions at least once a week. Each child could be accompanied in the water by as many as two adults, so usually either Kate or I joined Shirley and Zachary in the pool.

Zachary loved the water, splashing and kicking, bobbing plastic balls and little rubber duckies, and skimming across the surface in the grip of one or the other adult. Kate and I could focus mainly on his innocent pleasure and temporarily repress our anxiety at this bizarre social arrangement, but the situation highlighted a growing concern about Zachary's honesty. He consistently chose Kate over Shirley, twisting and squirming and moaning and reaching for Nan until Mom reluctantly handed him over and then tried to entice him back again. At Shirley's apartment, Kate could usually duck the issue by hurrying off to the restroom or the kitchen, but in the pool there was no place to hide.

We tried to make light of Zachary's mother-rejection, pointing out that most small children opt for Grandma over Mommy; Grandma is the rare, exciting, over-indulgent adult in his life, compared to boring old Mommy who's around all day, every day. This explanation was not entirely fatuous; we had seen such behaviour in grandchildren before, though not to the extent displayed by Zachary. Shirley mewled, "I know," and we hoped and prayed that she meant it.

Friday, March 7, 2003

From my journal:

> When Kate came out of the bedroom and Zachary looked up at her, his face lit up with pure joy. I realized that at this time in his life, his "love" was entirely based on his own needs. Anyone who consistently met those needs over a significant period of time would be greeted with this joyous face. But one of the two people who were greeted in this way by Zachary was Kate, and it gave me great hope that he would grow into a good and loving person, guided at first by Kate's pure joy in loving him. The other person who lit up Zachary's face was Shirley, and I hoped that when she finally was taken away from him and sent to prison, his loving grandma would meet his most basic needs and he would not feel the loss of his mother for very long nor very deeply.

Thursday, March 20, 2003

Kate and I drove Shirley to an appointment with her psychiatrist, Dr. John Doucet. At Shirley's request, we all went into his lobby to show off the baby after her consultation. After introductions, the conversation meandered into their children—how many, how old, what they were doing. Later, Kate said she wanted to scream at Shirley, "At least you have children, you wicked bitch!" Doucet seemed uncomfortable talking about children in our presence, but couldn't quickly break off the conversation.

Tuesday, March 25, 2003

On a shopping trip to the Avalon mall, Shirley asked to borrow my pocket knife to remove tags from a pair of shoes.

From my journal: "I obliged, but thought again how much damage I could do before anyone could stop me. As usual, I didn't do anything, and probably never would. I figured that, even if she isn't extradited and we have to move to Canada, I could not harm her because they would take me away from Zachary. And he needed Kate and me more than I needed to stop Shirley."

Saturday, March 29, 2003

From my journal: "In honor of our thirty-fifth wedding anniversary, I took Kate breakfast in bed; a fried egg on toast, sliced tomato, and coffee. I couldn't greet her with 'Happy Anniversary'; just 'Anniversary'. After breakfast, we celebrated the old-fashioned way. Pleasant, but the earth still didn't shake. Not surprising; it had not shaken in a long time."

CHAPTER 25
WAR

Once again Kate and I clammed up as we sat in Shirley's living room, at her request, to "talk about a serious issue." "Issue" became "issues" as she rambled on.

She had began to make arrangements for joint discussions— between her, Kate, and myself—about Zachary's future. She wanted these discussions to take place under the professional eye of a psychologist named Dr. Michelle Sullivan and she wondered whether there had to be boundaries on these discussions. For example, if she eventually went to trial, she was concerned about Zachary learning later on that we had testified against her.

She asked, "would we be able to forgive and forget later on?" It was unclear who was included in "we" and what might be forgiven and forgotten, but Kate and I stayed in ice mode, requesting no clarifications. Our best guess is that she meant: *could she later forgive us for testifying against her?* Second best: *could we forgive her for killing our son and join forces with her for Zachary's sake?* Either way, Madden was right—she was "effing nuts." Still, there was nothing we could take into court and use to separate her from Zachary.

Had she known that we were okay, Shirley told us, we could have joined her in the delivery room for Zachary's arrival, but at that time she feared we might kill her and the baby to avenge Andrew's murder.

She went on to say that her friends had wrongly accused Kate and me of trying to take Zachary away from her and she knew how hard it was to shake a false accusation. Carol Ross never came around to trusting us, nor did many of Shirley's friends. Only Zachary's godparents, Penney and Phillip, had decided that we were good people.

As an example of errors in the American documentation, Shirley mentioned her telling me about "*gum* and tissue paper," versus the quote in the Case Record: "*gun* and tissue paper."

That was way over the line. I said, "Stop, Shirley! Stop it! We should not be talking about this!"

She had an appointment with her custody lawyer so the discussion came to a halt. I drove her downtown to Cynthia's office, leaving Kate to look after Zachary. In the car she reiterated that her family, including her mother, had shown no interest in Zachary, except that her other children wanted a relationship with their half-brother. I told her that, when he was in our care, anyone who came forward could see him, including her mother. She said, "I don't think there's much chance of my mother changing." To myself, I noted the irony: today, she openly acknowledges her mother's disinterest in the baby; months ago, in Family Court, she had complained that the non-removal order impeded visits to Zachary's maternal grandmother.

NITS AGAIN

About a week after this bizarre exchange, Jackie received a letter from Randy Piercey soliciting our support in his fight to save Shirley from extradition:

April 4, 2003

Rose and Brazil...
Attention: Jacqueline Brazil

Dear Madam:

Re: My Client: Dr. Shirley Turner
Your Clients: David and Kathleen Bagby

I represent Dr. Turner in relation to the extradition
request against her by re: United States of America.

Various documents filed against Dr. Turner by the United
States refer to allegations attributed to your clients. I am
concerned that perhaps your clients did not actually make
the statements and the statements should be excised from
the documents at Court. My concern comes from two
sources:

1. One of the other people who allegedly made state-
    ments to the American authorities was a Heather
    Arnold. At the Extradition Ms. Arnold testified that
    while she did speak to the Americans her statements
    to them differed from what they reported she said. If
    the Americans were prepared to alter Ms. Arnold's
    words, then perhaps they have altered your clients'
    words.

2. My client informs me that your clients have been very
    supportive of her. They have supplied some of the
    baby's needs and have even driven Dr. Turner to some
    appointments. Their present attitude and helpfulness

toward Dr. Turner are not consistent with what the Americans allege they said about her. Dr. Turner categorically denies making any of the statements which the Americans say the Bagbys attribute to her. These statements are as follows:

a) Affidavit of Constable Glen Noseworthy in support of Provisional Warrant for Arrest: "Shirley Turner informed Kathleen Bagby, Andrew Bagby's mother, that Ms. Turner's attorney advised her to go to Canada and that Ms. Turner did not intend to return to the United States."

b) Case for Extradition paragraph 18: "David Bagby, Andrew Bagby's father from Sunnyvale, California, is expected to testify that he spoke to Shirley Turner on November 27, 2001 and that she stated that the gun and tissue paper were hers. Shirley Turner further told Mr. Bagby that her attorney told her to get in her vehicle and go to Canada and that she was adamant that she would remain in Canada. Shirley Turner claimed that she walked away from all of her belongings in Iowa."

If your clients did not say these things to the American authorities I can use the fact that the authorities lied in the documents in my attempt to stop Dr. Turner's extradition. I therefore request that you review these matters with your clients to the end of supplying me with written confirmation from them that they did not say what the Americans allege.

Yours truly,
Randolph J. Piercey

Piercey's first issue, Heather's testimony, was summarized in the Case Record in a way that could be interpreted as linking two unconnected ideas. This could have been "nefarious" (Piercey's word) on the part of the American authorities, or it could have been the inadvertent result of summarizing a long statement covering many topics. Under Piercey's examination at the extradition hearing, Heather readily acknowledged that the two ideas were not connected; given the opportunity, she would have willingly said so again, to a Pennsylvania jury.

Kate's testimony, the second item on Piercey's list, was in direct contradiction to Shirley's version of their conversation, and Kate was not going to change her testimony. Hence, a jury would have to decide which of the two witnesses was more credible, assuming that Shirley took the stand at her trial.

And finally, my testimony was summarized incorrectly in the Case Record—I reported that Shirley said "gum" and the Record said "gun." Perhaps the Americans did this nefariously, or perhaps it was due to a simple miscommunication in a long distance telephone call covering many topics. Like Heather, I was aching to clarify the discrepancy (nefarious or not) for a jury.

In context, each discrepancy on Piercey's list was a minuscule portion of the case against Shirley. In her dreams, Kate and I would renounce our testimony as summarized in the Record, thus confirming her thesis that the entire document was a work of fiction. Then Piercey would probably use this opening to challenge every syllable, requesting that all witnesses be brought to Canada to corroborate their testimony before an extradition court. In effect, hold a trial in Canada hoping to forestall one in Pennsylvania.

It was our theory—Jackie's, Kate's, and mine—that, in addition to slowing the extradition process, Shirley wanted to link the criminal case to our custody battle, couched in terms of our honesty: could she trust us to look after Zachary's best interest if we told lies about her in the criminal record? More bluntly, it was a feeble attempt at blackmail: *Renounce the lies and you can have Zachary, if and when I go to prison.* And she started to back up the threat with action.

Outward displays of the slip in détente began three days later. At 2 p.m. on April 7, we appeared at Shirley's door, as planned, to pick up Zachary for the afternoon. Nobody answered the bell so I called Shirley's son's apartment to see if he knew where she was. Shirley answered the phone. She had taken the bus to his place, meant to call us earlier, and been on the phone with Cynthia and Randy. "Sorry I didn't call earlier. You can pick up Zachary here if you like...."

She had been mostly courteous since getting out of jail, so I said something like, "No problem. We'll be over in a few minutes."

Shirley was still cordial when we picked up Zachary and took him to a five o'clock meeting with Jackie, where he amused himself by exploring her office while we pondered how to answer Piercey's letter. Kate and I wanted to say nothing and let him sweat what we might say on the stand. We wouldn't lie, but he didn't know that. Jackie wanted to consult a criminal lawyer, Bill Collins, about what to do, because this was not her field of expertise. That's one of the things you pay a lawyer for: to be cool and careful when you're angry and reckless. Kate and I agreed to Jackie's consulting with Collins.

From Jackie's office we drove to Shirley's apartment to drop off Zachary, and she rambled through another bizarre dissertation.

She was having difficulty parting with Zachary and thought she had been too generous with our visiting hours. She didn't want us to take Zachary to visit our friends, especially Heather Arnold and Rana Mercer. It wasn't necessary for him to meet our friends. The visits should be time spent with us. She appreciated our gifts and generous time, but had nothing to give us in return except time with Zachary. She wondered if we were co-parenting or sharing custody. We could not take his father's place; we were only his grandparents. She wanted to discuss these issues directly with us, in consultation with psychologist Michelle Sullivan, but had been unsuccessful in making an appointment. Cynthia considered these issues to be psychological rather than legal. If there wasn't this *situation* hanging over us, or if *her* mother took Zachary out, she would know where he was at all times. Her friends and family were still not comfortable with us and did not trust us, and she wanted to clear everything between us so that we could be trusted.

I suggested that these were all really legal issues in the end and so we needed to pass them through the lawyers. Kate and I went home and started writing everything we could remember, but we were interrupted by a tearful telephone call from Shirley.

If we had to go through the lawyers, then we would have to stick to the current visiting schedule. (We had been visiting about twice the hours per week called for in the Consent Order.) She had difficulty accepting rides and things from us (despite having done so since Zachary was three weeks old), as she had always been independent. She was uncomfortable having us present for Zachary's regular doctor visits and would cancel tomorrow's noon appointment with Dr. O'Dea.

I offered to drop off Zachary's car seat at her house so that perhaps Loraine, instead of Kate and me, could take them to the doctor.

She called back in a few minutes: she would need the car seat, but not before tomorrow morning. She wanted to know where we took Zachary at all times; it was just common courtesy that we keep her informed. We couldn't have any more visits until this issue was settled. "I thought you cared about my children," she cried, "and now it looks like you only care about Zachary."

In a measured voice, I said, "Shirley, you are over the line. Talk to Cynthia about this."

She hung up on me.

Kate and I finished our notes and went to bed for a much-needed soothing cuddle. She took a sleeping pill and crashed for the night, but my sleep was sporadic.

From my journal, April 7, 2002: "Among the dozens of ideas that rattled around in my head was a horrible image of going to Shirley's apartment and finding both her and Zachary dead. There was no way to prevent such a monstrosity, but I couldn't get to sleep."

PUNISHMENT

The next day marked the definite end of détente and the beginning of our punishment for non-compliance with Shirley's demands. I knocked on her door. She opened up, coldly said, "Good morning," and didn't have Zachary on her arm.

First whipping: not even a quick hello with our darling baby.

Aiming for a neutral tone and probably failing, I said, "Good morning," and handed her the car seat. She said something like, "I'll be looking for work in a month and, if I find a job, I would still like to consider you for babysitting, but I have to know that I can trust you first."

Second whipping: no Zachary even if she found a job. Also, our status had dropped from grandparents and near-partners in Zachary's care to mere babysitters.

We walked away, got in the car, and drove home to find a message from Shirley requesting that we return her spare apartment key, and noting that "I'm going to be out most of the day and going to be away for most of the weekend."

Third whipping: no Zachary today or over the weekend.

We reported all this to Jackie, who would inform Cynthia, who would perhaps remind her client that there were limits, clearly delineated in the Consent Order, to Shirley's power.

I called Shirley in the evening to check on Zachary and to confirm tomorrow's 9 a.m. scheduled visit. She reported that he was good and agreed to a visit. We hashed over the schedule of upcoming visits and our next overnight in particular. She slipped in another implied threat: "I only had the one concern about the overnight and that's easily resolved if you guys let me know where he's going to be."

Fourth whipping: no overnights without disclosure of Zachary's whereabouts.

I ignored that and summarized the plan: Thursday from two to six and Saturday overnight.

I told her that Jackie had her spare key, but that I would retrieve it and give it directly to her. She sarcastically said, "It won't do much good with Jackie if I need it."

We hung up but she called back a few minutes later. She had forgotten her plan to be out of town this weekend, so there could be no overnight on Saturday. We agreed to visits on Thursday and Friday instead.

She suggested that we not take him swimming until he was over his cold. "I'm not trying to dictate. He is my son... for my own peace of mind... common courtesy... I want to know pretty much where he is... I'm not going to say what you can and can't do, but I want to know."

I said that it pretty much made sense, but I wanted the lawyers to know what we were doing.

Shirley called back a few minutes later with more complications. Shirley's younger daughter was coming to town on Good Friday and that affected overnight visits. "I want you to be my number one choice for babysitting…things have steam-rolled out of control…I would do this with any babysitter…because car accidents do happen."

She had cancelled all her appointments for this week because she didn't have a babysitter. "I don't want to totally cut Kate out of the babysitting game—her and Zachary love each other," she laughed. "And she's a good babysitter, I think," she laughed again.

Fifth whipping: no extra Zachary this week.

When we picked up Zachary at noon the next day, Shirley was cold. She deposited everything outside her door. I transferred it to the car. She dressed Zachary and brought him out to Kate and said something I partially missed, so I asked, "Did you say you don't want us to give you any more formula or diapers for Zachary?"

Like a pouting adolescent, she sniped, "If we're going to do everything under court order, I want this under court order, too. I have enough money to buy Zachary's things!"

We took Zachary home for a four-hour visit.

CHAPTER 26
EMOTIONAL OCTOPUS

Andrew can't tell us precisely what transpired between him and Shirley in the days and minutes before his death. A year and a half later, Shirley gave me a pretty good idea what their final conversations must have been like. I, like Andrew, had the audacity to resist her wishes and she was not going to put up with it. She telephoned three times during our four-hour visit and several more times over the next few days. Kate tended Zachary while Shirley flooded me with words, a blizzard of words, desperate to convince me that we should bypass the lawyers and meet with Dr. Sullivan immediately.

Kate and I recorded these telephone conversations, as either party was free to do under the Consent Order.

The first call came as soon as we arrived home, but it was only a quick discussion of Zachary's food, sleep, and ongoing cough.

The second call was the beginning of a verbal wrestling match with the same emotional octopus to which Andrew had succumbed. I have transcribed several key portions here, enough to convey Andrew's and my insoluble problem. The entire conversation lasted two days over several phone calls, and our dear son must have endured dozens of these before exasperation compelled him to reject her entirely, thus signing his death warrant.

SHIRLEY: How's he doing?

ME: He's fine. [I told her what Zachary was doing.]

SHIRLEY: Cynthia called. She talked to Jackie, and Jackie's making a big issue about you guys not getting an overnight this Saturday. I thought we were very clear on the next few visits. Jackie was very upset that you didn't have him last Saturday or this Saturday.

ME: I don't want to make it a big issue. I don't want to go exactly by the schedule; it's too inflexible. [We went over the upcoming visits we had agreed to earlier.]

SHIRLEY: Maybe you should let Miss Brazil know that if there are things we're having problems with, there is no point taking up other people's time and your money on stuff that we're not even having problems with. It's hilarious to me, and it also made me very angry. I'm glad I calmed down enough to call you and clarify it. Now I know that you didn't have a big fuss about it.

I told Cynthia, 'That is so ridiculous, and how much time over and above the Consent Order have they been having. I don't think they're complaining that they haven't had enough time with Zachary'.... I'm glad I got it clarified with you. It's obvious that it's Jackie who has got the problem. This is why I have a problem dealing with lawyers so much.

There has been a lot of uncomfortable feeling, maybe miscommunication, or misinterpretation on both our parts. I'm as guilty of that as the next person. Cynthia would like us to reconsider getting some help with that with a mediator at the court or with Dr. Sullivan because letting it go is going to cause more hostility and not be in Zachary's best interest.

In my letter [to Dr. Sullivan] I'm saying that I want you guys to be honest. I'm not saying that you haven't been. Even Randy's letter doesn't say that you have been dishonest. I have told all my friends how good you are. We wouldn't lie about how much we care about this child. I have to convince everyone of that, and we have done a good job as well in that we have been very good to everybody.

We have taken all this good and for some reason some little thing now has made this seem so bad, and I'm really sorry if you think that I've been thinking bad things about you and Kate. I haven't. I have been struggling for Zachary's sake to make things so smooth with all my friends and the family that I have here.

I don't know where to go from here, other than a full court battle with a judge having to decide on access. At this point I'm ready to move out of St. John's just to get away from it because it's really upsetting me. I don't want to do that and Cynthia said 'Don't make rash decisions'. I checked with Randy and I could go live on the West Coast for the next six months if I so choose. [When Jackie heard this later, she exploded: 'Who the hell does she think she is?! She can't go wandering off to the West Coast without changing the Consent Order'!]

Maybe I'm overreacting. If me, you, and Kate can't talk at some arena with a third person there, because I think going back and forth between the lawyers is creating more turmoil and more fuss, for me and for Zachary. I'm having to stick to a Consent Order now, and I just feel really hostile, which I hate.

I was really upset when you took him today because I feel like the day you saw him at UFC [our first visit with Zachary at Unified Family Court]. I don't know if he's okay with you. I know you're not going to hurt him, but I don't know if he needs me. I don't know what you're saying to him. I just want you to love him and to do what's best for him.

ME: Listen. We will do what is best for Zachary. We will not hurt Zachary, period. You understand?

SHIRLEY: I know you don't *want* to, you don't *intend* to, but if we don't get help, we don't *know* if we're doing what's best. I know *I* don't, and I'm his *mother*.

ME: You don't like this answer, but I'm going to give it to you again. The reason we go through the lawyers is so that we don't have these meltdowns and emotional scenes. We do it coolly, calmly, through the lawyers. Let them hash out what we want. Understood?

SHIRLEY: I want more help with that. I don't just want the lawyers. I don't think they're going to necessarily do what is best for Zachary. They're going to do what we want, and what about if we're acting at cross-purposes? A big court battle isn't best for Zachary. I thought we were doing things so well, without having everything laid out in black and white. I didn't feel like this when he used to go for visits with you. And I can't consent to more time right now, feeling this way. Yet I was happy with you seeing him every day the way things were before. And coming and visiting at my home. How can *this* be better?

ME: [I was aching to say: 'You're the dipshit that took us out of cooperation mode! Just pull your head out of your butt, step back two weeks, and all this nonsense will disappear'! But I toned it down.] As far as I'm concerned, we can go right back where we were two weeks ago and start again.

SHIRLEY: Well, that's encouraging. So you're not totally given up on getting some more help from somebody.

I was way overmatched. She had spent her life meandering through these *structureless debates* masking as *adult discussions*, purportedly in search of some noble goal; in our case, "what's best for Zachary" (in Andrew's, it was no doubt "our relationship"). In fact, she was in single-minded pursuit of her own personal goal—control over all the lives she touched—and she was prepared to carry on the discussion till the telephone company went broke. As in our first conversation four years before, I finally lied to get off the phone: "I have to go pick up Kate at church."

She finished with, "I hope I don't have to say 'I told you so' in a month."

GUN/GUM

As planned, Jackie consulted with criminal lawyer Bill Collins on whether, and how, we should respond to Piercey's letter. On his advice, we decided to answer with the simple truth, and then keep marching. If Shirley turned really nasty or consistently cut our hours with Zachary, we would apply for a Family Court date and go into full battle mode. Jackie's letter to Piercey read:

April 11, 2003
Attention: Randolph Piercey

Dear Sir:
Re: Your Client: Shirley Turner
Our Clients: David and Kathleen Bagby

Further to your correspondence of April 4, 2003, we have reviewed same with our clients and Mr. Bagby advises that he stated to the police "that the **gum** and the tissue paper were hers." We have advised the crown attorney, Michael Madden, of same. In all other respects, the Bagbys' testimony as stated in your correspondence remains unchanged.

Thank you for your attention to this matter.

Yours truly,
Jacqueline Brazil

Light whippings continued throughout this period, in the form of missed telephone connections to arrange visits and general rudeness compared to our previous interactions. Jackie, Kate, and I met frequently, planning a Family Court application to formalize the additional hours to which we had grown accustomed. But once Piercey received Jackie's letter, the "bad" Shirley slowly morphed back into the "good" Shirley. We guessed that she considered my gun/gum clarification a major victory and was rewarding us, her errant children, for our good behaviour. Or perhaps she had grown so dependent on our instant babysitting service that the inflexible alternative was terribly inconvenient. Whatever the explanation, her demeanour steadily improved through the second half of April.

MONEY TALK

Until this freeze in relations, Kate and I had provided all of Zachary's diapers and formula, plus most of his other baby needs—wipes, cream, shampoo, and so on. Even with our relations improving, however, Shirley still did not agree to resume accepting baby supplies from us without an emotional scene.

In an early morning telephone call on April 28, she cried and moaned about Zachary nearly running out of food and diapers. She had sold his changing table and some toys to raise a little money, but was running low again and had only a day or two's supply left. He had received some Christmas money from our family and friends, which Shirley now wanted to use for his immediate needs. I told her that we had not yet decided what to do with that money, but had asked Jackie about using it as seed for a college account. I also told Shirley again, firmly, that we would ensure Zachary's physical needs were met.

She complained of feeling like a twelve-year-old asking us for his basic necessities. She wanted to work and earn the money to buy his things herself. I said that I couldn't help her financial situation, but that she, Kate and, I agreed on one thing—Zachary would want for nothing. I offered to bring food and diapers and clothes to her door. She suggested that we might go together to buy him a coat and some other clothing, in addition to food and diapers. She wanted to check with Cynthia first and call us back. We hung up the phone, and then Kate and I worried about what might happen to Zachary if she suffered a complete breakdown.

STRATEGIC DECISION

Jackie, Kate, and I carefully considered taking Shirley's recent irrational behaviour into court in an attempt to extricate Zachary from her clutches, but decided against it for several reasons.

First, she would be notified immediately if we applied for removal of the child from her care, which would certainly throw her into a raging frenzy, possibly resulting in exactly the outcome we were trying to avoid.

Second, if she didn't kill him outright but lost the case in court, she would probably retain visitation rights, though her visits would probably be supervised. However, a determined adult could kill or severely injure a baby in seconds, before an access supervisor could intervene. Appalling as it may seem to consider such brutality so analytically, it had to be done: grip the baby by the head and twist sharply. He wouldn't have the neck muscles to resist. He would either be dead or a quadriplegic.

Third, if she won the case and retained physical custody, she would still be holding the hostage *and* she would have no doubt about our worst fear, which would then be her greatest weapon against us.

Fourth, she may never have considered killing Zachary as punishment for our failure to comply with her wishes, and we would be putting the idea into her head.

And finally, if a formal documented accusation of premeditated murder didn't set off official alarms, why would the hand wringing of distraught, probably prejudiced, possibly malicious grandparents make any difference?

Jackie has strongly advised against my revealing the following in public, but it is a significant part of this story and therefore must not be omitted. My hatred for Shirley Jane Turner always peaked during Kate's meltdowns: "I want my Andrew! I want my son! How can he be gone?! How could she kill my beloved son?!" *That bitch almost certainly killed my son, and now I have to stand by and watch while she slowly kills my true love.*

Kate's only escape from her worst episodes of despair was two sleeping pills. Sometimes, as she finally relaxed beside me and slid into deep slumber, I gave serious thought to killing Shirley. I could have slipped my arm from under Kate's head and left her unconscious. I could have appeared at Shirley's door with some plausible excuse. I could have strangled her when she opened up. I could have gone back home to bed and

Kate would never have known I was gone—she would pass a lie detector test and possibly get custody of Zachary. He would be out of danger. Kate would have a solid reason to live. I would almost certainly end my days in a Canadian prison.

I could fantasize about killing Shirley, but I could never rouse myself to transform the fantasy into action. Besides, I wanted to be with Zachary as he grew up.

Hope and pray for peace and harmony just a little while longer, and keep marching.

CHAPTER 27
SURRENDER

On April 4, 2003, in Shirley's living room, she casually told us that the Federal Minister of Justice had delayed his Surrender Order decision from April 12 to May 18. She was obviously pleased. Kate and I both kept a straight face and made no comment. We should have been accustomed to delays by this time, but inside we both seethed, again.

This delay was to allow American authorities time to provide formal assurances that no death penalty would be imposed. Since the extradition of Charles Ng in 1991, Canada had tightened its policy: *no* extradition without concrete assurances that the death penalty could not be carried out.

On May 15, again in Shirley's living room, she casually told us that the Minister had delayed his decision from May 18 to June 9. For Kate and me, it was the same response, different month.

This second delay was the result of good timing on Piercey's part; he made written submissions to the Minister on May 12, leaving insufficient time for their evaluation before the May 18 Surrender Order decision. In these submissions, Piercey took the position that, not only should there be no chance of a death penalty, there should be no extradition at all. His submissions were not public record, but their main points were later summarized in Justice Minister Martin Cauchon's response to Piercey:

> In your recent letter, and in the letters received from individuals writing letters in support of Dr. Turner, it is indicated that Dr. Turner opposes surrender on the grounds that:
>
> - The evidence presented by the Americans against Dr. Turner is "*entirely circumstantial*";
> - Dr. Turner will not receive a fair trial in the United States, both because of her forced reliance on the public defender system and the unfavourable media attention this case has received in Canada and the United States;
> - Dr. Turner is the mother of four children, will not receive [bail] in Pennsylvania, and consequently, will be away from her children for a lengthy period of time; and
> - Dr. Turner is a Canadian citizen who has contributed greatly to her community where she is highly regarded and could make a valuable contribution to Canadian society as a doctor, teacher, and human being if her surrender were refused.[1]

Kate and I didn't know the contents of Piercey's submissions. We just waited for the new deadline, becoming increasingly anxious as June 9 came and went.

From my journal, June 10, 2003:

> Every time the phone rang, Kate did a near meltdown and my gut cinched up. Finally at about two o'clock, Francine

Blais called from Ottawa and said that the Minister had ordered Shirley Turner surrendered to the United States. Blessed relief! Andrew was still dead, but this was as good as things could get this side of Pennsylvania.

I asked if Shirley would be arrested again and Francine went to find out, promising to call me back in a little while. Kate gave Jackie the news using the cell-phone—we didn't want to tie up the regular phone until Francine had called back. In about a half hour she called and said that Shirley's release on bail from the November order would probably stay in effect, so she would probably not be re-arrested. Oh, well. Compared to the Surrender Order, we considered this a minor setback.

We mused over the implications of the decision, but decided not to do anything until we were certain that Shirley would be arrested...I called Shirley to see about visits for the rest of the week...She asked if we wanted to come and spend a little time with Zachary, as we had been denied a couple of visits over the last few days. We readily agreed, and arrived at around seven o'clock.

It was a surreal experience, with the three of us play-ing with Zachary, laughing at his toddling antics, giving him a bath, feeding him, and generally behaving like a normal family. Meanwhile, his mother was one major step closer to imprisonment and his grandparents were delighted at the prospect. Shirley put a good face on it, serene, accepting, resigned. Kate and I were even more civil than normal, if that's possible, ensuring that we could not be accused of gloating. And Zachary simply enjoyed himself, which was the goal we all shared. He walked a lot, kicking his four rubber balls all around the apartment. And they were deliberate kicks, not accidents. A couple of times he walked around to the other side of a ball to be in position to kick it back towards the centre of the room.

Minister Cauchon's letter summarized Piercey's main points, quoted above, and then addressed each one. In summary:

Essentially, you and others argue that Dr. Turner should not be surrendered since the evidence against her is circumstantial...barely any evidence exists...the evidence that does exist is flimsy...I am mindful of the fact that the Honorable Chief Justice Derek Green...committed Dr. Turner for extradition based on this evidence. Consequently, had Dr. Turner been charged in Canada... she would have been committed to face trial in Canada... based on the evidence tendered by the United States...It would not be unjust or oppressive, or "shock the conscience" to permit the United States to try her on this evidence.

[Regarding] the assertion that Dr. Turner would not receive a fair trial due to being unable to retain a private attorney and adverse media attention, it is important to keep in mind that surrender to an extradition partner whose criminal justice system does not have all the procedural safeguards of the Canadian criminal justice system would not, in itself, violate the principles of fundamental justice....If Dr. Turner is not able to afford the services of a private attorney to conduct her defense in Pennsylvania, she will be entitled to a public defender. She will be entitled to present a defense and call evidence....With respect to alleged unfavourable media reports…Dr. Turner will be entitled to take such steps as Pennsylvania law permits to ensure that she is tried by an impartial jury…I am not satisfied that Dr. Turner will not receive a fair trial.

[Regarding Shirley's status as a mother and a valuable contributor to Canadian society] It is certainly tragic when children, through no fault of their own, are separated from their mother.…However…surrendering her…would not…be unjust or oppressive…for the following reasons:

- The offences alleged against her are extremely serious;
- Dr. Turner should not, like any individual in Canada with dependent children, avoid prosecution for that reason;
- In Canada, parents, like Dr. Turner, with dependent children are refused bail or convicted of a criminal offence and sentenced to a period of incarceration;
- If Dr. Turner were convicted of first-degree murder in Canada, she would be sentenced to imprisonment for life without eligibility for parole until she had served twenty-five years of the sentence;
- Dr. Turner will have the opportunity to present her personal circumstances to the Pennsylvania courts during her bail hearing and to the trial judge upon sentencing if convicted;
- *It is important that Canada not be a safe haven to fugitives from justice, including its citizens. Dr. Turner chose to reside in the United States and only returned to Canada following the death of Dr. Bagby* [emphasis added];
- Canada's treaty commitments and the following basic tenets of our legal system should be respected: indi-

viduals, including Canadian citizens, who choose to leave Canada leave behind Canadian law and procedures and must generally accept the local law, procedure, and punishments which the foreign state applies to its own residents; justice is best served by a trial in the jurisdiction where the crime was allegedly committed and the harmful impact felt; and extradition is based on the principles of comity and fairness to other cooperating states in rendering mutual assistance in bringing fugitives to justice.

The remainder of Minister Cauchon's letter to Piercey dealt with the differing classifications of murder in Canada versus the United States,[2] the differing penalties associated with these classifications, and with death penalty assurances. On the issue of classification, he had several options on how to describe the charges against Shirley in his Surrender Order and wrote, "I have decided that my surrender order will specify the Pennsylvania charges of criminal homicide and first-degree murder."

On the issue of a possible death penalty, he wrote, "I have therefore signed a conditional surrender order…subject to the receipt of sufficient assurances…that the death penalty shall not be imposed or carried out against Dr. Turner."

TWO DOWN, FOUR TO GO

Down at Jackie's office, we all raised a glass of very good Chardonnay to a very good decision, and we marvelled at the audacity of Shirley's silliest argument: *I'm a good mother and a good Canadian, so I should get away with murder!*

But this was only the second of six steps, with probably another year to go.

From Kate's journal, June 12, 2003: "Can I live on one more year with no end in sight? David says I can—focus on Zachary's first day of kindergarten—with us taking him."

CHAPTER 28
COUNSELLING

Jackie and Linda were both adamantly opposed to our participation in any sort of joint counselling with Shirley. We had already jumped through every hoop she put in front of us, but this one was unacceptable, given its underlying purpose: to engage us in a discussion of Andrew and the murder case. Kate and I agreed to resist Shirley on this point, but were still concerned about showing Zachary peace and harmony.

Shirley's position was formally stated in a June 6, 2003 letter from Cynthia to Jackie. In part:

Dr. Turner believes that it would be in Zachary's best interests if all parties were to obtain professional counseling in two primary areas: (a) direction as to how best to present Zachary's unique reality to him, now and as he grows, and how both sides of the family can strive to act in Zachary's best interests and in a spirit of mutual cooperation; and (b) direction as to what sort of access would be in keeping with Zachary's best interests should Dr. Turner find herself in custody again, either here or in the United States. We understand that relations between the parties are much improved from April when your clients indicated that they were no longer interested in counseling. We are therefore hopeful that they are prepared to reconsider their previous position in this regard.

Jackie had verbally requested an explanation of Shirley's questioning of our honesty, which Cynthia provided in the same letter:

We understand that your clients wish to have clarification as to why my client was questioning their trust and honesty as the relationship was deteriorating in March–April month. Dr. Turner advises that she was having difficulty reconciling the content of the statements attributed to the Bagbys in the Extradition documents with her own position. Dr. Turner continues to maintain her innocence and specifically disputes the notion that she attempted to flee the jurisdiction in the U.S. The Bagbys' statements are contrary to Dr. Turner's position and she was having difficulty foreseeing Zachary having a stable relationship with both sides in light of their opposing views. We believe that this particular circumstance demonstrates the need for counselling in the area of how to appropriately present Zachary's situation to him without the conflict resulting from the differing views of the parties filtering down to him.

This letter clarified Shirley's position quite well. She believed that it was in Zachary's best interest for his mother and grandparents to "act…in a spirit of mutual cooperation." Toward that goal, we would have to agree on his family background; his "unique reality." She maintained her innocence in Andrew's murder, denied that she fled to Canada, and would not change her position. Therefore, Kate and I would have to renounce our testimony implying flight and acknowledge Shirley's innocence in Andrew's murder. Joint counselling would provide an appropriate forum for this reconciliation of our "opposing views."

Our response was contained in a July 2 letter from Jackie to Cynthia:

> [The Bagbys] are not prepared to participate in counselling sessions with Dr. Turner. The Bagbys cannot discuss their son with your client at this point. It would be very traumatic for them and it is likely inappropriate in the context of the criminal case.
>
> However, they are prepared to pay for 2 one-hour sessions with Dr. Sullivan if your client would like to meet with her individually. The Bagbys understand that your client has some concerns with respect to Zachary's "unique reality" and specifically with the issue of access with his mother in the event that she is incarcerated.
>
> Zachary is thriving despite the incredible circumstances into which he has been born. All sides are to be commended for this fact. The Bagbys are quite confident that Zachary will continue to thrive if he continues to see a stable relationship among his caregivers. Given the unknown outcome of the criminal justice process and his young age, it seems premature for the parties to seek joint counselling at this point. Perhaps the issue can be revisited at a later date.

That was the last formal communication between Shirley and us regarding counselling.

CHAPTER 29

BIRTHDAY PARTIES

On July 16, two days before Zachary's first birthday, we drove Shirley from shop to shop searching for margarita mix; she was planning a birthday barbecue and wanted to serve something a little different to the adults. Kate and I didn't mind; we would have accompanied her on a quest for eye-of-newt, if that's where Zachary was.

Throughout the search, she chattered away and we first heard about a man she was dating; a medical technician who she had met in a bar on George Street. We wondered if he read the papers.

The margarita search was successful and so was the party. Loraine was there with her grandson. Shirley's drinking buddy made an appearance, as well as her younger daughter, her son, and his girlfriend. The adults enjoyed the margaritas. Kate socialized. I overcooked the hamburgers and hot dogs, and then glued my eye to the camcorder, filming Zachary's exploration of the patio.

He was in toddler heaven, wearing nothing but a diaper on a warm summer day, ignoring his toys and his family and concentrating on a critical examination of old lawnmower parts. All things round were fascinating, so a wheel was his greatest find.

At one point, sitting on his well-padded bum, he very deliberately set the wheel on its edge, studied it carefully for a moment, and then pushed it over. Wobbling to a stop, it made that diminishing *whump-whump-whump* sound, which he had never heard before. That was very cool, but he tried and tried and failed to make the wheel stand up again. He finally gave up the effort, pushed himself to his feet, and squatted to pick up his treasure. When he stood back up, its weight threw him slightly off balance, forcing a couple of awkward steps backward and giving me a giggle fit. He kept his feet and his hold on the prize, which he then deposited in the ice chest, next to the margaritas.

Two days later, on Sunday evening, Shirley asked us to look after Zachary for an hour while her friend took her for a drive. We applied Rule One and appeared on her doorstep in five minutes. Apparently they couldn't tear themselves apart after their drive, because an hour later she called again to ask if we would keep the baby overnight. To us, a two-part gift: more time with Zachary and the hope that some romantic companionship might keep her spirits up. We wanted her as mellow as possible until the cuffs finally snapped into place again.

The following day we hosted a second birthday party for Zachary, at Shirley's suggestion, at McDonald's. The guests got along well enough. Those in attendance included Loraine's daughters and their children, Shirley's daughter and her two friends, their mother, and Penney and Phillip, in addition to Shirley, Kate, me, and Zachary. He was adorable in a little safari outfit from his big sister in Toronto. Everyone enjoyed a meal and soft drinks and then started opening gifts.

From Kate's journal, July 21, 2003:

Zachary very clingy to me.... Then gift opening—disaster hit—Zachary very fussy with Shirley and she put him down and he came straight for me.... Shirley said to Zachary, "You are one year old and you should be more independent. You can't cuddle all your life. If you want your grandma, let her open gifts with you." She went off to the corner saying, "He likes her more than me." [She] was on the phone to who-knows-who and crying. Jeannie and Jamie comforted her.

I felt utterly miserable.... Wendy looked at me with sympathy. Phillip winked. The atmosphere could be cut with a knife. Finally gifts opened—Zachary walked off... and she picked him up—he cried and wanted to come back to me so I walked away to the bathroom. Jeannie came in and squeezed my shoulder...

The party mercifully ground to a close. Most of the guests said "Goodbye," and "Happy birthday, little guy," and left. The plan included a piñata bashing in our backyard, but as I started up the engine Shirley declared, "I'm going home. We can do the piñata in our driveway."

Her daughter said, "We should tell Penney and Phillip." They were heading out of the parking lot on their way to our house.

Shirley said angrily, "Maybe they want to go to the Bagbys' anyway!"

We flagged down Penney and Phillip and told them the change in plans.

In Shirley's backyard, the children bashed the piñata and scrambled for the candy, and we went home. Kate was miserable.

From her journal: "My soul bleeds for Zachary, so innocent—yet causing this new chaos. It is so easy to see how Shirley could murder...she is wicked, evil, cold, dangerous..."

On the phone the next day, Loraine told Kate: "You were very hurt. My daughter Jeannie is very upset....She doesn't deny Shirley's love for Zachary, but said 'Zachary reaches out and loves Mrs. Bagby with his whole heart and soul....Shirley has no warmth with Zachary—Mrs. Bagby exudes warmth to him'....Speaking as a psychiatric nurse [Loraine worked at the Waterford Psychiatric hospital in St. John's] Shirley gives as much as she can give....However, with Shirley it is all 'Me first'. I have come to realize this....You and David are Zachary's rock and he needs you more than you need him. You have to take the hurt and pain....Zachary is damned lucky to have you....You must continue doing what you are doing."

Obviously we had reached common ground with Loraine. However, she did not regret her support for Shirley, as she felt that Shirley was desperately in need of a friend and she could minister to that need. She, like Kate, had a very strong faith— "I know that God is with you"—and considered her ministry to Shirley an act of Christian charity, which I'm sure it was.

Kate said, "Without God, and Christ's representatives on Earth, we would be floundering. I consider you in that long list [of Christ's representatives]."

"You'll make me cry," Loraine replied, and before hanging up the phone, told Kate to call if we needed her.

Four days after the McDonald's disaster, Shirley said to Kate and me, "You know Monday wasn't your fault. I over-reacted and got sentimental because Zachary rejected me for you. I meant to mention that before now. Definitely not your fault—neither of you did anything wrong." Kate and I just nodded.

CHAPTER 30
THE STRETCH

Shirley's two appeals would be heard together at the Court of Appeal on Duckworth Street on Andrew's thirtieth birthday, September 25, 2003. Kate and I settled into a state of low anxiety, mildly optimistic but always reminding ourselves: it ain't over till she's in Pennsylvania; and even then, it won't be over. A whole new set of legal nits, thrown up by a new lawyer on a new battlefield, will keep true peace and contentment just out of reach for several more years. Realistically, our grandson would probably be in school before a jury spoke. But don't worry about that; take each step individually and get through it. The "bad" Shirley remained in her lair. We spent a great deal of time with the "good" Shirley and her dear little boy. Zachary days were sweet relief.

ANOTHER REJECTION
Unknown to us, Shirley's new relationship, which had peaked early with the first two dates ending in his bedroom, had deteriorated dramatically. His friends told him who she was, prompting him to read some articles on the web about Andrew's murder. Shirley's boyfriend told her that he wanted to

end the relationship—to be just friends from that point on—and her rejection response pattern kicked in: random telephone calls at all hours of the day and night.[1] When he answered the phone, Shirley said that she only wanted to talk, and then apologized for calling so much, but the calls kept coming. After about a week of this, the man called the police to ask if anything could be done. He was told that, because Shirley wasn't threatening him, there was nothing to be done. Shortly after that, he made his position very clear to Shirley: "Fuck off calling me!"

That drove Shirley to the next level; she told him that she was pregnant with his baby, called him an "immature asshole," and demanded that he help her with the baby: "Grow up and be a fucking man." She told him that she had an appointment for an abortion, then left a message that she had cancelled the appointment, and later a message saying that she had suffered a miscarriage. The next day, she called and said that it hadn't been a miscarriage—only spotting—and she was happy to be pregnant. She wanted to meet with him and talk about an abortion, but he refused to meet with her, offering instead to help with the pregnancy and support, but declining to have any relationship with Shirley. He proposed to deal with the pregnancy through lawyers, and steadfastly refused to have any more direct contact with Shirley.

Occasionally Shirley brought up Andrew's name in these conversations and assured her ex-boyfriend that she was innocent of his murder. She said that Andrew had been obsessed with her, calling her all the time and wanting to see her, but that she had only considered him a friend. The irony of this accusation was not lost on him, given Shirley's hundred-plus phone calls to him over a five-week period.

THE BIG BABY POOL

High thin clouds scattered the sun's light softly, evenly, over the Bowring Park kiddie pool. It was huge compared to the indoor Aquarena baby pool, but it was only a foot deep, so Zachary could easily stand up on his own. Walking and running, however, presented a problem that was, like most of his experiences, new. Water resistance held his legs back while he thrust his body forward at normal speed, and the laws of physics would not be denied: he fell on his face. His arms weren't long enough to reach the bottom and push his head up out of the water, but Shirley was right behind him to pick him up and set him back on his feet, as he sputtered and blinked the water out of his eyes.

Kate and I didn't go into the pool; she watched from a deck chair while I ran the camcorder. A couple of times I thought Shirley was a little slow to pull Zachary's face out of the water, but he didn't seem to mind. He was having a blast wading and splashing in this enormous new bathtub. Shirley was soon bored with following him around and picking him up, so she took him to the adult pool, which was far too deep for him to stand up. He was immediately bored with being held and cried and reached for Kate.

After they dried off and dressed, we drove Shirley and Zachary home. He was asleep when we arrived, but Shirley woke him to wave bye-bye to his grandparents. Kate's departures always upset him, so she was quietly furious at Shirley for putting him through that unnecessary trauma. He was sitting on his mom's arm crying for his nan as we hurried to the car and drove away.

The following day, Sunday August 17, 2003, sometime in the afternoon, Shirley picked up thirty Ativan tablets at a pharmacy using a prescription written on July 15 by her psychiatrist, Dr.

John Doucet. She spent the rest of the day at her apartment writing letters.

At 11:38 p.m., Shirley telephoned a friend from her apartment. She wasn't home, but Shirley left a message stating that she was at her ex-boyfriend's house with Zachary, they would stay the night, the man was in the bathroom, they were "working things out and talking," and she had some "interesting surprising things to tell" her friend the next day.[2] Shortly after making this call, Shirley strapped Zachary into the infant seat in her adult son's car and left home.

At about 12:45 a.m. on Monday, August 18, she stopped at an old age home in Conception Bay South and asked directions to Job's Road, off Fagan's Road, telling a home care worker that she was looking for her ex-boyfriend's house. The worker knew the area well and gave accurate directions. She also noticed that "the lady kept looking behind her while talking to me and I could see a car seat in the back seat but I didn't see anybody else in the car."[3]

Shirley's ex-boyfriend worked for an ambulance service, located on Pine Tree Road a short distance from his residence on Job's Road. The precise sequence of Shirley's actions—once she located his residence—can't be determined. She stuffed a photograph of herself between the rear door and the door frame of an ambulance located in the ambulance service's parking lot. She placed a used tampon and two photographs—one of herself in bra and panties, and one of herself and Zachary—under his car, which was parked in his driveway. She ran her son's car into the roadside ditch a short distance from her ex-boyfriend's house. She attempted and failed to get the car out of the ditch. She fed Zachary some of the Ativan tablets, probably washing them down with baby formula. Carrying Zachary, she walked north along a footpath to the coastal road, which was separated from the water by a rocky beach. She followed this road east to the Foxtrap Marina.

A night watchman at the marina headquarters thought he heard "crying like a baby crying" at around 2:30 or 3 a.m. He turned down his radio "to make sure what [he] heard" and went outside where "It was very dark and raining very heavily." He saw "a person—one person, who was short, [he] th[ought]—walking near the picnic tables." He called out, "Is anyone there," and heard no answer. He "couldn't tell if the person was male or female because the person was back-on to [him] and it was very dark." He watched the person walk away into the black night.

There is no certain way to determine Shirley's access path to the ocean, but the coastline to the west of the Foxtrap Marina main wharf, paralleling the coastal road, is a rocky beach; to the east, a wharf lined with boats. Hence, "Most probably, from the end of the main wharf of the Foxtrap Marina at or about 3 a.m. on Monday, August 18, 2003, Dr. Shirley Jane Turner, clutching her thirteen-month-old son Zachary to her bosom, jumped into the North Atlantic Ocean, murdering him and killing herself."[4]

CHAPTER 31
NOTIFICATION

Zachary had been dead for perhaps half a day when Constable Tim Walsh, who had helped track Shirley when she first arrived in Newfoundland, sat in our living room and told us what the police knew: Shirley Turner's son had reported that she and Zachary were missing. They had left home before midnight in his car, which was found in a ditch in Kelligrews, about twenty minutes from St. John's. The media had been notified so that a public be-on-the-lookout announcement could be made. When was the last time we had seen Shirley Turner?

We briefed Walsh on our recent contacts with Shirley and Zachary and he left.

Jackie rushed to our apartment as soon as we called. She helped us write a police statement listing everyone we could think of who had contact with Shirley. Jackie took our statement to Royal Newfoundland Constabulary headquarters.

We paced the floor and imagined the best and the worst. Maybe she's making a run for it. Her chances of escape are slim; everybody in Newfoundland knows her face. It's an island—there aren't many ways to get off, unless she has significant money stashed somewhere and she can hire a small boat. Not likely. If she's tried it, she'll almost certainly be caught and locked up, and Zachary will be safe. Or maybe she finally flipped out completely and...don't go there! Wait. Wait. We know how to wait...

The media announcement did not help locate Shirley and Zachary, but it was nonetheless very effective; friends started to call. Some dropped by. Some left after a few minutes. Some stayed, among them Father Chris. Every few minutes we stopped pacing, took another deep breath, let it out slowly, and started pacing again. Time is meaningless when you have no control.

Jackie returned from the police station, but didn't stay long. Constable Walsh called and asked to speak to her. I handed over the phone and resumed pacing and breathing.

Walsh told Jackie that he had left his coat at our house and asked if she would bring it to the station. Jackie was about to protest that she should stay with us when Walsh repeated the request with a definite urgency in his voice: "Jackie! Please bring me my coat!" She took the hint and hung up the phone. On the way out the door with the coat under her arm, she quietly said to Father Chris, "I think you should stay." Kate and I, pacing and breathing, noticed none of this.

About seven o'clock a car pulled up out front. Walsh and Jackie got out. I saw them through the window and opened the door before they knocked. As they stepped into the hallway, Jackie said, "The news is not good," and my brain started to melt again. I'm not certain whether she or Walsh said it, nor do I remember the precise words, but I heard: "The bodies of a woman and a baby have been found on Manuels Beach." I think there were more words, but they were lost to me. I had to move and had nowhere to go. I think I stepped forward and back and left and right, and turned circles, and moaned, and then exploded in another primitive screaming protest. Just like before: "Andrew's dead! He's been murdered!" Now: "Zachary's dead! He's been murdered!" I kicked a hole in a door and screamed again. Father Chris tried to bring me back to reality. I don't remember his words. I screamed at him, "Not now!" He told me later that he tried to get me focused on Kate, who had collapsed in a heap on the floor, moaning, "I can't bear any more. I can't take it."

I could not focus on anything. I don't remember if I went to Kate. I have no idea how much time passed.

Walsh (I think) said that the bodies had not yet been positively identified. We all knew who they were, but someone had to make a formal identification. Kate wanted to see Zachary.

Walsh drove. Jackie rode shotgun. Kate and I in the back seat.

Outside the morgue we saw Piercey sitting in a car, waiting to identify Shirley. Constable Noel Stanford met us at the door and led us through some hallways. Outside a room, he stopped and told us that we couldn't touch the baby. Forensics. Evidence. I'm not sure what he said.

On a nod from us, he opened the door to a small room with a gurney against the opposite wall. A tiny body, surrounded in ruffled white cloth. One step in and his face was clearly visible over the ruffles. A second passed, no more. Kate started forward. Stanford and I, one on each arm, turned her back to the door. Kate's legs stopped working. Stanford tried to keep her on her feet. I said, "Let her down," and followed her to the floor, she on her back, me straddling. No words that I can recall, just primitive despair. No time. No thought. Just feeling.

Walsh drove us to Heather and Matt's house. More primitive despair. Far too much wine, but what difference could that make? Some sleep, I think. I can't recall.

CHAPTER 32
NEXT

A living organism does the best it can with its given situation. If a root encounters a stone, it grows around it. If a fox can't find rabbits in one valley, it moves to the next. If your child is murdered, you take care of your grandchild. If that grandchild is murdered…

The day after Shirley and Zachary washed ashore on Manuels Beach, Deputy Chief Medical Examiner Dr. Charles Hutton conducted autopsies on both bodies and confirmed that the cause of death was drowning. He "issued the death certificates as homicide-suicide,"[1] but pointed out that "suicide is a difficult thing to prove…there has to be clear and compelling evidence that a suicide has occurred with the exclusion of all other causes." Hence, Constable Stanford continued his investigation of the deaths. Shirley's attempt to cast her ex-boyfriend as a double murderer turned out to be a feeble one, but Stanford had to be certain before making his final report.

Despair never left us. Kate and I relearned thought and speech. With renewed thought came renewed rage; not just at Shirley, but at the blindness—the wilful blindness—of those in positions of power who refused to stop her. They must be told exactly what they had done and we no longer had any reason to keep quiet. We would start with a press conference and go from there. While Constable Stanford completed his investigation, I wrote a press statement.

The first draft was unreadable—the ravings of a lunatic. With a great deal of help from Kate, Jackie, and John Ennis, I hammered it into a structured speech. Barbara and Virgil, our neighbours from our home in California, had come to Newfoundland for a short visit, but had arrived too late to meet Zachary. They also helped review the statement. When it was ready, we waited. We knew how to wait, but I was nearly insane with fury at Judge Welsh, Madden, Piercey, even that goddamned solid stone building masquerading as a house of justice.

Crazy fantasies bounced around in my skull, mostly centred on Welsh, the last person in a power position. I momentarily considered killing her, in retribution for her assistance to Zachary's murderer, but I was not so consumed by the righteousness of my outrage that reason could not prevail. Killing Welsh may have provided some fleeting barbaric satisfaction, but it would also inflict horrendous long-term damage on her family and friends, and I knew what that felt like. Whether or not she deserved punishment, those who cared about her were utterly innocent. Besides, the death penalty is far too high for arrogant pedantry; Welsh did not deserve to die. Neither did Madden, Piercey or any other official who had wilfully or negligently ignored the danger posed by Andrew's killer. I waited for Constable Stanford to do his job.

On September 1, 2003, the RNC issued a news release that stated, in part, "The investigative team from the Major Crime Unit are satisfied of no third party involvement in this tragedy. Accidental cause has also been ruled out as the evidence indicates that Shirley Jane Turner was responsible for her own death as well as the death of her son Zachary Turner."

Jackie arranged a conference room at Atlantic Place for Wednesday, September 3, at 11:30 a.m. She would act as the moderator and cut off questions if things got ugly, or if we got too tired or too excited. Danette and another friend in the publishing business, Karen Dawe, informed all their media contacts that we would hold a press conference. I printed twenty copies of our statement. We waited for Wednesday.

I was in the shower on Wednesday morning when Kate came into the bathroom with the phone and said, "It's Jackie. We can't hold the press conference!"

I turned off the water and Kate handed me the phone. Jackie said, "Technically, there is still a publication ban in place. You can't hold the press conference."

I blew up: "Fuck 'em! If they want to lock me up for talking while they let murderers walk around free, just fuck 'em!"

Jackie took a deep breath and sighed, "How did I know you'd say that?"

The precise legal situation was unclear, but this was conceivably a career-ender for Jackie. She could not counsel a client to violate a court order, either by advising us to hold the conference or by accompanying us to the conference, since that could be construed as supporting our action. Another in a long list of bitter ironies: decent people fret over the implications of speaking in public, while the judiciary of one of history's most civilized nations ignores the implications of a corpse with five extra holes in it.

Judge Green had set Monday morning for a hearing in which the publication ban would be officially lifted and Jackie asked that we wait until after that to hold our press conference. I could not do that. We had held our tongues for nearly two years, watching the battle from the sidelines, twisting in agony each time a judge let Shirley's lawyer insert another delay, while our baby was dust and his killer held our baby's baby hostage. We had held our tongues another two weeks to be absolutely certain that Stanford's investigation would reveal no surprises. I was nearly straitjacket material, uncertain if I'd even know my own name in a week's time.

Karen Dawe also had lots of experience in media relations, but she seemed more like a fight manager. She seated Kate and me on one side of the conference table, the side nearest the door, and placed all the other chairs on the other side. She took possession of the handouts—the written statement that I would read—so that all eyes would be on Kate and me until I finished reading.

At eleven thirty I began reading the statement.

From my journal, September 3, 2003: "It was one of the most emotional experiences of my life—not in a league with seeing Andrew's or Zachary's dead body—but I had so much pent-up anger that I needed all my concentration to keep from slipping into a pure maniacal rage. I nearly lost it several times, but paused to regain control and went on. Kate offered to read the rest for me once, but I declined."

The content was simple enough. In fact, it was a very short form of this book—a chronological narrative, followed by a plea for change:

I have no idea what happens when Canada asks the
United States to return a fugitive. It may be just as
appalling as what we have seen here. It's wrong anywhere
it happens.... We know that Shirley Turner's family must
be in agony right now, just as we are, but these things have
to be said.

We believe that Shirley Turner bears 100 per cent of the responsibility for the murder of our son, Andrew.

We believe that the system helped her to kill our grandson, Zachary. [I summarized the story, including the names of Justices David Russell and Gale Welsh, who let Shirley out on bail in December of 2001 and January of 2003, respectively.]

Nobody will ever know exactly how Shirley Turner convinced herself that it was okay to kill a baby, anybody's baby, but particularly her own baby, and I don't care how she did that. It doesn't matter how she did that.

What matters is that we knew from the record of the extradition case that she was almost certainly a monster. We knew, and we can't see how the judges and lawyers involved in the extradition could not have known. And still we left her free on the streets.

I summarized the evidence against Shirley in the killing of Andrew. Then I lambasted the surety system: "They'll take a signature from somebody who doesn't have a dime. Somebody with a negative net worth. Somebody living on student loans. Somebody who couldn't pay that money without robbing a bank."

I lambasted Piercey's Authority-to-Proceed argument: "In effect, Mr. Piercey said, 'Let's don't even find out if this person did that monstrous crime, because some letters on a piece of paper are wrong.'"

I put premeditated murder in perspective: "This is not a possible car thief or a possible burglar, or even someone who might have killed accidentally. This is a very special category of person who can set out to deliberately kill another. Plan the steps to kill someone, and then carry out the plan, step by step, to make someone die!"

I briefly described the other people who had an official connection to Shirley—Betty Day of the Department of Social Services, social worker Susan Green, and psychiatrist/surety John Doucet—and asked that they look in hindsight for indications of danger: "We're not asking this to crucify them. They would never have needed to consider these questions if the legal system had done its most basic job and locked her up."

My statement finished with a naive pitch for immediate changes in bail policy:

> It is obviously too late to do anything for our grandson. Can anything be done to prevent the next Shirley Turner from killing the next Zachary? Are there others out on bail now who are accused of premeditated murder? If so, you District Attorneys and Crown Prosecutors, please go back into court and make applications to revoke their bail. And you judges hearing those applications, please, please, please, keep Zachary in mind, too, while you're poring over the criminal codes and case law. You have it in your power to prevent the next Zachary.

I was drained and Kate looked as bad as I felt. We took questions. Heather took notes. NTV news broadcaster Darrin Bent asked what was probably the most telling question of the day: were we aware that no psychological evaluation had ever been asked for or performed on Shirley throughout the extradition process?

At some point Karen announced, "One more question." It was asked and answered and we stood up to leave. The swarm began. Would we agree to be interviewed? Yes, but we had no idea where or when. We moved out the door and into the elevator with several reporters still clinging to us. Out of the elevator and into Jackie's office. The reporters stayed out in the hallway.

As if by magic, dear Karen produced a written schedule of our upcoming television and radio interviews, two that afternoon and two more the next morning, including notes on the interviewer and his or her style.

Dear Linda Rose broke out the Chardonnay. We only had a sip; mustn't appear drunk on television.

Dear Jackie, who had been right down in the trenches with us throughout this nightmare, was sick with worry that we might be basket cases by now. We were, but it was the lesser of two evils—holding it in would have been much worse.

From my journal, September 3, 2003: "The relief in Kate and me was a drug. I felt like I would be able to sleep again, for the first time since Shirley murdered Zachary. I also felt like we had started on another major quest for something worthwhile. After we lost Andrew to Shirley, and Zachary to a combination of Shirley and the system, the best we could possibly get out of the situation was to try and prevent the next Shirley Turner from killing the next Zachary."

That's life. Not the cliché, but literally: living organisms seek the best outcome available in any situation. Kate and I would much rather have taken Zachary home to California and raised him as our own child, which, in spirit, he had been, and still was. That option was taken away. This quest would have to do.

CHAPTER 33
MOTIVE

Initially Kate and I had been determined to understand the outcome of a trial, if one ever took place in Pennsylvania. But Shirley had run to Canada and our focus had shifted to extradition; we were determined to understand its outcome, while also paving the way for Zachary's new life. Now, with both those avenues closed, we must thoroughly understand what went wrong. Not just the shallow observation that a person in a position of power knew Shirley Turner was probably dangerous and still set her free, but a deeper insight into the theory behind letting probable killers go free.

Judges Russell and Welsh are not alone; persons accused of criminal offences are normally released on bail in countries with a legal tradition based on English common law. Even those accused of offences involving extreme violence are routinely turned loose on the general population, which largely consists of decent non-violent people; that is, people who do not initiate violence, but only resort to it in response to the violence of others. We are the most vulnerable targets of bullies, rapists, and murderers.

LESTER POWELL MURDER

On May 17, 2003, at around two-thirty in the morning, nine-teen-year-old Josephine Vivian stabbed twenty-one-year-old Lester Powell in the chest near the RCMP detachment in Fort McMurray, Alberta. Vivian had left home that night with a hunting knife in her bag. She and her companion, Travis Paquette, had an argument on the sidewalk. Powell and his friend happened along. Words were exchanged. Vivian placed the point of her knife four inches into Powell's chest, where it pierced his heart.

Through a plea bargain, Vivian was convicted of manslaughter. Her intoxication at the time of the killing worked to her advantage: under the law, a severely intoxicated person is deemed to be unable to form the *intent* to kill, and intent is an essential element for a murder conviction. With credit for time served awaiting trial, Vivian was sentenced to eighteen months and released on September 17, 2005. Lester Powell is dead forever; Josephine Vivian's life is interrupted for a total of twenty-eight months. If she kills again, which she is statistically inclined to do, her next victim's murder will have been entirely preventable by the state.[1]

When Vivian's sentence was announced in the courtroom, Powell's mother, Maureen, said of the judge: "He's just a man in a black robe with more education than me." Then she hurdled the rail and attacked Vivian. Officers pulled her off before any-one suffered serious injury.

BLACK ROBES

A judge is not a god; he or she is just a person "in a black robe with more education" than most of us. Presumably it is their education that leads them to these decisions. Perhaps if I earned a law degree I would understand these decisions and maybe even agree with them. I'm a little too old to pursue a degree in law, but I'm reasonably intelligent and capable of independent research and thought. I have set myself the task of understanding the law of bail in Commonwealth legal culture so that I can effectively argue against its current application to persons accused of murder.

GRIEF

But why do I care? Why must I understand how judges think about those accused of murder, and in particular how Russell and Welsh thought about Shirley? This quest for understanding is an essential part of the grieving process.

Kate and I have participated in several organized activities designed to help us cope with our loss. From each, we took something of value; and in return, I hope, gave something of value to others coping with their losses.

Parents of Murdered Children (POMC) was created in 1978 by Robert and Charlotte Hullinger, whose nineteen-year-old daughter Lisa was beaten to death by her ex-boyfriend in Germany. The Hullingers knew no one who had shared their dreadful experience, had no one with whom they could speak freely about their anger and despair, and wanted to help others faced with this terrible ordeal in the future. The organization grew dramatically, which in itself is both a dreadful and a hopeful commentary on our species.

There is a POMC chapter in San Jose, near our home in California, and we attended meetings whenever we weren't in Newfoundland. Not only did we meet other parents, but also aunts, uncles, brothers, sisters, daughters, sons, and friends of murder victims. We heard tales of justice dispensed by courts, and tales of unfathomable injustice dispensed by the same courts. We acquired some insight into the process of criminal law, as viewed through the eyes of survivors who had already been down the path we expected to tread in Pennsylvania. And we learned one fundamental truth about grieving after murder: it's okay to say exactly what you think and feel. Vomit it right up there! You can growl, "I should have killed that fucking bitch when I had the chance!" and nobody in the room will think the less of you. Nobody will consider you nuts, or overreacting, or out of control. Nobody will think, "Now, hold on, that's not right." They've all felt exactly the same way about the monster that deprived them of their loved one.

Kara, founded in 1976, derives its name from the Gothic word for "care," and provides compassionate support to those who are grieving a death or facing a life-threatening illness. Kate and I joined a group session composed entirely of parents who had lost a child to death. Ours was the only murdered child in the group, but we learned another important lesson: it doesn't matter how old you are, how old your child was when he or she died, or the particular manner of your child's death; the hole in your heart never heals over. You can function in life, but you are doomed to fall far short of that contentment which had once been available to you.

Soon after our return to California following Andrew's murder, Kate and I began regular counselling sessions with clinical psychologist Dr. Christine Chang. These sessions have continued to this day, interrupted of course by our twenty-seven-month residence in Newfoundland. In these sessions, we have addressed virtually every aspect of this nightmare, but one issue has come to dominate our discussions with Dr. Chang: Kate's torturous feelings of guilt at not having saved Zachary. Logically, we know that we did everything possible within the law to keep Shirley mellow and wait out the legal delays. But every day our guts—especially Kate's—remind us that our beautiful baby grandson is gone, in part because we failed to act.

I believe I have followed to its conclusion every possible logical thread of this issue, and I have found only one way in which I could have ensured Zachary's life: kill Shirley Turner. For me, the analysis is over. I deeply regret my failure to act in my grandson's best interest, but I do not dwell on my guilt.

Kate, on the other hand, frequently slips into self-recrimination: "If only we had pushed harder in Family Court.... Maybe we should have gone public early and complained to the press.... We should have enlisted Penney and Philip as allies..." She has repeatedly flogged herself with dozens of these questions, but on analysis each one leads to the same result: as long as Shirley held the "hostage" (Dr. Chang's word), we were powerless to save Zachary. Any action on our part was likely to result in his death even earlier than it actually occurred. Our only consolation is that he knew true love, if only for the brief span of his life.

In Newfoundland, Kate and I enrolled in group sessions with Dr. Rick Singleton, head of Pastoral Care at the Health Sciences Centre in St. John's. Again, we were the only survivors of murder in the group, but grief is not a contest. It is very personal and very intense for the griever. The loss of one's eighty-five-year-old mother to a natural death is ample cause for grief among those who loved her.

Dr. Singleton's vivid images depicting a model for grief gave me a deeper understanding of my own situation. My explosions, upon learning of Andrew's and Zachary's deaths, were the result of multiple emotions—anger, despair, fear, hatred—all felt simultaneously. And the intensity of each was greater than I had ever experienced it before. It was, as Singleton put it, like overlaying different coloured transparencies, one on top of the other, with each colour saturated to its maximum—the deepest possible red, green, blue, yellow. An emotional funny bone; all nerve endings suddenly enervated simultaneously.

The most important insight I gained from Dr. Singleton was the absolute requirement for *understanding* as the first step in the grieving process. I believe this explains my compulsion to know how judges think about those accused of murder. "Educated people in black robes" won't cut it. I might defer judgment on cancer treatment to an oncologist, based on his extensive and highly specialized knowledge of that narrow field of medicine, but justice is not a deep mystery. Most of us learned the basics as small children—Kate and I hammered the nonviolent message home to Andrew as a boy—and the rules change very little with age: don't hit people, don't steal, tell the truth; and if you don't follow the rules, there will be a price to pay. The people in black robes have read a great many books and loads of case law on *the legal process*, but they have no monopoly on understanding *justice*. Kate and I cannot progress to the next steps in our grieving process—some minimal level of acceptance, peace, and contentment—until we understand the principles behind those black-robed decisions.

CHILD DEATH REVIEW (CDR)

The day after our press conference, the government of Newfoundland and Labrador issued a news release that stated, in part:

> Gerald Smith, Minister of Health and Human Services, today indicated that he has requested a full report on the health and community services provided to Dr. Shirley Turner and Zachary Turner. The minister will forward this information to the Child and Youth Advocate with a

request that the Advocate report back as he considers
appropriate.

"I have been given every confidence that our policies
were properly applied and good judgment was used,"
stated Minister Smith.... For reasons of confidentiality,
the report will not be made public...[2]

Mr. Lloyd Wicks, a retired provincial court judge with a
long history of dealing with troubled youth, was the first to
occupy the newly created office of Child and Youth Advocate in
the province of Newfoundland and Labrador, and this was
likely to be the highest profile case his office would handle during his tenure. Zachary's beautiful little round smiling face and
his death at the hands of his mother "became, without question, the story of the year [2003] in [Newfoundland]."[3]

Wicks first had to decide whether there was sufficient cause
to initiate a Child Death Review—a formal investigation to
determine precisely why baby Zachary Turner had died. That
was a clear "Yes," but since the office was new and his staff was
new, he didn't know how to conduct a CDR. Officials in the
province of Saskatchewan had done approximately a hundred,
so Wicks consulted with them to learn the process and to train
his staff.

Kate and I met with Wicks and psychologist Dr. Michele
Neary, his staffer assigned to the CDR, several times and came
away convinced that they were sincerely dedicated to doing a
good job on this task. We decided to stay in Newfoundland
until its completion, so that we would be present to review the
results. Once again, we found ourselves trapped in our compulsion to understand, and waiting on others to complete a task
before we could get on with rebuilding a life.

CHAPTER 34
USEFUL LIMBO

While Wicks and Neary got up to speed on the process of a Child Death Review, Kate and I made several quick trips to take care of some emotional chores.

Shirley's death effectively ended the case against her in Pennsylvania, so Lieutenant Weaver, Trooper McElfresh, Kate, and I watched as a young police officer brought Andrew's personal effects from the evidence room. Kate lost it. Her baby was reduced to a laptop computer, Palm Pilot, lab coat, stethoscope, and some miscellaneous odds and ends in cardboard boxes labelled HOMICIDE.

Kate wanted to see police photos of the crime scene. I didn't. I cannot account for this difference between us. Grief is very complicated and very personal.

McElfresh brought out several of the least horrific images, including one of Andrew lying in the parking lot with an array of police cars and officers far in the background. The mother in her wanted someone to go to him, but of course it was a crime scene, so they had kept back to avoid contaminating evidence.

Back in Tyson Research Park, we and our Missouri relatives repeated the ceremony of nearly two years before, spreading

Zachary's ashes over the ground to soak into the soil with those of his father.

Back in Upnor churchyard, we and our English relatives dug another hole in the family grave and placed a part of Zachary with his father and his great-grandparents. While entering this ceremony in the church log book, the vicar noticed that it was exactly two years ago this day—December 19, 2001—that we had placed Andrew's ashes in that grave with his grandparents.

Back in Newfoundland, we had practical chores to do. I collected court documents and literature on murder and the criminal justice system, and started writing this book, using Andrew's laptop computer. Kate—along with Barbara St. Onge, whose sister, Brenda Gillingham, had been murdered by her ex-boyfriend—organized a group of murder survivors in St. John's. They called it Victims of Homicide and modeled it loosely on POMC. And, in contrast to our reticence of the previous two years, we never turned down an interview request by anyone in television, radio, or print media. We were determined that those in positions of authority—those with the legal power to stop Shirley Turner—be reminded as often as possible of the catastrophic results of their wilful inaction.

WARNING SIGNS/WHERE IT WENT WRONG

By far the most complete media coverage of Zachary's story was done by Chris O'Neill-Yates of CBC Television. After a get-acquainted meeting at our apartment, she convinced her boss to produce a series of television documentaries entitled Warning Signs and Where It Went Wrong. This series included one comprehensive report that aired on *The National*, plus four shorter segments that aired on the local Newfoundland news show *Here & Now*.

Kate and I spent most of a gruelling day in front of a camera describing our involvement with Shirley, with Zachary, and with the two legal battle fronts: extradition and custody. We also provided Chris with over four hours of raw video footage of Zachary, plus lots of still photos of both Andrew and Zachary.

Chris interviewed Heather Arnold about her fear of Shirley Turner: "The two months she was in Clarenville was the first time I ever felt any peace…and when she was let out again… things went back to being [Heather was choking back her tears at this point] very hard." Heather described finding Shirley on her doorstep in the middle of the night shortly after her escape to Newfoundland: "For the next forty-five, fifty minutes, [Shirley started] to berate me, and rail about how she should have been involved in the funeral service [for Andrew at the medical school] and how I could as easily have murdered Andrew as she could have." Heather had informed the police of her fear, but she was apparently the only one who did: "A lot of people didn't speak up because of the fear, I think…with her strolling around, for all intents and purposes free as a bird, it's hard to bring yourself to want to speak out."

Chris included some file footage of Gerald Smith, Minister of Health and Human Services, mouthing a "policies and procedures" mantra at a press conference: "My understanding is that proper protocols were followed. I have asked my officials to…follow up…to see, in fact, that all the proper protocols had been adhered to."

Ken Eckhert and Chad Burkhart, Andrew's medical school buddies, described the erratic and confrontational behaviour they had witnessed in Shirley throughout her relationship with Andrew. Chad said, "I found her to be a very in-your-face type of individual. She always needed to be the centre of the crowd....She would become very, very angry with Andrew and other people around her if she didn't get to go to the bar she wanted to go to, or didn't know where Andrew was all the time."

Ken said, "We all thought she was nuts...we all collectively said...actually pulled Andrew aside and said 'You have to end this'!"

Penney and Phillip, who had signed as surety for Shirley's release in January of 2003, were both extremely reluctant to speak to Chris on camera. Penney, however, finally overcame her anxiety and agreed to be interviewed. She did an excellent job of exposing the lax procedures of the surety process. "It was just a matter of Phillip going into the courthouse and signing a piece of paper and he was on his way again...it was very simple...there were no instructions...our bank books weren't checked...to make sure that we could put up the money."

After Shirley had been free on bail for several weeks, Penney and Phillip began to notice Shirley's affinity for the local bar scene. She had also become quite argumentative, Penney said, and they began to regret their decision to put up bail. "I really wanted nothing else to do with her. You couldn't even talk to her; it was just her way or no way."

A surety has the right to cancel the obligation at any time for any reason, but Penney and Phillip were not informed of that right when they signed up. "We would like to have revoked bail, but we weren't aware that we could do that....If we had known that...we would have done it in a heartbeat."

Had any of her sureties known of this right and exercised it, Shirley would have had to find a replacement surety or go back to jail. Or, what seems more likely to this cynical observer, a judge would simply have reduced her surety requirement to whatever she could meet, and put her right back on the street.

The point so clearly made in Chris's documentary was that the entire surety system is a farce; there is a pretension that money is involved, while in practice the only thing that matters is a signature, and authorities take no pains to ensure that the signature is backed up by money.

Chris took a cameraman to Pennsylvania and interviewed State Police Lieutenant Robert Weaver and Assistant District Attorney Judi Petrush. Petrush expressed her dismay at Shirley's release on bail: "She was a person that could not handle rejection…she behaved in a violent and extreme manner when faced with rejection." Weaver expressed his surprise that the sureties "actually didn't have the money."

Ivy Burt, Director of Child, Youth and Family Services, sounded like the prototype bureaucrat when Chris asked why her department had not responded to our concerns about Zachary's safety: "There's no standard that says we have to report back." Then she stepped behind the twin bureaucratic cloaks of policy and confidentiality: "You're asking me to comment on the details of a specific case and it's not the policy of the department to do that."

Chris drove the point home: "But in a police statement, a Child Services employee says, 'A review of internal files shows no indication of threat to do harm by Shirley Turner, or any suicidal tendencies'. Yet the American prosecutors were explicit on this point. They said that Turner had attempted suicide in the U.S. when another man had left her and there were restraining orders against her here in Canada." On this last point, Chris was referring to Shirley's residency supervisor from medical school, who had first-hand experience of her hostile behaviour. This supervisor had no connection to the criminal case against Shirley, but he had asked to be included in the no-contact list of her bail release conditions. His request was granted.

Kathleen Kufeldt, an expert in the field of child protection, went before the CBC camera and weighed in on our side: "Somebody, somewhere, forgot that their son had died; that this baby's father could no longer speak for his son....I think that those grandparents should have been allowed to speak for the father's side of the family." Regarding the lack of cooperation among the various government agencies involved with Shirley Turner, Kufeldt added, "Each particular part of the system sees its mandate narrowly...child protection...police... the justice system...but in the meantime, you have a child—in this case, it was Zachary—slipping between the cracks."

Chris's series of reports went on to win the 2004 Award for Excellence in Journalism from the Newfoundland and Labrador branch of the Canadian Bar Association. Kate and I were very pleased for her, and grateful for the fine job she did, but mainly we were gratified that the atrocious circumstances surrounding Zachary's death had received such extensive and effective public exposure.

WRONGFUL CONVICTIONS

In the early 1990s three men in Newfoundland were convicted of murder and later exonerated. The government of Newfoundland and Labrador hired Antonio Lamer, retired Supreme Court of Canada Chief Justice, to head a commission of inquiry to identify the causes of these wrongful convictions and to recommend appropriate compensation for the victims and preventive measures for the future. The commission hearings, commonly called the Lamer Inquiry, were open to the public, so Kate and I took advantage of this opportunity to gain additional insight into the criminal justice process.

Of the three cases examined by the Lamer Inquiry, we learned the most about Gregory Parsons. On January 2, 1991, when he was nineteen years old, he discovered the body of his mother, Catherine Carroll, in her upstairs bathroom. She had been slashed with a serrated kitchen knife over fifty times and police investigators had quickly settled on Parsons as their prime suspect. He was convicted of his mother's murder in 1994, but appealed and was awaiting a new trial when DNA evidence exonerated him and led to the arrest of the actual killer, Parsons' boyhood friend, Brian Doyle. Lamer's task was to determine what caused Parsons' wrongful conviction.

From the back of the room, over several weeks, Kate and I listened as Parsons' lawyer, Jerome Kennedy, mercilessly hammered on witness after witness, especially the police investigators and Crown prosecutors who had perpetrated this injustice on his client. Kate and I agreed that, even allowing for Kennedy's self-righteous over-the-top rhetoric, he made a very strong case for police tunnel vision as the primary culprit in Parsons' prosecution and wrongful conviction. (It was a very complicated case and there were other issues on Kennedy's list, including possible judicial incompetence regarding admissibility rules for hearsay evidence, and possible police and prosecutorial misconduct. Thorough analysis would require another volume or two.)

In his final report, Lamer agreed with Kennedy: "The investigation and prosecution of Gregory Parsons became a 'runaway train', fuelled by tunnel vision and picking up many passengers along the way."[1]

NO MALFUNCTION HERE

Greg Parsons' attorney at his 1994 murder trial had been Kennedy's law partner, Bob Simmonds. On September 5, 2003, two days after our press conference, Simmonds was interviewed by Jeff Gilhooly on *The St. John's Morning Show* on CBC Radio, and had this to say about our public expression of outrage at Shirley's release on bail:

> Gilhooly: How do you feel about the way the Shirley Turner case was handled?
>
> Simmonds: I guess we have to start off by saying…there's no doubt that this was horrific.… The grief and anguish these…grandparents must be going through…must be unimaginable for most of us. Their concerns, their grief, their anger with the system—very understandable. Having said that, that does not mean the system malfunctioned here…[2]

This last point strikes me as equivalent to a statement with which Simmonds could not possibly agree: Greg Parsons' concerns, his grief, his anger with the system—very understandable. Having said that, that does not mean the system malfunctioned in convicting him of his mother's murder.

But I was not surprised by Simmonds' seemingly cavalier dismissal of Zachary's life. I was, instead, reminded of author Gavin de Becker's description of the O.J. Simpson defence team: "paid advocates in service of just one man."[3] Simmonds could not very well endorse Kate's and my outrage over Shirley's bail release, since he may have to stand up in court the next day and argue the opposite position if he were retained by a client accused of murder.

The question of whether "the system malfunctioned" is this simple: Parsons was raked over the coals by the legal system, and it was right and proper—even imperative—that an inquiry be conducted to determine exactly how that injustice occurred, and to initiate corrective action to reduce the probability of a recurrence. Ditto for Zachary.

BAIL VERSUS PRESUMPTION OF INNOCENCE

During the Lamer Inquiry, Kate and I wondered if public sympathy for the victims of these wrongful convictions had influenced the judges in Shirley's bail decisions. Since then, we have become convinced that there was little or no connection; the law of bail in Canada clearly favours release.

EDWARD SHAW MURDER

Through our involvement in the Victims of Homicide group, Kate and I met many other Newfoundlanders who had lost a loved one to murder. But more to the point of this book, we soon learned of another bail-release murder case. On March 28, 1994, John Cousins and Derek Allen, high on alcohol and hashish, stabbed Marvin Squires to death. While free on bail pending trial for that murder, John Cousins stabbed another man, Edward Shaw, over sixty times. Shaw's death, like Zachary's, was facilitated by a legal system wilfully unconcerned about the implications of Marvin Squires' agonizing end, and quite content to allow Cousins a repeat performance.

EDWARD LAWRIE MURDER

The liberal bail-release policy was carefully explained to us by a judge at the conclusion of a bail hearing in July 2004. Laura Abbott was accused of running over her boyfriend, Edward Lawrie, with her car on July 14, 2004. Initially, the charge was attempted murder, but Lawrie died two days later and the charge was upgraded to second-degree murder. Several members of Kate and Barbara's Victims of Homicide group, including myself, attended the Abbott bail hearing on July 21. In contrast to Shirley Turner's original bail hearing in December 2001, the Crown Prosecutor argued in open court against Abbott's release. She lost the debate.

Before issuing his decision to release Abbott, Judge Robert Hall acknowledged the presence in the courtroom of we Victims of Homicide members, and took a few moments to deliver a short civics lesson on the basics of Canadian bail law:

> I cannot help but note the interest this matter has generated amongst others. I just wanted to read the provisions of the Criminal Code insofar as they relate to detention in custody. Contrary to what many people think, the judges don't make the laws. Judges interpret laws. Criminal law of this country is legislated by the Parliament of Canada, the people that we elect to represent us... [Criminal Code] Section 515 deals with bail, and Subsection 10 deals with the grounds on which the detention of an accused person in custody is justified. And it says this:
>
> For the purposes of this section, the detention of an accused in custody is justified only on one or more of the following grounds.
>
> And the first one—you've heard it called the primary ground—is where the detention is necessary to insure his or her attendance in court in order to be dealt with according to the law. In other words, that the accused person simply isn't gonna take off and not show up for trial.
>
> The secondary ground is where the detention is necessary for the protection or safety of the public, including any victim of or witness to the offense, having regard to all of the circumstances including any *substantial* likelihood that the accused will, if released from custody, commit a criminal offense or interfere with the administration of justice.
>
> And then the third ground... is where the detention is necessary in order to *maintain confidence in the*

administration of justice [emphasis added], having regard
to all of the circumstances, including the apparent
strength of the prosecution's case, the gravity of the
nature of the offense, the circumstances surrounding its
commission and the potential for a lengthy term of
imprisonment.

Those are the factors that I as a judge have to consider
based upon the evidence that comes before me. I have no
authority or right to add into that any additional grounds
that I might think to be appropriate.

Those are the things that I have to consider, and it's a
heavy burden, because I have to balance those considera-
tions with the very, very fundamental principle that one is
innocent until proven guilty in a court of law.[4]

After Judge Hall ordered Abbott's release and court was
adjourned, the media, which knew of our new Victims of
Homicide group, was anxious to hear what Kate, Barbara, and
I had to say about the decision. The following day, St. John's
Telegram reporter Bonnie Belec summarized the three bail criteria, just as Judge Hall had done, and then wrote the
following:

It is this third requirement that drew criticism Thursday
from members of the group Victims of Homicide....
"Maintaining confidence in the administration of justice—I can't prove it but I bet there's a whole bunch of
people who don't feel very confident right now about the
administration of justice," said David Bagby, whose grandson was murdered by a woman who was out on bail
awaiting extradition to the United States to stand trial for
the murder of Bagby's son.

"And anybody who went to (murder victim) Edward Shaw's funeral or my grandson's funeral would have no confidence right now in the administration of justice. The legal system keeps doing it.

"Edward Shaw is dead because the legal system let (two-time convicted murderer) John Cousins out and he killed Edward Shaw while on bail. My grandson Zachary is dead because the legal system let Shirley Turner out pending extradition for the murder of my son. The legal system does not respect even the potential of violence from somebody who's accused of murder," said Bagby, who is one of the founders of Victims of Homicide.[5]

Judge Hall did me a favour. He crystallized for me the precise goal of this book: instigate changes in law to prevent release on bail of persons accused of murder. Toward that end, I have set out to acquire a basic understanding of the principles and procedures of Canadian criminal law, and especially of bail law. The remainder of this book consists of this layman's analysis of the law of bail, application of the Canadian Charter of Rights and Freedoms to bail and, finally, an argument to deny bail to persons accused of murder.

CHAPTER 35

THE LAW OF BAIL

In researching murder and the law, and during the writing of this book, several themes emerged which are not directly on point; that is, they are peripheral to the subject of bail release for persons accused of murder. For the reader who is interested in a broader historical, cultural, and legal context for the treatment of murder, I briefly address these peripheral issues in appendices, which are referenced at the appropriate places in this chapter.

PROBABILITY IN THE LEGAL CONTEXT

Each step of the criminal justice process involves an evaluation of probability of guilt. At the arrest stage, police need only convince a judge that there are *reasonable and probable grounds*[1] to believe the accused committed a crime. At the subsequent Preliminary Inquiry, a judge raises the bar somewhat; he or she reviews both the police evidence and defence evidence, and determines *whether a properly instructed jury could reasonably convict the accused based on the evidence presented.*[2] At the end of a trial, in which the prosecution and defence present the most detailed examination of evidence by the legal system, a jury must apply the highest standard of proof used in law; they must decide whether they are convinced of guilt *beyond a reasonable doubt.*

This issue of probability of guilt was succinctly stated by former Stanford University law professor Herbert Packer in his book on criminal punishment: "A criminal case, or any lawsuit for that matter, necessitates making a judgment about past events. Like any historical reconstruction, such a judgment is not a matter of certainty but rather one of probabilities."[3]

The implicit application of probability estimates that must occur at each major step of the criminal justice process does not appear to extend to bail decisions for a person accused of murder.

BAIL PEDANTRY

Kate and I witnessed first-hand some of the pedantry (arbitrary adherence to rules and forms) of courtroom bail analysis, which seems to pervade the literature and judicial writings. For example, in a 1990 decision discussing public perception of bail release, Quebec Appeals Court Justice Jean-Louis Baudouin suggested,

> that the public often adopts a *visceral and negative reaction to crime and criminals*... such a view cannot dominate the conception of the public interest. A more *sophisticated* view is required... certain *inconveniences* with respect to effectiveness in the repression of crime [are] the price that must be paid for life in a free and democratic society... the application of the presumption of innocence, even with respect to [bail], has the effect that people, who may later be guilty of even *serious crimes*, will be released for the period between the time of their arrest and the time of their trial. In other words, the

criterion of the public perception must not be that of the *lowest common denominator*. [emphasis added][4]

Long before Andrew was murdered, Kate and I had a "visceral and negative reaction to crime and criminals," and so did everybody we knew (except Shirley, who had no particular reaction to the murders at the World Trade Center on September 11, 2001). Andrew's murder obviously magnified the effect dramatically—brought it right into our kitchen—but the basic reaction was already there, born of empathy for the victims of violent crime we would see in the news. Decent people are *supposed* to be "visceral and negative" about "serious crimes." Such visceral empathy is not the "lowest common denominator;" it is perhaps the most significant sign of our humanity. What sort of "sophisticated" barbarian reacts to a murder with a big yawn and a "what else is new?"

The task of the criminal justice system when a murder occurs is not to disparage this natural visceral response, but to intercept its natural reaction, which is personal vigilante-style justice. Courts should replace this vigilante justice with a careful, reasoned search for truth (did the accused do the crime?) while simultaneously recognizing that decent people are entitled to be both intellectually and viscerally outraged at murder, and to be protected from the "inconvenience" of a second murder while a court unravels the truth.[5]

I shall now attempt to briefly distill the basic principles underlying bail policy, so that I can both intellectually and viscerally attack their current application to murder cases.

APPEARANCE FOR TRIAL

In English law from the thirteenth to the eighteenth century, the only significant issue in the granting of bail was "the likelihood of the accused's appearance for trial,"[6] and the precursor of today's surety system was the usual means to ensure appearance. Family or friends took charge of the accused and obligated themselves financially if they did not produce him for trial. The gravity of the offence was partially taken into account: "Bail was a matter of right with respect to misdemeanours, but discretionary [at the judge's pleasure] for offences classified as felonies."[7]

Canadian bail law closely tracked English law until shortly after Confederation when "the Federal Government made bail discretionary for all offences.... As with British law, the Canadian jurisprudence initially recognized the probability of the accused's attendance in court as the sole determinant of whether bail ought to be granted."[8]

The current statute, as Judge Robert Hall read it to our Victims of Homicide group at Laura Abbott's bail hearing words this criterion for pre-trial detention as: "(a) where the detention is necessary to ensure his or her attendance in court in order to be dealt with according to law."[9]

PUBLIC INTEREST/FURTHER OFFENDING

A 1947 English burglar (a Mr. Phillips) with a long history of burglaries was granted bail pending trial for a burglary and burgled again while awaiting his burglary trial. A subsequent English Court of Appeal decision on Phillips delivered a scathing rebuke of "magistrates who release on bail young housebreakers."[10] The Court declared that "in nineteen cases out of twenty it is a mistake." The Phillips decision, and others like it, "opened the door to an explicit and honest consideration of factors other than the likelihood of the accused appearing for his or her trial."[11]

With the Phillips case in mind, and after lots of academic studies and hand-wringing, the Parliament of Canada passed the Bail Reform Act of 1972. Its most important feature relative to Shirley's bail release was the addition of "specific criteria for the determination of an accused's suitability for release [including] consideration of the 'public interest' and the prevention of further offending."[12]

Twenty years later, the Supreme Court of Canada ruled that "the 'public interest' [criterion] was impermissibly vague"[13] and therefore did not constitute "just cause" [under the Charter] for denial of bail to an accused awaiting trial.

The current law on this criterion reads: "(b) where the detention is necessary for the protection or safety of the public, including any victim of or witness to the offence, having regard to all the circumstances including any substantial likelihood that the accused will, if released from custody, commit a criminal offence or interfere with the administration of justice."[14]

CONFIDENCE IN THE ADMINISTRATION OF JUSTICE

Four years after the "public interest" criterion was declared unconstitutional, Parliament amended the Criminal Code to add a third criterion for denial of bail:

(c) on any other just cause being shown and, without limiting the generality of the foregoing, where the detention is necessary in order to maintain confidence in the administration of justice, having regard to all the circumstances, including the apparent strength of the prosecution's case, the *gravity* of the nature of the offence, the circumstances surrounding its commission and the potential for a *lengthy term of imprisonment* [emphasis added].[15]

When Judge Hall read this paragraph to us, I thought a charge of murder (the gravest) with its nominal sentence of life in prison (the longest) should automatically make Abbott a prime candidate for denial of bail. Hence, I thought, failure to deny bail would surely result in a loss of "confidence in the administration of justice." What a simpleton I was to focus on the only two concrete aspects of this criterion. The rest of it is pure smoke, effectively leaving the decision up to a coin toss by each individual judge. Gary T. Trotter, then a law professor at Queen's University, didn't think much of this new criterion either, suggesting that it "would appear to be purely political. It is sure to be struck down."[16]

In short, current Canadian bail law for domestic crimes allows for detention of an accused only on three grounds: one, to ensure attendance at trial; two, for the protection or safety of the public; and three, to maintain confidence in the administration of justice.

EXTRADITION IS A LITTLE DIFFERENT

Bail release pending extradition is covered by a different section of the Criminal Code—the one that deals with bail pending appeal of a domestic conviction. As we heard during Shirley's extradition bail hearing, this section requires the accused to establish that: the appeal is not frivolous, the accused will appear in court, and detention is not necessary in the public interest.

Judge Welsh declared that frivolousness of appeal was not an issue during extradition, leaving only appearance in court and the public interest. Chances are that if Welsh had denied bail to Shirley based on the public interest, her decision would have been overturned on appeal since the Supreme Court had already declared this criterion to be "impermissibly vague."

That leaves the centuries-old "appearance in court" as the only effective criterion for denial of bail in an extradition case.

For my argument, the key issue is the same in both the domestic and extradition cases: people accused of murder anywhere in the world are probably very dangerous and should be treated with extreme caution until guilt or innocence is determined.

DANGEROUSNESS AS A BAIL CRITERION

A bail release decision is "an exercise in risk assessment,"[17] with the second domestic criterion—the protection or safety of the public—"largely consumed by this issue."[18] In assessing this criterion, judges routinely consider the following factors: the prior criminal record, the current bail or probation status, the strength of the evidence, the nature of the offence, and the stability of the accused.[19]

At her January 2003 bail hearing, Shirley had no prior criminal record and had abided by the conditions of her previous bail release for nearly a year, so the first two factors worked in her favour.

Shirley's appeal of Judge Green's Committal Order argued that the evidence against her was "flimsy." Madden argued that it was strong. Judge Green ruled that it was enough to go to trial. Call this factor, strength of the evidence, a tie; it's not my main issue.

Hence, only the last two factors clearly worked against Shirley: the nature of the offence and her record of emotional instability. Madden chose not to push the issue of Shirley's emotional instability, but he did argue strongly that the nature of her offence ("just about the most serious...extreme violence") justified denial of bail. He lost that debate. I hope to win it here.

CONVICTED KILLERS ARE DANGEROUS

The Canadian National Parole Board published a twenty-five-year study of 11,783 persons who were convicted of homicide (first- or second-degree murder, or manslaughter), sentenced to prison, and later released on parole. Of these, thirty-seven subsequently committed another homicide. That did not seem like very many killers, until I compared this homicide rate among parolees to that of the general population of Canada, where an equivalent group of 11,783 persons chosen at random would have committed about two homicides. That is, parolees committed homicide at a rate approximately seventeen times that of the general population.[20]

SO ARE MOST ACCUSED KILLERS

The Research and Statistics Division of the Canadian Department of Justice published a twenty-eight-year study of 1,137 persons accused of homicide in Toronto. Of these, 85 per cent actually did the killing. Hence, the danger factor for someone accused of homicide is approximately 85 per cent of seventeen, which is fourteen.[21]

EMPIRICAL VACUUM

It seems intuitively obvious that both a convicted killer and an accused killer are statistically much more dangerous than the average person, and I believe this intuition is borne out by the published data quoted above and derived in Appendix C. In the first edition of Trotter's book on bail, he notes that "the criminal law is often analyzed in an empirical vacuum."[22] (Trotter's second edition briefly discusses the literature on dangerousness and its assessment in individual cases by mental health professionals and actuaries, but concludes that they "are not very successful in determining who is likely to be dangerous in the future."[23])

BEGGING THE QUESTION

In his book, *The Limits of the Criminal Sanction*, Herbert Packer primarily confined his bail analysis to an empirical vacuum: "to speak of the possibility that the accused may commit further crimes if left at large is to beg the question; for it has not yet been determined that he has committed any crime at all."[24] But in the next paragraph, Packer acknowledged the obvious: "The problem of what to do with 'dangerous' people who have not been convicted of committing a crime is a troublesome one."

Having acknowledged the "troublesome" problem, Packer then focused on the specific threat of an accused engaging in witness tampering, destruction of evidence, "or otherwise [impeding] the preparation of the case against him."[25] Such threats, he suggested, "can be dealt with in other ways [besides detention]: by giving witnesses police protection, by placing the accused under an injunction backed up by the contempt power, by providing criminal penalties for tampering with witnesses, and the like....At the first concrete sign that the accused has engaged in obstructive activities, it is altogether proper to seek to confine him on the basis of proof that obstructive activities have taken place."[26]

Packer didn't say whether this confinement for "obstructive activities" had to be based on proof beyond a reasonable doubt, as in a trial. Presumably such proof would be required, since obstructing justice is a crime. But, since the accused must be considered innocent until proven guilty of this second crime (as well as the first) he must be entitled to bail release while awaiting his second trial, "for it has not yet been determined that he has committed any crime at all."

Furthermore, for someone initially charged with murder and released on bail, Packer's "first concrete sign" of "obstructive activities" is quite likely to be a second corpse. Suppose

Shirley Turner had drowned only Zachary and not herself, and that police had built a case against her and laid a charge of murder in the death of her baby. Would she be entitled to bail pending the outcome of that trial? How many corpses should an actual killer be allowed to create before authorities declare, "Enough, already! We have to secure this person, guilty or innocent, while due process runs its course. One more corpse would be unacceptable." I submit that one corpse should be enough; there should never be a second corpse.

York University Adjunct Professor James C. Morton and Barrister Scott C. Hutchison, in their discussion of pretrial detention "for the protection or safety of the public," echo Packer's logic: "[such detention] is directed at detaining persons whose acts show that they constitute a menace to society. But the acts that constitute a menace are the very acts that amount to the alleged criminal offence. If we assume that the prisoner is innocent [then this ground for detention] falls by the wayside."[27] The only valid ground for detention, they claim, is to insure that the accused appears at trial. Like Packer, Morton and Hutchison then acknowledge the troublesome problem and, for some murder cases, identify the solution: "It would be the height of folly to release, say, a dangerous psychopath who has been caught in the act of murder simply because he is likely to appear at his trial."[28]

Morton and Hutchison do not say how a court is supposed to identify "a dangerous psychopath" in order to avoid the "folly" of releasing him. Since it is the police who normally conduct criminal investigations and would therefore know the most about the accused, police information would seem the logical source for evidence of "a dangerous psychopath." But everywhere else in the discussion of bail, an impenetrable blanket of presumed innocence is thrown over police information so that it carries no weight whatsoever until the case reaches trial.

DANGEROUS PSYCHOPATH?

"Many of the characteristics displayed by psychopaths…are closely associated with a profound lack of empathy (an inability to construct a mental and emotional 'facsimile' of another person)"[29]—Robert D. Hare from *Without Conscience: The Disturbing World of the Psychopaths among Us*

In 1962, Milwaukee pawnbroker David Hurwitz tried to cheat Butch Bosket out of fifty dollars, so Butch stabbed him once in the chest and five times in the back. The chest wound pierced Hurwitz's aorta. William Locke, another customer in Hurwitz's shop, tried to intervene, so Butch stabbed him six times in the chest. Both victims died and Butch was sentenced to life in prison.

Twenty-two years later, having earned "a bachelor of arts degree 'With Highest Distinction' [and having] become the first inmate ever elected to Phi Beta Kappa,"[30] Butch had a small army of supporters on the outside lobbying for his release on parole. They wrote that he "was a 'model individual' who was being held in prison 'without any rational basis',"[31] and that he was "the perfect example of what a person can accomplish in the vein of individual rehabilitation. His educational achievements as well as his emotional stability are solid proof of this fact."[32] His enthusiastic supporters finally won Butch his parole.

He moved in with his girlfriend, Donna Bernhagen, and her twin six-year-old children, Mathew and Kristin. Several *days* later, having spent over two *decades* convincing authorities that he was safe, Butch began regularly raping the little girl. The child's grandmother noticed the resultant bruising and her subdued demeanour and notified authorities.

Butch was arrested two months after being paroled and was facing return to prison as "an ordinary sex offender"[33] rather than his accustomed status as "a big-time professional criminal, a bank robber, and a killer."[34] He conned Bernhagen into buying some guns and helping him escape from the county jail, but when the two were cornered by police, Butch shot his girl-friend, then himself, in the head. Both died instantly.

The moral: if Morton, Hutchison, Packer, and any other legal theorists want to identify a dangerous psychopath, they must look at the objective evidence of his behaviour when he's not being watched; not the behaviour he wants his evaluator to see. For Butch, the last time he wasn't being watched he exploded in fury and stabbed two men to death. Everything after that—all those years of study and "model individual" behaviour—was a façade designed to get himself out of prison. If such single-minded long-term dedication to an apparently impossible goal seems implausible, consider the strength of his motivation (it was his only chance at freedom) and his level of distractions (he had nothing else to do with his time). However, Butch's core concern—what was in it for him—never altered in all that time, nor did his utter disregard for the pain of others. He was quite happy to put a six-year-old child through hell to satisfy himself sexually or to gratify some sick lust for control over a vulnerable human being.

Given that Butch succeeded in hiding his true nature for two decades in order to get out of prison, what challenge would there be for such a monster to hide his true nature long enough to get through a bail hearing? Not much, if his evaluator is willing to disregard dead bodies and observe only what the subject wants him to see.

WAS SHIRLEY A DANGEROUS PSYCHOPATH?

Throughout the extradition process, a psychiatric evaluation of Shirley was never discussed in open court. During our custody battle strategy sessions, Jackie, Kate, and I considered asking the Family Court to order an evaluation of Shirley in the hope that she would show some indication of danger to herself or others. We decided not to make the request for fear that Shirley, with decades of experience at manipulating people, would pass with flying colours and then forever be able to wave the report in our faces: "See, I'm sane and safe; a psychiatrist said so!" Meanwhile, the objective evidence of her danger to herself and others was already in the court records, but smothered under presumption of innocence.

CHAPTER 36

PROPOSAL

I suggest a genuine life sentence—no parole—for anyone con-victed of murder,[1] and denial of bail to anyone accused of homicide (murder or manslaughter), for the same reason I'm against capital punishment: to minimize the risk of innocent death.

PROPOSED BAIL CRITERIA FOR ACCUSED KILLERS

At a minimum, bail should be denied to anyone accused of first-degree murder (killing with intent and planning). This denial should apply, not only to a domestic murder charge, but to an extradition process based on a foreign murder charge—a foreign corpse should raise the same emergency alarm as a domestic corpse.

Bail should also be denied to anyone accused of second-degree murder (killing with intent but without planning). The victim is just as dead and so will be the next victim if the accused once again forms a spontaneous (unplanned) intent to kill before the trial. Those accused of manslaughter (killing without intent, either due to momentary "rage, terror, or des-peration," or due to "criminal negligence or recklessness"[2]) should also be denied bail for similar reasons; the victim is just as dead, and so will be the next victim if the accused once again becomes angry, scared, desperate, negligent, or reckless before the trial.

The dangerousness of persons convicted or accused of the above three crimes—first and second-degree murder, and manslaughter—is documented in the studies conducted by the Canadian National Parole Board and the Canadian Department of Justice quoted in the previous chapter and described in detail in Appendix C.

OTHER POTENTIAL NO-BAIL OFFENCES

I suggest that at least two more crimes be included in the list of no-bail offences. The first is attempted murder where the intent to kill was there, but the skill or luck of a successful murderer was lacking. The accused might get it right if given a second chance. For the legal system, this is a rare opportunity to prevent a first killing. The second is aggravated assault (assault with "serious bodily injury," or with a "dangerous or deadly weapon"[3]). This seems like another name for attempted manslaughter. The victim has only a bit of luck to thank for his life. It's another opportunity to prevent a first killing.

Any Criminal Code offence that results in a corpse, or would result in a corpse but for a little luck, belongs on this list. However, I don't know the Code well enough to identify all of these potential no-bail offences. For the remainder of this chapter, I will focus on accused murderers.

CHARTER CHALLENGES

If these proposed measures were enacted by Parliament today, they would be challenged in court tomorrow based on claims of Charter rights violations.

Reasonable Bail/Just Cause

An accused murderer who is denied bail would argue first that his right under Charter Section 11(*e*) "not to be denied reasonable bail without just cause" had been violated.

I submit that his statistical dangerousness constitutes "just cause" to detain him "for the protection or safety of the public" (the second criterion for detention) until his trial.

Presumption of Innocence

The accused would also argue that, under Charter Section 11(*d*), he must be "presumed innocent until proven guilty according to law in a fair and public hearing by an independent and impartial tribunal." This presumption of innocence, he would claim, implies that he is no more dangerous than the average man on the street.

I submit that his presumed innocence applies at the trial stage of the process, where the burden of proof will lay on the prosecution (as it should), and he will reap the benefit of any doubt about his guilt (as he should). But until trial, and in sharp contrast to the average man on the street, there are "reasonable and probable grounds" to believe he murdered someone and is therefore "probably" much more dangerous than Mr. Average. Recognition of that potential danger is not a violation of presumption of innocence. In order to violate presumption of innocence, the accused would have to be sentenced to a long term of imprisonment, and pre-trial detention is not long-term imprisonment.

Arbitrary Detention

The accused might argue that his right under Charter Section 9 "not to be arbitrarily detained or imprisoned" had been violated.

I submit that detention of an accused murderer is not "arbitrary;" it is based on "reasonable and probable grounds" to believe that he or she is a murderer. To be arbitrary, the detention would have to be based on random selection from the phone book, or on some other method unrelated to the evidence of "reasonable and probable grounds."

Fundamental Justice

Charter Section 7 might be the accused's next tack. It provides the right "not to be deprived of [life, liberty, or security of the person] except in accordance with the principles of fundamental justice." In my limited readings, I never came across a complete definition of "principles of fundamental justice." Perhaps the phrase is analogous to "reasonable doubt," in that it is generally considered to be self-explanatory. It seems to encompass such maxims and concepts as "laws may not be too vague,"[4] "the adversarial nature of the trial process,"[5] and "an accused is not called upon to demonstrate his or her innocence."[6] In short, fairness to the accused.

In this vein, the accused may argue that "pretrial detention [hampers his] ability to assist counsel in the preparation of his or her case. While incarcerated, an accused person will be unable to track down potential witnesses and gather evidence to support the defence."[7] This was the strongest practical argument I encountered in support of bail release for an accused murderer, or any other accused, and it is a compelling argument.

Trotter addressed some aspects of this problem, suggesting that "Pretrial detention should be as burden-free as is consistent with appropriate security...pretrial detainees should be permitted unlimited counsel and family visits, liberal access to telephones and writing materials, and the right to wear the clothing of one's choice. These small 'privileges' are all consistent with the accused person's innocent status at the bail stage of proceedings."[8]

I submit that authorities *must* devise a solution to this problem, presumably incorporating the relatively burden-free policies like those suggested by Trotter and that this solution should be applied to accused murderers. If there is no solution, then *every* accused—including serial killers, terrorists, and multiple repeat offenders—*must* be released on bail. Otherwise, he or she is being wilfully deprived of a fair trial. And if even one wilfully unfair trial is tolerated, then we're headed back towards the tyrannical torture dungeons of the middle ages and the Charter is no better than toilet paper.

One final point related to extradition: if pretrial detention is such an onerous policy that it cannot be applied even to an accused premeditated murderer, then perhaps Canada should abrogate its extradition treaties with those European democracies where "pretrial detention is generally the rule instead of the exception."[9] The return of a fugitive to face detention and trial in one of these presumably unfair European democracies should not be tolerated by a nation devoted to the principles of fundamental justice.

Limits on Charter Rights

The Charter enumerates the basic rights of everyone in Canada. These rights "are not, however, absolute. It may become necessary to limit rights and freedoms in circumstances where their exercise would be inimical to the realization of collective goals of fundamental importance."[10] Charter Section 1 gives Parliament the opportunity to place limits on Charter rights and lays down the conditions under which these limits may be justified: "The *Canadian Charter of Rights and Freedoms* guarantees the rights and freedoms set out in it subject only to such reasonable limits prescribed by law as can be demonstrably justified in a free and democratic society."

For all the reasons outlined above, I submit that legislation ordering pretrial detention for accused murderers is not a *limit* on any Charter right (there is "just cause," the accused is still "presumed innocent" where it counts—at trial, it is not "arbitrary," and it can be done "in accordance with the principles of fundamental justice.")

However, if such detention were deemed to be a limit on one or more Charter rights, I submit that the limit is justified under Section 1. That is, pretrial detention of accused murderers, if enacted into law by Parliament, would be: reasonable, prescribed by law, and demonstrably justified in a free and democratic society.

Obviously, if Parliament enacted such a law, it would meet the requirement to be "prescribed by law." I need focus, therefore, only on the other two requirements for a limit on a Charter right or freedom, and these were generally discussed as one in the literature that I have read.

Reasonable and Demonstrably Justified

Before enacting a measure that limits a Charter right or freedom, Parliament must have a clear objective for the measure. Supreme Court of Canada decisions have laid down two criteria for determining whether such a measure is acceptable.[11]

First, Parliament's objective must be "of sufficient importance to warrant overriding a constitutionally protected right or freedom." To be "sufficiently important," the objective must "relate to concerns which are pressing and substantial in a free and democratic society."

Second, the measure to achieve the objective must be "reasonable and demonstrably justified." This justification is determined using a "proportionality test" in which the Court must "balance the interests of society with those of individuals and groups."

There are three components to this "proportionality test:" one, the measure must be "rationally connected to the objective;" two, the measure should impair "as little as possible" the right or freedom it limits; and three, "there must be a proportionality between the *effects* of the [measure]" and its intended objective.

Using the Supreme Court's terminology: "measure" is pretrial detention of accused murderers, "objective" is prevention of second killings by *guilty* accused murderers awaiting trial, and "effect" is the pretrial detention of *innocent* accused murderers awaiting trial.

Marching through the Supreme Court's criteria, I make two submissions. The first is that everyone in a "free and democratic society" is entitled to government protection against criminals—especially against murderers, since their crimes cause the most damage to their victims. In fact, such protection is one of the primary functions of government—perhaps *the* primary function of government.

The damage that is inflicted by a murderer on his victim, on his victim's loved ones, and on his victim's community, is devastating. But the damage that is inflicted by a murderer *who has been identified by government and allowed to repeat his crime* is even more devastating than a first killing. Not only are the second victim, his loved ones, and the community crushed again, but confidence in government's ability to do its job (and interest in doing its job) is severely undermined among those innocent citizens whom government is charged with protecting.

The "objective" of preventing both the repeat devastation of a second killing, and its ensuing loss of confidence in government, constitutes "concerns which are pressing and substantial in a free and democratic society."

My second submission is that pretrial detention is "reasonable and demonstrably justified" based on the three-part "proportionality test."

Pretrial detention (the measure) is obviously "rationally connected to" prevention of second killings by *guilty* accused murderers (the objective), since they cannot kill again while in detention.

Judge Gale Welsh ordered Shirley Turner to appear in court. Rather than obey that order, she drowned herself and her baby. The court did not, because it could not, force her compliance with its order. Hence, thanks to Shirley, it is quite obvious that a court order is a demonstrably ineffective "measure" for controlling accused murderers on bail-release, and, therefore, cannot achieve the "objective" of preventing second killings. If Parliament, with infinitely more research capabilities than my own, were to discover an effective measure (short of detention) to meet the objective, then I suggest they enact that measure into law. In the meantime, pretrial detention impairs the accused's rights and freedoms "as little as possible" while achieving the objective.

This is the crux of the issue: "there must be proportionality between the effects of the measure and its intended objective." Obviously it would be ludicrous to hold a jury trial for everyone accused of a parking violation, and even more so to detain all such accused in custody pending trial for fear of a second offence. Such a measure would surely fail the proportionality test because detention of the innocent is so much more onerous than a second parking violation by the guilty. But how can the suffering caused by temporary detention of an innocent accused murderer (the effects) be compared to prevention of permanent death of an innocent second victim (the objective)?

The innocent accused awaiting trial in detention surely suffers greatly from the severe restrictions on his liberty. He also suffers, perhaps, from the loss of income, and no doubt from the sheer boredom of jailhouse life. His family and friends, too, surely suffer daily from the lack of him in their lives. (These effects should be mitigated as much as possible using the liberal visitation and communication policies suggested by Trotter.) However, once acquitted, the innocent accused has an opportunity to rebuild a life—to rejoin family and friends, and to re-establish a career. The suffering of his detention will presumably never be forgotten, but in the perspective of his entire life, its significance should diminish over time.

The innocent bail-release murder victim, by contrast with the innocent pretrial detainee, suffers permanent loss of everything. He has no life to salvage. He does not rejoin family and friends, and he does not re-establish a career. If it can be said that the dead suffer through lack of life's pleasures, he suffers immeasurably more than one who is temporarily incarcerated and later released. In the perspective of his entire life, the significance of his murder is immediate, overwhelming, and permanent.

The suffering of a murder victim's family and friends is (unfortunately) Kate's and my area of personal expertise. Shortly after Andrew was murdered, his good friend Kurt Kuenne (pronounced like Kenny) foresaw Kate's and my long-term problem and gave us each a desk clock inscribed "You Still Have Children. Love, Kurt." He was right. We need to focus on the living, and I think we are doing that. In fact, this book is dedicated to the living—those potential bail-release murder victims who have a right to keep on living. Kate, too, is focused on the living. She has undergone the training and is now acting as a child advocate within the justice system, and I expect to join her in that endeavour once this book is finished.

We are salvaging some of life's pleasures from this double wreckage—spending a great deal of time with friends doing normal things. But each of life's pleasures is clouded by the absence of Zachary (also, of course, by the absence of Andrew, but his murder could not be prevented by the State and is therefore not relevant to the issue at hand). When we see a small child running through the mall or playing in the park, we enjoy his exuberance, but he is not Zachary. When Kate babysits a friend's grandson, she enjoys nurturing his developing personality, but he is not Zachary. The gap in our souls cannot be filled. The reminders are everywhere. They cannot be switched off.

EPILOGUE

CHILD DEATH REVIEW

Kate and I stayed in Newfoundland for nearly a year, waiting for completion of the CDR. In September 2004, however, with the completion date still not firm, we went home to California with a promise from Mr. Lloyd Wicks, the Child and Youth Advocate, to inform us as soon as the report was ready so that we could return to Newfoundland and make public comment when it was released. Our only weapon in our quest for change was our voice and we intended to use it at every opportunity.

To assist Dr. Michele Neary in her review of Zachary's death, Wicks assembled an Advisory Council of five highly respected practitioners of various professions.[1] Neary's report was in the final stages of production when, in March 2005, Wicks retired for reasons unrelated to the CDR. Shortly thereafter, Neary resigned for reasons that were never made public. At about the same time, the Advisory Council was disbanded and the CDR was on hold pending stabilization of management at the Office of the Child and Youth Advocate. The underlying reasons for this disintegration of the CDR process did not matter to Kate and me, but the resulting delay in release of the report was distressing, to put it mildly.

In May 2005, Mr. Wicks' successor, retired judge James Igloliorte, hired Winnipeg forensic pathologist Dr. Peter Markesteyn to conduct a Review and Investigation into Zachary's death. Dr. Markesteyn engaged the services of St. John's attorney David C. Day, Q.C., and together they produced a report, which was released on October 4, 2006.

The 1,165-page "Turner Review and Investigation" is a three-volume set. Volume I details the events leading up to Shirley's murder of Zachary, including her interactions with family and friends, with Kate and me, and with various departments of government, both provincial and federal. Volume II systematically analyzes the performance of each department, identifies errors and omissions, and recommends systemic changes and specific follow-up actions for improving performance in the future. Volume III contains appendices. Kate's and my anguish over the long delays is trumped by the quality of this report. It is exactly what we had hoped for and it was well worth the wait. By the way, there should be no negative inference drawn concerning Dr. Michele Neary's almost-completed but unpublished report. It may well have risen to this standard of excellence.

"NO NAME, NO BLAME"[2]

In his review, Markesteyn stresses, "it is not my intention to attribute blame or to scapegoat any one individual."[3] Accordingly, the review names no names, but instead refers to those who dealt with Shirley by their titles or their relationship to Shirley.

COMMUNITY SERVICES

The review identifies Shirley's risk factors—past and current child abuse, past suicide attempts, current suicide indicators (she was on suicide watch nearly all the time she was incarcerated in Clarenville), emotional instability in past and current broken relationships (including telephone harassment, stalking, and a charge of first-degree murder)—and assails Child, Youth and Family Services (CYFS) for three things: failure to thoroughly investigate these factors, failure to effectively apply these factors using its own formal Risk Management System, and focusing almost entirely on providing supportive services for Shirley to the exclusion of child protective services for her younger daughter and Zachary.

The responsible regional director is quoted, stating "that we were going to consider this as an ongoing long-term protective intervention file."[4] But, the report notes, "It is unfortunate that the workers on the front line, who were in direct interaction with Dr. Turner, were never apprised of protection concerns at higher levels."[5] This regional director, Elizabeth Day—who was informed of Kate's and my concern for Zachary's safety by Jackie Brazil on June 17, 2002—did the honourable thing and resigned her position shortly after release of Dr. Markesteyn's report.

HEALTH SERVICES

The review examines Shirley's interactions with two psychiatrists: Dr. John Doucet and Dr. David Craig. Kate and I lodged a formal complaint against Dr. Doucet following Zachary's murder, and I describe his interactions in a later section of this epilogue and won't summarize Dr. Markesteyn's findings here. There is one issue, however, that should be noted. Dr. Markesteyn lacked the statutory authority to compel Dr. Doucet to meet with him, and Dr. Doucet declined an invitation to voluntarily answer questions. Hence, the review recommends, "That the Department of Psychology and/or Psychiatry at Memorial University of Newfoundland (MUN) complete a psy-

chological autopsy on Dr. Shirley Jane Turner."[6] A "psychological autopsy" is "a 'quality assurance' activity, the main goal being
to learn whatever lessons could be learned from the case in the
hope of improving the care of future patients."[7]

Dr. Craig examined Shirley when she was incarcerated at
Clarenville Women's Prison from November 15, 2002, until
January 7, 2003. The review notes that Dr. Craig,

> placed her on suicide watch but took her off all medica-
> tion.... During her time in the Correctional Centre,
> Shirley Turner's behaviour was disruptive and disturbing
> to her fellow inmates.... What remains particularly trou-
> bling to me [Markesteyn] is the failure of community and
> psychiatric services to consult with one another. Clearly,
> the impetus for such consultation should come from the
> community services system. Nevertheless, I would have
> expected that within psychiatric services there might be
> some concern for the safety and security of a child as
> young as Zachary.[8]

FINANCIAL SERVICES

The review summarizes the financial support received by
Shirley and notes several instances of her fiddling the government out of several hundred dollars, but found nothing
remarkable.

CHIEF MEDICAL EXAMINER

Regarding responsibility for conducting child death reviews,
the review recommends, "That the Medical Examiner's Office
establish and conduct Child Death Reviews, chaired by the
Chief Medical Examiner, with multi-disciplinary membership,
including the Child and Youth Advocate."[9]

Autopsy results for Shirley and Zachary are summarized in the review. Of particular interest to Kate and me is the following analysis of Zachary's toxicology report (provided by Dr. Milton Tenenbein, professor of pediatrics and pharmacology at the University of Manitoba): "A serum concentration [of Ativan (Lorazepam)] of 1.2 mg/Litre is very high. It is approximately 100 fold greater than the therapeutic concentration. I would expect with such a finding to be severely obtunded and in marked coma. As there are no precedents of fatalities from the ingestion of Lorazepam, in the absence of other drugs, it would seem that this child was the victim of drowning. At the very least, he did not suffer."[10]

OFFICE OF THE CHILD AND YOUTH ADVOCATE

The review questions whether the Advocate's office had sufficient information prior to Zachary's death to consider initiating a review "to determine whether his rights and interests in any respect were or could be in jeopardy, either because of the persona of his mother, Dr. Turner, or the—potentially destabilizing—impact of her critical legal dilemma on the mother's parenting capacity...Whether or not a request for assistance was received, the Advocate's Office is empowered... to decide whether to conduct a review."[11]

JUSTICE SERVICES

Dr. Markesteyn, as the designate of a provincial government agency, was constitutionally precluded from examining federal officials—the Federal Minister of Justice or his legal counsel— or any judge, federal or provincial. This did not, however, deter him from asking a series of pointed questions on Shirley's bail release that he would like to have put directly to federal officials and judges.

Regarding the December 12, 2001, bail hearing in which federal counsel did not oppose bail, did federal counsel request any investigation of Shirley's background prior to the hearing? On what basis did federal counsel consent to bail? What steps did federal counsel take to be certain that sureties "were financially capable of paying the amounts they signed for,"[12] and "understood their responsibilities as sureties, including the obligation to 'bring in' Dr. Turner if any of them had reason to believe she breached a condition of her 'bail'?"[13]

"Generally," Markesteyn asked, "why didn't federal counsel insist under section 522 of the Criminal Code that Dr. Turner remain in custody unless and until she established to the Justice that she should be released?"[14]

"I ask whether a Court may, solely on the basis of the submissions and consent of federal counsel and defence counsel, release a fugitive who, under section 522 of the Criminal Code, must be held in custody unless s/he 'shows cause' why being held in custody is not justified."[15]

Regarding the January 2003 bail hearing at which "federal counsel opposed release [but] called no evidence to support opposition to Dr. Turner's release,"[16] the review posed the question, did federal counsel request any investigation of Shirley's background, including (for example) examination of her record of incarceration at Clarenville Correctional Centre "during which she was under some form of suicide watch and admitted to 'suicide attempts' historically?"[17] Did federal counsel take steps to investigate Shirley's affidavit in support of her bail application? Why didn't federal counsel appeal the Court's decision not to consider frivolousness—a decision that directly contradicted "another Court of Appeal Justice some two years earlier" who *had* considered frivolousness in an extradition bail case?[18]

Is public confidence in the administration of justice by the Court of Appeal maintained "when a Justice of the Court releases someone usually resident in the United States, who (although not convicted of an offence) has been committed to custody—after the Trial Division heard evidence in 2002 of her involvement in the circumstances of a murder—to await the federal Justice Minister's decision whether to surrender her to the United States to be tried for the murder?"[19]

Because Dr. Markesteyn could not legally pursue answers to these questions, the review recommends "That the Child and Youth Advocate, after having determined who is legally entitled to conduct a Judicial Review (acting along with the authority of the Federal Government), do so in order to fully examine how the justice system functioned in relation to Dr. Shirley Turner and hence affected the rights and interests of Zachary Turner."[20]

In summarizing the bail issue, the Review notes that "had Dr. Turner not been released on 'bail' on 12 December 2001 or on 10 January 2003, my Review would have been unnecessary. Zachary would be alive today."[21]

After reading the review, I was struck once again by the lack of proportion that pervades the system that is supposed to deal with murderers. If only a few people had done their jobs properly in the various government agencies that dealt with Shirley, she might well have been incarcerated *without a trial*, not because she probably committed first-degree murder, but because she slapped her children, abandoned her children, made harassing telephone calls, or faked a suicide attempt.

DR. JOHN DOUCET

On December 5, 2003, three and a half months after Zachary's murder, Kate and I wrote a letter to Dr. Robert Young, registrar of the Newfoundland Medical Board, the professional body overseeing physicians in the province of Newfoundland and Labrador. We summarized our story—from Andrew's murder through Zachary's murder—and finished with:

> On December 12, 2001, Dr. Doucet signed as a $65,000 surety to obtain Shirley Turner's release from custody pending the outcome of her extradition hearing.
>
> We question the ethics of a psychiatrist acting as a surety for his client in a legal proceeding. We question his ability to objectively evaluate his patient's mental and emotional state while acting as a surety in a legal proceeding.
>
> We request that the Newfoundland Medical Board inquire into Dr. Doucet's actions in relation to Shirley Turner, and that the Board provide a written summary of its findings.

The Newfoundland Medical Board, which has since been revamped and renamed the College of Physicians and Surgeons, investigated our complaint and formed a tribunal to hear the evidence. The tribunal's eighteen-page March 16, 2006 decision stated (in part):

> By providing the surety, the Respondent, Dr. Doucet, added a dimension to the doctor/patient relationship which ought not to have been created.... Any physician who involves himself to such a degree in the legal affairs of his patient is stepping outside the boundaries of what a reasonable physician should do in providing clinical care. In the opinion of the Adjudication Tribunal, the provision of such a surety was wrong and should not have been done.... In conclusion, by providing a surety to his

patient, Shirley Turner, Dr. John Doucet engaged in professional misconduct which is conduct deserving of sanction...[22]

On April 10, 2006, the tribunal announced the sanction to be imposed on Dr. Doucet, which had two key elements. First, he was ordered to "obtain medical treatment and counseling in the form of therapeutic peer consultation with a psychiatrist.... A focus of the therapeutic sessions shall be the circumstances under which Dr. Doucet agreed to act as surety for Shirley Turner."[23] Second, he was ordered to "pay a part of the costs incurred by the College in the amount of $10,000."

After the final sanction was announced and the hearing was adjourned, Dr. Doucet said only this to the media waiting in the hallway: "I just want to say I'm disappointed in the decision and we have to consider our future. Thank you."

My comments to the media were more extensive. The key points: "I would like to have seen something a bit more severe, but that probably wells from a bit of vindictiveness. Objectively, I think: mission accomplished.... What the College has done is hand physicians a weapon—a defensive weapon—they can use the next time a monster like Turner tries to get them to do something they shouldn't be doing."

SURETY PROPOSALS

On December 10, 2003, three months after Zachary's murder, Kate and I wrote a letter to the Minister of Justice and Attorney General of Canada, Martin Cauchon, briefly summarizing our story and suggesting several measures for improvement of the extradition process. We made three proposals regarding sureties.

First, if the accused is released on bail, it should be required that actual money (rather than signatures) be deposited with the court. In Turner's case, eight different people signed as sureties, but nobody had to deposit money, or even show that they had the amount of their surety. At least two were clearly incapable of producing the money if required (one worked at a minimum wage job and lived in subsidized housing, and another was heavily in debt on student loans).

Second, require that sureties read the detailed charges against the accused. In Turner's case, at least one surety was only vaguely aware of the charge against her and accepted ner version of the story. They were shocked when, after Zachary's murder, they learned the details. This point is especially important if there is a press ban in effect.

Third, require that sureties be informed of their right to revoke bail at any time. At least one of Turner's sureties would have done so, had they known they could.

Cauchon did not respond to our letter, so on April 14, 2004, we wrote to his successor, Irwin Cotler. We enclosed a copy of our December 10 letter, and asked that Mr. Cotler respond to the issues we raised therein.

On April 22, 2004, Cotler responded. His letter was very kind and thoughtful, briefly summarizing the extradition process and the general principles underlying bail and sureties. He then wrote, "It may be helpful for you to know that the administration of justice falls within the purview of the provinces. As such, you may wish to direct your concerns regarding the selection of sureties in Newfoundland to the attention of the Honourable Tom Marshall, Minister of Justice and Attorney General of Newfoundland."

On June 21, 2004, we wrote to Tom Marshall, summarizing our story and enclosing the sequence of letters to date. We finished with, "Please consider implementing the enclosed suggestions from our December 10 letter, and please consider collection of the money currently owed by Shirley Turner's sureties, listed above. Public knowledge of such a collection, in conjunction with stricter requirements for assuming the role of surety, would significantly decrease the chance of another Shirley Turner slipping through the cracks and murdering another thirteen-month old baby."

Kate and I agonized over this suggestion to call in Shirley Turner's sureties. We had come to know Penney and Phillip, Loraine Mercer, and Shirley's son fairly well, and we considered them to be very decent people who got manipulated by a monster. We did not want to see them hurt. In the end, however, we concluded that the prevention of another bail-release murder was the top priority.

On July 14, 2004, Marshall responded to our letter, stating (in part): "While The Honourable Mr. Cotler was correct in stating that the administration of justice falls within the purview of the provinces, I must advise that provincial prosecutors had no involvement in Ms. Turner's case, and that any issues involving her bail or sureties were dealt with by a federal prosecutor.... Any attempt to collect money from the sureties is the responsibility of the federal Department of Justice, not the provincial."

On July 24, 2004, we added Marshall's letter to the pile of enclosures and once again wrote to Cotler, finishing with: "Hence, we are requesting that you consider pursuing such collection, for the reasons indicated in our June 21 letter."

On December 16, 2004, Cotler responded. Regarding surety collection, he wrote:

> It is within my jurisdiction as Attorney General of Canada to institute forfeiture proceedings against the sureties of a person sought in extradition proceedings who has failed

to comply with the conditions of release. You are quite correct that forfeiture proceedings against sureties are important in ensuring that the public is aware that persons who offer themselves as sureties are undertaking important and consequential obligations. However, the amount of money pledged by a surety cannot be forfeited to the Crown without a court order. In forfeiture proceedings, the court has the discretion to refuse forfeiture. The extent to which a surety is at fault in failing to prevent the breach of the bail is relevant, and the court may remit the entire sum to the surety, even if default by the accused or the person sought for extradition is established.

Dr. Turner breached a term of her bail when she took Zachary's life. My agents in the Atlantic region, who are entrusted with the discretion to commence forfeiture proceedings against sureties, could have commenced forfeiture proceedings against Dr. Turner's sureties. After carefully considering whether such proceedings were appropriate, my agents concluded that in this most tragic case, they were not. My agents considered that Dr. Turner's most heinous act of killing Zachary was not something that would have been reasonably foreseen by her sureties, or by anyone else who was observing Dr. Turner closely, since she had convincingly portrayed herself as a good mother.

In such circumstances, it would be doubtful that a judge would find the sureties remiss in their supervision of Dr. Turner, and punish them by ordering forfeiture, particularly when one of the sureties was Zachary's brother. At the time, it was felt that forfeiture proceedings would have further traumatized an already traumatized community. I can assure you that in deciding not to commence forfeiture proceedings, all competing interests were considered, and that the final decision was not undertaken lightly.

Kate and I left the issue at that.

After Shirley was released on bail in January 2003, Mr. Madden told Kate that, if Shirley failed to appear in court, the State would go after the sureties even if it took ten years.

I characterized the surety system as a farce. I rest my case.

NET RESULT

The greatest personal change in Kate and me since Andrew's murder, aside from the huge gaps where our precious child and grandchild should be, is overwhelming regret. A miserable, sick longing for a second chance to do the right thing: kill Shirley Turner to save Zachary. (See Appendix A for a brief historical perspective on the issue of personal versus institutional responses to murder.)

Kate is an avid reader of fiction and came across a quote from Anthony Trollope's novel *Barchester Towers*. I believe it explains why I did not kill Shirley: "A man in the right relies easily on his rectitude and therefore goes about unarmed. His very strength is his weakness. A man in the wrong knows that he must look to his weapons; his very weakness is his strength. The one is never prepared for combat, the other is always ready. Therefore it is that in this world the man that is in the wrong almost invariably conquers the man that is in the right, and invariably despises him."

Responses to my declaration of regret at not killing Shirley—among family, friends, acquaintances, and even strangers—vary dramatically, and the pattern is very simple and quite predictable: the better they knew Andrew, the more likely people are to agree. Family and long-time friends—especially those who grew up with Andrew as an integral part of their lives through grade school, high school, college, medical school, and career—are nearly universal in their assent.

On the other end of the spectrum are responses like "Then you'd be no better than Turner," and "Do you think you'll ever get to forgiveness?" and "You're too good a person to do a thing like that."

To become "no better than Turner," I would have to become a murderer myself; that is, I would have to kill an innocent person. But as a murderer, Turner was among the least innocent of depraved human beings, so killing her would not have been murder in my moral book. It would have been more like a repugnant but obligatory service to humanity.

Forgiveness of murder is God's prerogative, if there is a God. Among mortal humans, however, the greatest right of forgiveness belongs to the one suffering the greatest harm. For the murder of Andrew, that would be Andrew. Suppose that, just after Shirley fired the first shot at his chest, we could freeze frame and get an opinion on forgiveness from him: "Look, Andrew, in a few milliseconds, that slug suspended in front of Shirley's gun is going to slam into your chest. It's going to hurt like hell, worse than anything you've ever felt before. Very quickly, another slug will hit you in the face and come out the back of your head. Shock will have started to set in, but you will still feel that second slug ripping through hundreds of nerve endings. You will spin halfway around and fall face down. Three more slugs will tear into you in the next few seconds, two near your rectum and one in the back of your head, and within a few minutes you will bleed to death. There is no way to avert this fate. Shirley Turner has determined, through some strange calculus that is comprehensible only to her, that you are not worthy of continued existence. The question is: do you forgive her terminating your life about forty years short of its natural end?"

Assuming a normal life expectancy of about seventy years, Zachary's loss was nearly twice Andrew's. Try the same mind experiment with him: "Zachary, your mother is about to step off this wharf and take you with her into the cold black water below. She has decided that you should never know your ABCs, Newton's law of gravity, orgasm, Shakespeare, Bart Simpson's smart-ass humour, or romantic love. In another few seconds, you will inhale water instead of air, and you will experience a terror normally reserved for combat troops and skydivers with tangled parachutes. How do you feel about your mother? Should she be forgiven for depriving you of all but one year of your natural life?"

We can't know Andrew's and Zachary's answers to these questions because a murderer deprives his victim of everything, including the ability to forgive. I know what my answer would be, given the chance to pass judgment on my murderer.

The suggestion that I am "too good a person" to kill someone bothers me a great deal. Zachary was in extreme danger, I was aware of the danger, I knew that the authorities responsible for his protection were aware of the danger and refused to take action, and *still* I did not save his life. The brutal truth: I was not a good enough person to kill Shirley Turner.

Kate's and my bloodline is finished, so it is not possible for us to suffer another assault of this magnitude. However, if it were possible, and if there were a recurrence, I would not hesitate a second time to counter the attack myself, if the government once again refused to perform its most basic function. Ditto for Kate. In addition to sacrificing Zachary on the altar of presumed innocence, the criminal justice system has converted two decent, non-violent people—myself and my true love—into potential killers.

SCHOLARSHIP FUNDS

After Andrew's murder, Kate and I wanted to leave the Latrobe Area Hospital with something of lasting significance in Andrew's memory. His boss, Dr. John Bertolino, suggested an annual scholarship to support medical students who were specifically interested in Andrew's field, family practice. The selected students would be given a small stipend for living expenses and provided with room and board for a month of on-the-job training during their summer break from medical school. By working closely with family practice physicians in a clinical setting, they could provide valuable service to Bertolino's team, while at the same time determining whether the family practice specialty was right for them. Kate and I agreed, and the Dr. Andrew Bagby Family Medicine Scholarship Fund was created.

After Zachary's murder, nearly two years later, a similar fund was established at Memorial University of Newfoundland, under the title Dr. Andrew Bagby and son Zachary Andrew Memorial Bursary.

Both funds are supported by public contributions, which may be sent to the following addresses:

Dr. Andrew Bagby Scholarship Fund
LAH Charitable Foundation
Latrobe Area Hospital
121 West Second Avenue
Latrobe, PA 15650-9905
USA

Dr. Andrew Bagby and son Zachary Bursary Fund
Scholarships and Awards
Memorial University of Newfoundland
St. John's, NL A1C 5S7
Canada

ACKNOWLEDGEMENTS

Except for a few words and phrases suggested to me by reviewers of the manuscript, the content of this book is mine. The spirit, however, is entirely shared by my wife, Kate. We are in virtual lockstep in our thoughts and feelings about this tragedy that overwhelmed our lives. My name is on the cover, but it is our story.

Dr. Elliott Leyton, professor of anthropology at Memorial University of Newfoundland, read an early draft of the manuscript and, in effect, gave me a grade of incomplete. I had mixed fact and conjecture, which would confuse the reader and seriously weaken the story. I fixed it. He introduced me to his literary agent, Beverley Slopen. She found a publisher, Key Porter Books, and the result is represented in the pages you hold in your hands.

Kate's and my lawyer, Jackie Brazil, was right beside us throughout most of this ordeal. Her familiarity with the facts of the case has given this book a review that has confirmed my own recollection, but she also caught several important misconceptions and filled in several important details that I had missed during the living of these events.

Judi Petrush, assistant district attorney of Westmoreland County, Pennsylvania, and Trooper Michael McElfresh of the Pennsylvania State Police ensured that I got the facts right surrounding the murder charge that lies at the root of the story. Constable Noel Stanford of the Royal Newfoundland Constabulary ensured that I got the facts right surrounding the subsequent murder/suicide.

Carol Harrison, my editor at Key Porter, was the first to cast a professional, critical eye on my telling of this story, generating dozens (possibly hundreds) of valuable suggestions, most of which I incorporated. We agreed to disagree on some issues of tone and style. I am curious to see how readers react.

Kate and I are blessed with loving families and with a huge circle of friends. Their emotional support was, and remains, critical to our day-by-day survival. They are too numerous to mention by name here, but I'll single out two as examples.

Kate's brother David, a retired social worker with a huge heart and some professional insight into the grieving process, understood at the outset Kate's need for an open ear. David has provided a place for Kate to unload her pain and anguish whenever she felt the need, which in this case was often.

Our old friend, Carol Stein, has strong opinions on most issues and shares these opinions freely. When we told her that Shirley was pregnant with Andrew's child, she immediately grasped the situation and declared, "You've got to go get that baby!" We replied, "Yes, Carol, that's the plan."

APPENDIX A
MURDER PREVENTION AND RESPONSE

Every problem has two fundamental aspects: prevention and reaction. What can be done to prevent future murders, and what should be done when prevention fails and a murder occurs? In the United States, the murder rate ranges up to twenty-six times that of most major industrial nations,[1] so a great deal has been written about the causes and prevention of murder in the United States.

PREVENTION

According to anthropologist Elliott Leyton the primary factor determining murder rates is cultural attitudes towards violence. For contrasting examples of these attitudes, Leyton looks at two cultural icons, one English (where the murder rate is very low) and one American (where the murder rate is very high). English superhero James Bond kills only when he has to, while American war hero John Rambo takes out a whole town because the sheriff won't let him buy breakfast at the local diner. And American audiences eat it up, oblivious to the suffering of dozens of innocents Rambo leaves in his wake. To correct this culture of violence worship, Leyton suggests, there must be a movement "to reinforce the civilizing process, using the major cultural forces of our time—the mass media, highly qualified daycare personnel, the schools, and a reinforced or redesigned family—to re-implant in youth a genuine compassion for others and a repugnance for violence."[2] Leyton does not, however, strike a hopeful note for the future: "But a cynical culture has rendered repugnant to the modern ear the essential aims of 'character building'…"[3]

In his book *All God's Children*, Fox Butterfield chronicles the history of six generations of the Bosket family men, beginning with Aaron, a South Carolina freed slave. Aaron, who tried to "live lowly and humble" under the boot of post–Civil War white supremacy,[4] had a son called Pud, who refused to be "meek and humble like his father."[5] Like many of his black brethren, Pud modified the Southern white man's code of honour to produce his own variation: "Don't step on my reputation. My name is all I got, so I got to keep it. I'm a man of respect."[6] His rebelliousness led Pud into several scrapes with the law—petty theft, assault and battery, running moonshine, and gambling—but he never killed anyone. His progeny, however, grew progressively more violent, culminating in Willie, who shot and killed two men on New York subway trains at the age of fifteen.

Because he was a minor when he committed the crimes, Willie Bosket was released on his twenty-first birthday. He got married, went to college, and then was convicted (possibly framed) of attempted assault and sent back to prison. Willie was determined to become "the worst fucking nightmare the Department of Correctional Services ever had to deal with," and he succeeded.[7] He "engaged in a holy crusade,"[8] setting fire to his cell seven times, spitting and throwing urine on his guards, and finally plunging a shank—a makeshift knife—into the chest of guard Earl Porter, who miraculously survived the wound. In Willie's own words, "To this day, the only regret Bosket has

[Willie wrote about himself in the third person] is not having killed prison guard Earl Porter and spitting on his corpse—not because he was Earl Porter, but because he was the system."[9]

Willie may have been the worst of the Bosket family males, but he wasn't the only young killer in the big cities. "Between 1985 and 1994, homicides by fourteen- to seventeen-year-old males more than tripled.... Willie Bosket is no longer an anomaly."[10] Butterfield attributes this increase in murders by adolescents to a casting off of "long accumulated rules of self-control for an exaltation of the individual...We are now less religious...The family is being pulled apart...jobs are shrinking...We are less public-spirited and less willing to spend our scarce tax dollars on public schools to teach students to sit still, obey the teacher and learn useful skills..."[11]

Butterfield asks the reader to "imagine if you and your child were trapped in the inner city without the resources to escape, [and to] come up with policy recommendations. You might advocate more cops and jails. More likely, you would want programs that removed guns from the streets, created good jobs, built better housing and, in particular, made sure your son or daughter was surrounded by good, loving adults."[12]

Former Massachusetts Public Health Commissioner Deborah Prothrow-Stith echoes this sentiment in her book, *Deadly Consequences*: "More police in patrol cars, more street lights, stiffer sentences, and new prisons will not, I believe, prevent two young people from settling their differences with a firearm."[13] To combat the rising tide of violence, Prothrow-Stith argues for a "public health approach because it has worked in the past.... Following a massive twenty-year public health campaign the incidence of smoking has decreased by 30 percent...Americans no longer believe it is all right to drive when intoxicated....We have [convinced] millions of Americans to adopt [exercise and diet] in order to reduce their risk of heart disease and stroke. I believe that we can do the same thing for violence."[14]

These three authors—Leyton, Butterfield, and Prothrow-Stith—and presumably a great many more whom I have not encountered, are attacking the murder pipeline at its source, searching for long-term strategies to head off murder before it happens. It is obviously an admirable and daunting assignment, and potentially much more significant and valuable in the long run than my quest. However, even if solutions evolve that dramatically reduce the incidence of murder, it is a safe prediction (unfortunately) that the number will not reach zero any time soon. Hence, for the foreseeable future, North American society will be stuck with the problem of how to react when a Shirley Turner makes a corpse of an Andrew Bagby.

REACTION

Murder used to be considered a family problem. "Like much of Western Europe, England inherited the influence of Greco-Roman civilization. The Athenian laws encapsulated and expressed the dominant mentality of blood vengeance implicit in primitive societies... [W]hen a homicide had been committed in classical Athens, it was the responsibility of the victim's family to seek revenge according to the ancient laws of the blood feud."[15]

By the thirteenth century, the English view of murder had begun to diverge from the rest of Europe, with "the emergence of a distinctively English common law increasingly intolerant of blood feud and personal violence."[16] A system of royal courts developed, with "authority to bind over offenders to keep the peace."[17] This practice became known as "keeping the King's Peace. To some extent it was the state as the representative of society that became the victim of law violations, and not the private offended party, and the state took the initiative in seeing that justice was carried out."[18] Hence, in England, there was no longer any need for the outraged kinsmen of a homicide victim to exact personal retribution. As seventeenth century English jurist Sir Edward Coke phrased it, "Revenge belongeth to the magistrate."[19]

While England was, in a sense, nationalizing the practice of vengeance, it was also undergoing "what [social scientist Norbert] Elias has called the 'civilizing process', *the culturally programmed internalization of shame and fear*, of learned inhibitions about violence...transmitted from generation to generation through a variety of socialization techniques..."[20]

Two factors, then—one legal, one cultural—"worked together to keep the English murder rate low."[21]

The rest of Europe, by contrast, was much slower to relinquish private violence. Over a twenty-two-year period in the eighteenth century, the murder rate in Rome was approximately four hundred times that in London and Middlesex, which were "the most lawless part of England."[22]

Today, who cares about murder rates in England and Italy over two hundred years ago? I believe they offer the best objective evidence for the superiority of an institutionalized criminal justice system over private vengeance. If private vengeance were still the norm in our culture, I would have pursued and perhaps killed Shirley Turner, in retribution for the murder of my son. Perhaps then her son would kill me, my brother Pat would kill Shirley's son, whose sister would kill Pat, and so on, until conceivably both families might be wiped from the face of the earth. While it is open to rational debate whether railroad and health-care systems ought to be government or private institutions, surely the threat of such an appalling bloodbath weighs heavily in favour of government as the sole legitimate exactor of retribution.

APPENDIX B
JUSTIFICATIONS FOR CRIMINAL PUNISHMENT

Retribution was an accepted goal of criminal punishment in English law until at least the seventeenth century ("Revenge belongeth to the magistrate"), but it has fallen out of favour in modern legal thought. "Retribution in the sense of revenge has no place in modern sentencing law,"[1] and "[retribution] has no useful place in a theory of justification for punishment."[2]

Retribution has been replaced in modern times by the following six objectives for criminal punishment, which are listed in Section 718 of the Canadian Criminal Code:

> The fundamental purpose of sentencing is to contribute, along with crime prevention initiatives, to respect for the law and the maintenance of a just, peaceful and safe society by imposing just sanctions that have one or more of the following objectives:
> a) to denounce unlawful conduct;
> b) to deter the offender and other persons from committing offences;
> c) to separate offenders from society, where necessary;
> d) to assist in rehabilitating offenders;

e) to provide reparations for harm done to victims or to
    the community; and

f) to promote a sense of responsibility in offenders, and
    acknowledgement of the harm done to victims and to
    the community.[3]

MURDER IS A REALLY, REALLY BAD THING

The issue of justifications for criminal punishment does not
bear directly on my primary concern in this book (bail release
for persons accused of murder). However, I believe the lack-
adaisical treatment of both bail and sentencing in murder cases
is symptomatic of a more general problem: lack of respect
among modern legal thinkers for the damage inflicted by a
murderer. Regarding incapacitation as a justification for criminal punishment (that is, "lock up killers so they can't kill
again"), Herbert Packer notes that "very few murderers kill
again; [hence, the] incapacitative claim is weak."[4] In their book
Deadly Deeds, Robert Silverman and Leslie Kennedy note that
"violence, after all, accounts for only 8 per cent to 10 per cent of
Criminal Code violations in Canada, but violent crimes elicit a
much more intense response than either common delin-
quency... or property offences."[5]

These authors don't get it: property crimes are *irritating*;
violent crimes, especially murder, are *devastating*. You can take
everything I own and leave me standing naked in the wilder-
ness; but please, please, please don't harm my baby! John Walsh,
whose six-year-old son Adam was abducted and murdered in
1981, stated the issue perfectly: "If someone had walked in with
a rusted knife and said, 'I'm going to spend two days killing you
slowly with this blade. But after I do that, I will let your boy go',
I would have begged them."[6]

RESURRECT RETRIBUTION

In view of this appalling lack of humanitarian insight among legal thinkers, I am compelled to rebut the omission of retribution from the official list of justifications for punishment.

Hang around any bar, have dinner with friends, chat with the stranger next to you on an airplane, and, if the subject of violent crime comes up, you will eventually hear something like: "If anybody ever hurt my kid, I'd rip his goddamned head off!"

This popular attitude may have its roots in evolutionary factors; a species that would not defend and avenge its young is not likely to survive long in the wild.

There is definitely a tremendous psychological component to this urge for revenge, which may be based on pure selfishness. In depriving Andrew of everything he had, and everything he was ever going to have, Shirley also deprived me and my true love of our two most precious values: time with our child before we left this life, and assurance that a part of us, embodied in our beloved Andrew, would live on after we were gone.

It's probably also cultural. Growing up, most of us learned from our seniors that we're supposed to defend and avenge our young, so we practice what they taught us and pass it on to our offspring.

Whatever the source of my rage at my son's killer—evolution, psychology, culture—I do not apologize for it, and I resent its arrogant, pedantic dismissal by those who write the theory and practice of criminal punishment. Let them kiss the cold dead forehead of their murdered child before they tell me my rage has no place. These theorists are in denial of something very, very fundamental to the nature of humanity and this denial leads them to inflict additional excruciating pain on the innocent survivors of a murder victim. To wit: the release on parole of a convicted murderer while his or her victim is *still dead*. This practice effectively says to the victim's survivors, "The murderer is more valuable than his victim, your precious loved one."

LIFE WITHOUT PAROLE

In my calculus of justice, an actual murderer—as opposed to someone who is only convicted of murder in a fallible court-room—forfeits all rights, including the right to live. However, since the standard of proof for a legal conviction is (quite rightly) only proof beyond a *reasonable* doubt, rather than beyond *any* doubt, the state should acknowledge the possibility of error and refrain from carrying out the irreversible sentence of death. Instead, the sentence for murder should be life in prison without the possibility of parole. Unlike the death penalty, imprisonment provides the option of restoring free-dom to one who is erroneously convicted and later exonerated. (For some chilling accounts of erroneous death sentences in the United States, see Stanley Cohen's book *The Wrong Men: America's Epidemic of Wrongful Death Row Convictions*.)

Under a life-without-parole sentence, only one and a half of the six objectives for punishment listed in the Canadian Criminal Code would be applicable to murder.

One of these is to deter the offender and other persons from committing offences. The first half of this objective would be irrelevant to a sentence of life without parole, since the offender cannot commit a second offence while he or she is incarcerated. (If a convicted murderer commits a second mur-der while in prison, and there is no death penalty, life in solitary confinement seems the only reasonable insurance against yet a third murder by the same monster.) I can personally attest to the effectiveness of the second half of this objective—deterrence of "other persons." I am one of those other persons and, had I not been threatened with long-term imprisonment, I would have put my best effort into killing Shirley Turner.

The second objective is to separate offenders from society, where necessary. Since Andrew's murder, Kate and I have met dozens of survivors of murder victims, many of whom understandably crave the death of the monster who took away their loved one. Absent a death penalty, however, most would be reasonably content with a genuine life sentence. I submit that such a sentence is "necessary" to avoid inflicting additional emotional damage on these innocent survivors, who have already suffered a sledgehammer blow to their psyches. They are entitled to absolute assurance from the state that their loved one's murderer will never again walk free, and they are entitled to be free from periodic traumatic appearances before a Parole Board to plead over and over again for the justice they, and the dead victim, deserve from their government.

APPENDIX C
DANGEROUSNESS

This appendix contains calculations of two danger factors using data published by the Canadian National Parole Board, Statistics Canada, and the United States Bureau of Justice Statistics. First, persons *convicted* of homicide are compared to an equivalent group chosen from the general population of Canada. Then persons *accused* of homicide are compared to those convicted of homicide, and hence indirectly to the general population.

CONVICTED

Between 1975 and 1999, 11,783 people who had been convicted of homicide were released on parole in Canada.[1]

Of these 11,783 convicted killers, thirty-seven were subsequently convicted of another homicide.[2]

These thirty-seven repeat offenders killed fifty-eight victims (one parolee killed twelve people in a gang contract killing).[3]

The average delay between parole and the second killing was 21.6 months (ranging from two days to 11.9 years).[4]

This corresponds to a murder rate among parolees of 174 per hundred thousand per year (37/11,783 × 100,000 × 12/21.6).

During this same period, the murder rate for Canada as a whole ranged between 1.7 and 2.9, averaging about 2.3 per hundred thousand per year.[5]

If we stop analyzing at this point, we would declare that a convicted killer is about seventy-six times more likely to kill in the future than is someone chosen at random from the population of Canada (174/2.3). Such a declaration would drastically overstate the case because most murders are committed by males and few are committed by the very young or very old. Hence, in order to make a fair comparison against parolees, the Canada-wide rate needs to be adjusted for a reduced population consisting of adult males who are not too old.

In 2004, there were approximately 31.9 million Canadians, of whom 7.2 million were males aged twenty to forty-nine.[6] The homicide rate among these adult not-too-old males, therefore, was approximately 10.2 per hundred thousand per year $(2.3 \times 31.9/7.2)$.

Hence, a person convicted of homicide is roughly seventeen times more likely to commit a future homicide than is an adult male chosen at random from the general population of Canada (174/10.2).

Another way to state this comparison: if 11,783 males aged twenty to forty-nine were chosen at random from the general population of Canada and observed for one year, there would be about two killers in the group, compared with thirty-seven among the same number of parolees.

One more perspective: if the general population of males killed at the same rate as parolees, Canada would average over ten thousand homicides per year, rather than the six hundred or so that actually occur.

I suggest that authorities who compile recidivism rates should, as a routine step in their reporting, lay these rates alongside the basic offence rates for the population as a whole. Such a comparison would provide a better perspective on the risks associated with releasing, not just killers, but any convicted offenders.

ACCUSED

In a study of Toronto homicide cases between 1974 and 2002, the Research and Statistics Division of the Canadian Department of Justice reported that 1,137 persons were accused of homicide. Of these 1,137 accused, seven had their cases dismissed, 163 were found "not guilty," ninety-six were found "not criminally responsible by reason of mental disorder," 476 pled "guilty" without a trial, and 395 were found "guilty" at trial.[7]

Hence, for this twenty-eight-year sample, 77 per cent of those accused of homicide were eventually convicted (476 + 395 = 871, which is 77 per cent of 1,137). Assuming those who were acquitted had a danger factor of one (the same as someone chosen at random from the general population) and those convicted had a factor of seventeen (calculated in the previous section), the average factor for all 1,137 of the accused was 77 per cent of seventeen, which is thirteen.

If we add the ninety-six accused who actually did a killing but were found "not criminally responsible by reason of mental disorder," the danger factor for accused killers rises from thirteen to fourteen (476 + 395 + 96 = 967, which is 85 per cent of 1,137. And 85 per cent of seventeen is fourteen).

In summary, compared to the general population of Canada, a *convicted killer* has a danger factor of approximately seventeen, and an *accused killer* has a danger factor of approximately fourteen.

AN EQUIVALENT DANGER FACTOR FOR THE UNITED STATES

The danger factor for persons convicted of homicide in the United States is approximately twenty-two and is derived using an approach similar to that used above with Canadian data.

According to Bureau of Justice statistics, "released prisoners were arrested for homicide at a rate fifty-three times higher than the homicide arrest rate for the adult population."[8]

I believe this report somewhat overstates the relative danger of released killers, since it compares them with the entire adult population. Since males commit most murders, and few are committed by the very old, a more accurate danger factor can be calculated by comparing released killers to males aged eighteen to sixty-four. This group constitutes about 41 per cent of the adult population. Hence, the danger factor for paroled killers in the United States is approximately 41 percent of fifty-three, which is twenty-two.

NOTES

CHAPTER 1 MURDER

1. Clark Simpson, interviewed by Chris O'Neill-Yates in "Warning Signs," *The National*, CBC TV, on November 5, 2003.
2. Pennsylvania State Police Homicide Investigation Action Report of witness interview at 22:25 on 2001/11/06.
3. Pennsylvania State Police Homicide Investigation Action Report of witness interview at 13:00 on 2001/11/09.
4. Ibid.

CHAPTER 2 BACKGROUND

1. Rene Pollett, "In Defense of Shirley Turner," *The Telegram*, August 30, 2003. no page number.

CHAPTER 5 INVESTIGATION

1. Shirley Turner, interviewed by Corporal Randall D. Gardner of the Pennsylvania State Police, November 6, 2001.
2. Shirley Turner, interviewed by Sergeant Jerry Mann and Detective Robert Sellers of the Council Bluffs, Iowa, Police Department, November 6, 2001.
3. Ibid.
4. Quotes in this section are from a Pennsylvania State Police Homicide Investigation Action Report of witness interview at 18:39 on 2001/11/08.

5.   Vincent Bugliosi, *Outrage*, (New York: Dell Publishing, 1996) 288.

6.   Pennsylvania State Police Homicide Investigation Action Report of Heather Arnold interview on 2001/11/15.

7.   Pennsylvania State Police Homicide Investigation Action Report of witness interview at 17:55 on 2001/11/06.

8.   Pennsylvania State Police Homicide Investigation Action Report of witness interview at 10:28 on 2001/11/27.

9.   Pennsylvania State Police Homicide Investigation Action Report of witness interview at 11:28 on 2001/11/28.

CHAPTER 6 **ESCAPE**

1.   Ross and Herzog later provided affidavits to Shirley's Canadian lawyer during the subsequent extradition process. In her affidavit dated 2002/02/01, Herzog stated: "Dr. Turner weighed the pros and cons of staying in Iowa and decided to go to Canada." Herzog also stated: "Had there been a warrant issued for [Shirley's] arrest while she was still in the United States, I would have recommended that she surrender herself to lawful process as is my duty as an officer of the court."

CHAPTER 7 **LIMBO**

1.   Bonnie Belec, "Woman Arrested for Murder in U.S.," *The Telegram*, December 13, 2001, A1.

2.   Dr. John Doucet letter to Constable Noel Stanford of the Royal Newfoundland Constabulary, August 25, 2003.

CHAPTER 10 **NITS**

1.   Source for the extradition hearing information in this chapter is a transcript of *The United States of America v. Shirley Jane Turner*, May 27 and 28, 2002, in the Supreme Court of Newfoundland and Labrador, Chief Justice Derek Green presiding.

CHAPTER 13 **ACCESS**

1.   Source for the custody hearing information in this chapter is a transcript of David Franklin Bagby and Kathleen Daphne Bagby

(Applicants) and Shirley Jane Turner (Respondent), August 6, 2002, in the Supreme Court of Newfoundland and Labrador Unified Family Court, Judge Robert Wells presiding.

CHAPTER 15 **EXTRADITION HEARING**

1. Source for the extradition hearing information in this chapter is a transcript of *The United States of America v. Shirley Jane Turner*, September 19, 2002, in the Supreme Court of Newfoundland and Labrador, Chief Justice Derek Green presiding.

CHAPTER 16 **MORE NITS**

1. Source for the extradition hearing information in this chapter is a transcript of *The United States of America v. Shirley Jane Turner*, September 19, 2002, in the Supreme Court of Newfoundland and Labrador, Chief Justice Derek Green presiding.

CHAPTER 18 **ATP RULING**

1. Source for the extradition hearing information in this chapter is a transcript of *The United States of America v. Shirley Jane Turner*, October 22, 2002, in the Supreme Court of Newfoundland and Labrador, Chief Justice Derek Green presiding.

CHAPTER 20 **JAIL**

1. Source for the extradition hearing information in this chapter is a transcript of The United States of America vs. Shirley Jane Turner, November 14, 2002, in the Supreme Court of Newfoundland and Labrador, Chief Justice Derek Green presiding.

CHAPTER 21 **ICE MODE**

1. Notice of Appeal from Order of Committal Pursuant to the Extradition Act, filed in the Supreme Court of Newfoundland on 2002/11/15.

CHAPTER 22 **BAIL APPLICATION**

1. Source for this section is the combined Affidavits and

Interlocutory Application, dated December 30, 2002, in the matter of *Shirley Jane Turner (Applicant/Appellant) v. The United States of America (Respondent)*, submitted to the Supreme Court of Newfoundland and Labrador Court of Appeal.

CHAPTER 23 **BAIL HEARING**

1. Source for the bail hearing information in this chapter is a transcript of *Shirley Jane Turner (Plaintiff) v. The United States of America (Defendant)*, January 8, 9 and 10, 2003, in the Supreme Court of Newfoundland and Labrador, Court of Appeal, Judge Gale Welsh presiding.

CHAPTER 24 **DÉTENTE**

1. There was extensive discussion of possible decision sequences: should the Minister hold off his Surrender Order decision until the Committal Order appeal was settled (possibly obviating his need to make a decision), or should the Court of Appeal hold off its decision on the Committal Order appeal until the Minister's Surrender Order decision (possibly obviating its need to address the appeal). That was just the simple version. If the losing side appealed to the Supreme Court on either issue, the decision tree grew exponentially. And this was under the new *expedited* process. Perhaps the amazing thing about Charles Ng's case— decided under the old, slow process—is that it took *only* six years to get him out of the country.

CHAPTER 27 **SURRENDER**

1. Minister of Justice and Attorney General of Canada Martin Cauchon to Randolph J. Piercey of Kelly and Piercey, Barristers and Solicitors. June 9, 2003.

2. As I understood it, the real issue here was something called the "rule of specialty," easily the subject of another book or two. Briefly, it concerns the possibility that a requesting state could base its extradition request on one charge—robbery, for example—and later try the accused on other charges such as capital

murder. By this means, the requesting state could circumvent the perceived interference in its internal criminal justice system by its extradition partner. Obviously, this issue is closely linked to the death penalty question, in that Canada imposes its anti–death penalty policy on its extradition partners. This subject, too, could fill another few volumes.

CHAPTER 30 **THE STRETCH**

1. Royal Newfoundland Constabulary interview of witness on 2003/08/19.
2. Royal Newfoundland Constabulary interview of witness on 2003/08/29.
3. Royal Newfoundland Constabulary interview of witness on 2003/08/21.
4. Peter H. Markesteyn and David C. Day, "Turner Review and Investigation." Office of the Child and Youth Advocate Province of Newfoundland and Labrador. Volume I, p. 493. Except as noted, details of Zachary's last night are from Volume I, pp. 486–493.

CHAPTER 32 **NEXT**

1. Bonnie Belec, "No Accident," *The Telegram*, August 22, 2003, A1.

CHAPTER 33 **MOTIVE**

1. See Appendix C.
2. News Release, Government of Newfoundland and Labrador, September 5, 2003, available online at: http://www.releases.gov.nl.ca/releases/2003/health/0905n02.htm
3. Geoff Meeker, "Bagbys top newsmakers in 2003," *The Express*, December 30, 2003–January 6, 2004. no page number.

CHAPTER 34 **USEFUL LIMBO**

1. *The Lamer Commission of Inquiry Pertaining to the Cases of: Ronald Dalton, Gregory Parson, Randy Druken, Report and Annexes*, 2006, p. 171, available online at: http://www.justice.gov.nl.ca/just/lamer/.

2.   Bob Simmonds interviewed by Jeff Gilhooly, *The St. John's Morning Show*, CBC Radio, September 5, 2003.

3.   Gavin de Becker, *The Gift of Fear* (New York: Random House, 1997), 183.

4.   This is an excerpt from the Laura Abbott bail hearing before Judge Robert Hall on July 21, 2004 in the Supreme Court of Newfoundland and Labrador, Trial Division.

5.   Bonnie Belec, "Bail granted for murder suspect," *The Telegram*, July 23, 2004, A1.

CHAPTER 35 **THE LAW OF BAIL**

1.   Joel E. Pink and David C. Perrier, *From Crime to Punishment* (Toronto: Thomson Carswell, 2003) 69.

2.   Variations on this phrase appear throughout the Extradition Hearing transcript and also in Chief Justice Derek Green's written decision ordering that Shirley be committed into custody: Reasons for Judgment, Between The United States of America and Shirley Jane Turner, dated 2002/11/14.

3.   Herbert L. Packer, *The Limits of the Criminal Sanction* (Stanford, CA: Stanford University Press, 1968) 136.

4.   Gary T. Trotter *The Law of Bail in Canada*, 2nd ed. (Toronto: Thomson Carswell, 1999) 151.

5.   Appendix A very briefly summarizes the history of murder, and the response to murder, in our culture.

6.   Trotter, 2nd ed., 4.

7.   Ibid., 6.

8.   Ibid., 7.

9.   Criminal Code of Canada, Section 515(10).

10. Trotter, 2nd ed., 9.

11. Ibid.

12. Ibid., 12

13. Ibid., 23.

14. Criminal Code of Canada, Section 515(10).

15. Ibid.

16. Trotter, 2nd ed., 31.

17. Ibid., 48.

18. Ibid, 49.

19. Ibid., 136–143.

20. See Appendix C.

21. See Appendix C.

22. Gary T. Trotter *The Law of Bail in Canada* (Toronto: Thomson Carswell, 1992) 26.

23. Trotter, 2nd ed., p. 49.

24. Packer, 217.

25. Ibid.,. 218.

26. Ibid.

27. James C. Morton and Scott C. Hutchison, *The Presumption of Innocence* (Toronto: Carswell, 1987) 120.

28. Ibid., 121.

29. Robert D. Hare, *Without Conscience: The Disturbing World of the Psychopaths Among Us* (New York: The Guilford Press, 1999) 44.

30. Fox Butterfield, *All God's Children* (New York: HarperCollins, 1995) 249.

31. Ibid., 284.

32. Ibid, p. 285.

33. Ibid, p. 293.

34. Ibid.

CHAPTER 36 **PROPOSAL**

1. See Appendices B and C for supporting arguments. Appendix B addresses the justifications for punishment underlying current sentencing guidelines, and challenges their application to persons convicted of murder. Appendix C shows the derivation of danger factors for persons convicted of homicide, and also for persons accused of homicide.

2. *Dictionary of Legal Terms, 3rd ed.* (Hauppauge, NY: Barron's Educational Series, Inc., 1998).

3. Ibid.

4. Don Stuart and Ronald Joseph Delisle, *Learning Canadian Criminal Law*, 6th ed. (Toronto: Carswell, 1997) 45.

5. Pink and Perrier, 181.
6. Ibid.
7. Trotter, 2nd ed., 40.
8. Ibid, 41.
9. Trotter, 24.
10. Stuart and Delisle, 101.
11. Ibid., 102.

EPILOGUE

1. The members of the advisory council were Ken Barter, Ph.D., R.S.W., Professor at the school of Social Work, Memorial University of Newfoundland; G.G. Leahy, R.C.M.P. Assistant Commissioner (retired); Dr. Elliott Leyton, Professor of Anthropology (retired) and author of many books on murder; Stephanie L. Newell, LL.B., a member of the Newfoundland and Labrador Bar and Law Society, practising with the St. John's law firm of O'Dea, Earle; and Dr. Ted Rosales, pediatrician and geneticist in the Newfoundland and Labrador Medical Genetics Program.
2. Markesteyn and Day, Volume I, p. 50.
3. Markesteyn and Day, Volume II, 66.
4. Ibid., 73.
5. Ibid., 210.
6. Ibid., 229.
7. Ibid., 233.
8. Ibid., 256–257.
9. Ibid., 330.
10. Ibid., 326.
11. Ibid., 341.
12. Ibid., 49.
13. Ibid.
14. Ibid., 50.
15. Ibid.
16. Ibid., 51.
17. Ibid., 52.

18. Ibid., 53.

19. Ibid., 56.

20. Ibid., 57.

21. Ibid., 58.

22. Dr. Edmund Collins, Dr. Elizabeth Mate, Mr. Gerald Kean, Adjudication Tribunal Decision, College of Physicians and Surgeons of Newfoundland and Labrador, 2006/03/16.

23. Dr. Edmund Collins, Dr. Elizabeth Mate, Mr. Gerald Kean, Adjudication Tribunal Decision, College of Physicians and Surgeons of Newfoundland and Labrador, 2006/04/10.

APPENDIX A **MURDER PREVENTION AND RESPONSE**

1. Elliott Leyton, *Men of Blood: Murder in Everyday Life* (Toronto: McClelland & Stewart, 2002) 15. Male homicide rates in 1992 per 100,000 population: United States, 15.9; Italy, 4.8; Canada, 2.9; England and Wales, 0.6. Only Mexico (31.5) and Russia (24.9) were higher than the United States.

2. Ibid., 233.

3. Ibid., 230.

4. Butterfield, p. 44.

5. Ibid., 45.

6. Ibid., 63.

7. Ibid., 303.

8. Ibid., 304.

9. Ibid., 323.

10. Ibid., 325.

11. Ibid., 327.

12. Ibid.

13. Deborah Prothrow-Stith, *Deadly Consequences* (New York: HarperPerennial, 1993) 27.

14. Ibid., 28.

15. Leyton, 99.

16. Ibid., 100.

17. Ibid., 104.

18. Pink and Perrier, 2.

19. Leyton, 99.

20. Leyton, 3. Referring to Norbert Elias, *The Civilizing Process* (Oxford: Blackwell Publishing Ltd., 1994).

21. Leyton, xiii.

22. Ibid, p. 109. "In London and Middlesex...eighty-one people were convicted of murder in the years between 1749 and 1771, when in 'half that period Rome, a city only a quarter of the size of London, had 4,000 murders.'" Hence, the ratio of murder rates is $(4,000 \div 81) \times 2 \times 4 = 395$, which I rounded off to 400.

APPENDIX B JUSTIFICATIONS FOR CRIMINAL PUNISHMENT

1. Pink and Perrier, 295.

2. Packer, 38.

3. Reprinted in Pink and Perrier, 295.

4. Packer, 269.

5. Robert Silverman and Leslie Kennedy, *Deadly Deeds: Murder in Canada* (Scarborough, ON: Nelson Canada, 1993) 37.

6. John Walsh with Susan Schindehette, *Tears of Rage* (New York: Pocket Books, 1997) 144.

APPENDIX C DANGEROUSNESS

1. *Repeat Homicide Offences Committed by Offenders Under Community Supervision*, National Parole Board, November 1999, available online at: http://www.npb-cnlc.gc.ca/reports/pr101001_e.htm.

2. Ibid.

3. Ibid.

4. Ibid.

5. Statistics Canada, "Homicides," *The Daily*, Wednesday, October 1, 2003. Available online at http://www.statcan.ca/Daily/English/031001/d031001a.htm (accessed November 3, 2006).

6. Statistics Canada, *Population by Sex and Age Group*, 2004. Available online at http://www40.statcan.ca/l01/cst01/demo10a.htm (accessed November 3, 2006).

7. Myrna Dawson, "Criminal Justice Outcomes in Intimate and Non-
    intimate Partner Homicide Cases," Department of Justice Canada,
    March 31, 2004. Available online at http://canada.justice.gc.ca/
    en/ps/rs/rep/2004/rr04-6/ (accessed November 3, 2006).

8. Recidivism of Prisoners Released in 1994, Bureau of Justice
    Statistics, United States Department of Justice, available online
    at http://www.ojp.usdoj.gov/bjs/pub/pdf/rpr94.pdf (accessed
    November 3, 2006).